Martin Kirby is the former deputy editor of the *Eastern Daily Press*, is a regular contributor to a number of newspapers in the United Kingdom, and his first book, *Albion: The Story of the Norfolk Trading Wherry*, was published by Jarrolds in 1998.

No Going Back: Journey to Mother's Garden

MARTIN KIRBY

timewarner
paperbacks

A *Time Warner* Paperback

First published in Great Britain in 2003
as a paperback original by Time Warner Paperbacks
Reprinted 2003 (twice)

A CIP catalogue record for this book is
available from the British Library.

ISBN 0 7515 3548 6

Typeset by M Rules
Printed and bound in Great Britain by
Clays Ltd, St Ives plc

Time Warner Paperbacks
An imprint of
Time Warner Books UK
Brettenham House
Lancaster Place
London WC2E 7EN

www.TimeWarnerBooks.co.uk

To Maggie

. . . The light
That holds my eye
And lifts my face
And folds around me
A love
That tells me
I
Am
A
Lucky
Man

And our children Ella and Joe

Acknowledgements

This isn't of course, just our story. It also belongs to all of the following for their love and ceaseless support and encouragement: Earle and Eve Kirby, Beryl Whitman and our wonderful families, and loved ones Pat and Horace Kemp and David Whitman who have passed away but we don't feel have left us; Mac and Conxita and our good friends and neighbours across the valley; Quico and Enriqueta and the people of our mountain village; our close friends in England and around the world for whom the miles mean nothing; Billy Paulett, Amanda Blue, Will Millner and everyone at Ricochet; and Barbara Boote and the Time Warner Books team for believing.

My thanks, too, to my friends at the *Eastern Daily Press*, *Yorkshire Post*, *Daily Mail*, *East Anglian Daily Times*, and *Country Smallholding* magazine.

Spellings, to the best of our ability, are Catalan rather than Spanish.

Preface

mother's garden

I knew a man, an average sort of bloke in many ways, whose life seemed to be trundling along nicely into middle age. I haven't seen him for a couple of years, but back then, about the time he was approaching forty, he seemed 'set', if that's the right word. He was happily married. They had a young daughter and another baby was on the way. He had a good job and they lived in an old cottage in a pretty village. He'd worked his way up through the company he'd been with for twenty-odd years and, ever cautious, had been paying into a pension scheme all that time. They had about twelve years to run on their large endowment mortgage and, although they never had any savings, they ploughed what spare money they had into the house which they saw as their investment.

He liked his career, even if the hours were long. He made it to middle management by the time he was thirty, which meant a company car, parking space and the occasional vol-au-vent in the boardroom. He knew he'd have to move to another firm if he was to climb further up the ladder, but that wasn't his style. He felt appreciated and secure in what he saw as an increasingly unstable world. As I said, a fairly typical bloke, spending nearly two hours a day behind the wheel commuting, forever apologising for being late home, doing his best to help out at the village school, fiddling with a bit of DIY, drinking a little too much maybe, but reasonably healthy and apparently with a handle on his life.

By all accounts, they were thriving – just one among the countless happy families beating the common path through life.

Then, out of the blue, they stopped. They stunned friends and colleagues by announcing that, despite all they had, they'd decided to opt out and live a radically different life halfway up a mountain in Spain.

He, of course, is me – and this is how, and why, we made the journey to Mother's Garden.

Sowing the Seed

mother's garden

*T*here's a sign hanging just inside the broad and battered front door of our ramshackled farmhouse that reads 'DEU VOS GUARD'. On the day we bought our patch of Catalonia in northeast Spain a new friend who lives across the valley laughingly translated it as 'God Help You'.

Although it was only the year 2000, it seems an age since we signed on the dotted line, exchanged a fat cheque for the enormous old key more befitting a church, and realised that, after years of debating and dithering about changing our lives, we'd finally crossed the Rubicon. I glanced at that sign almost every day for months after our move. Sometimes it made me smile, but sometimes it seemed profoundly relevant when doubts about our sanity and sobriety and the chances of us making a go of our radically different way of life jangled the nerves, shortened the fuse and fostered 'What in hell's teeth have we done?' cold sweats.

But, boy, what an adventure.

I remember so well one day in the spring of 2001. I was standing beside the vegetable patch peeing on the compost and gazing idly up the valley at nothing in particular. I was finding it hard to focus. The dogs were having their usual early morning forage beside the bumpy track to the farm. Every blade of grass was smothered in thousands of unavoidable tiny snails that popped like bubble wrap as I'd walked across them. The birds were singing for all their worth and crisscrossing the wakening sky, while away to my left I could just make out someone, probably a boar hunter, moving through the pines on the ridge above the terraces of vines and olives. The church in the village half a mile away had just chimed seven and the whole scene was bathed in the honey light of dawn.

Unshaven for days and looking like a scarecrow in my torn jeans and tatty T-shirt, I stood there transfixed, blinking in slow motion and ruminated over some weird, indigestible facts. For the first time in twenty-two years I didn't have a job, unless you classed being a farmer's husband or a three-hours-a-week English teacher as gainful employment. I felt more content and together than at any time in my life, even though I was both mentally and physically knackered and (friends kept reminding me) 'doing something exceptionally brave' – a nice way of saying we were bonkers.

The fog-headed fatigue I put down in part to giving up the

ordered world of the office for a ride on the emotional roller coaster of full-time parenting, an exhilarating and frequently hair-raising trip with five-year-old Ella and ten-month-old Joe Joe at the controls. I was also attempting to write, to bodge some farm-scale DIY, to scavenge for firewood and generally do farmer Maggie's bidding until it was too dark to see where the rotovator was dragging me. Green-fingered Maggie grew up on a farm and it was in her blood, so she was the brain while I was a feeble excuse for the brawn. Every morning my 42-year-old body was as stiff as our ironing board and as reluctant to stand up.

But it was between my ears where the greatest risk of overload lay, not least because of the almost daily traumas of a linguistic imbecile making painful progress with Catalan and forever resorting to charades in an effort to be understood. It was a cast-iron recipe, if ever there was one, for a litany of sometimes alarming, sometimes farcical misunderstandings – like what will forever be known as the paella saga.

When new farmer friend Joaquim, who was selling us eggs before we got our own chickens, rang asking us all over to see his cattle and to have a spot of Spanish cuisine, I couldn't wait to tell Maggie.

'Do you mean his cattle sheds?'

'Yes, he definitely said the farm.'

'But his house is four miles away from the farm.'

'Well, he's always with the cattle and probably has some sort of kitchen there.'

'What time?'

3

'Saturday, about five, I think he said.'

'That doesn't sound right.'

'No, believe me, he definitely did say come for some paella. Brace yourself, though – it may include some of those plump snails we gathered on the veg patch and gave to him.' I explained that another new friend of ours, Marta, was invited too, then I bellowed up the stairs to Ella. 'Ella! Joaquim has invited us to eat with them on Saturday. Paella – but don't worry. I know you're not too keen on it – I think he said something about chicken too, though.'

Joaquim was all smiles as our car squelched to a halt in his cattle yard, and he beckoned us into the shed where all the senses except the taste buds went into overdrive. It was getting dark and the only half-decent shoes I owned were immediately swallowed up. He shouted '*palla*' and beckoned me to grab the other end of a bale of straw.

'P-pardon?' I asked as the colour drained from my cheeks.

'*Palla*!' he repeated, flashing his teeth. 'For your chickens.'

'Oh. Right. Er – *gracies*. Marvellous. Thank you very much.'

'When are we eating?' Ella asked Joaquim in perfect Catalan.

'*Qué?*'

'Ha ha! Just a little misunderstanding. Ella, be a darling and get in the car. Now.'

All I can say in my defence is that the Catalan words for straw and the famous Spanish rice, meat and seafood dish are remarkably similar. At least I picked up the word for chicken correctly.

You have to smile. What a berk. Yet despite all the trials, tribulations and cock-ups I'm about to relay, nearly three years on we're still here, doing it, living the life we talked about so much, in a place and at a pace we'd tried so hard to imagine but never got close. Time and time again since we moved lock, stock, springer spaniels and biscuit barrel from Britain we've been aware of how we turned our world upside down. But having done so, we've never been more conscious of every minute of our lives and those of our children which, basically, is the heart of the matter.

Our new home is called *L'Hort de la Mare*, which means Mother's Garden. It's scruffy but as solid as the seam of red rock on which it stands and we think it's utterly enchanting despite its many blemishes. So, it seems, does everyone who sees it. Both the farmhouse and terraced land need work – heaps of it – and beside the track an ugly broken-down cottage entangled with ivy tells us of other toils ahead. The main house, though, is dry and habitable, and, although the plaster is pitted and the brick floors are cracked, all we crave in practical terms is a bath instead of the shower.

The rendering on the outside walls is falling off too, but the mottled remains carry the glorious colours of countless seasons – a mellow Mediterranean mix of orange and yellow framing an ancient door beneath a weathered sundial.

We burn old hazel on the wood burner in the main downstairs room and on the open fire in the old kitchen, but for weeks after we arrived that first January we couldn't keep them going all night and the countless draughts meant we nearly froze. Joe slept in a bonnet and gloves and in the mornings the dogs left trails through the frozen grass as they bounded across the meadow. For more than a year all we had in the kitchen were a rusty little gas hob and an equally decrepit wall-mounted oven with a broken door that had to be wired shut. Both were here when we arrived and, because they worked and we were broke, we persevered with them until we salvaged a dirty but otherwise perfectly serviceable gas range from a derelict house in town. We cook on the open fire occasionally, too, and the outside bread oven works a treat for pizzas, fuelled by old vine cuttings that we also use to fire up the barbecue in the summer.

The lights dim when you plug anything in and we have to remember to switch on the pump once in a while to keep our water tank full. Our water comes from a well at the top of the land, while a ceaseless spring feeds our *balsa*, a huge circular reservoir which also serves as a swimming pool and is home to more than seventy goldfish, countless frogs and the occasional snake.

Mother's Garden is in a peaceful valley, a timeless landscape where the Romans once nurtured their precious vines and the prefects and merchants built their villas. It's also close to where the last battles of the Spanish Civil War were fought and the back wall of the farmhouse is scarred by bullet holes. To the east a mighty mountain range stands guard between us and the crowded coastline. Swarms of German cyclists whizz past occasionally, and we may see the odd touring car on our narrow, twisting road, but the Renault 4, beloved by rural Spaniards, still rules here. The bustle of the beaches and bars fifteen miles away has no bearing on this life. It might as well be a million miles away.

But although Mother's Garden may be off the beaten track, it's easy to find if you know a few local landmarks. We always advise family and friends that once they've reached the nearest town they should look for the road lined with plane trees that heads for the small mountain to the north which appears to be an almost perfect conical shape. The road will take you past the comfortably close Guardia Civil compound where you may glimpse a well-ironed national policeman in one of those distinctive black hats designed by someone keen on origami. It is one of the few places around here where you will see the Spanish (rather than Catalan) flag, in this case fluttering in glorious juxtaposition just a few feet in front of the flats where members of the force hang out their smalls and other washing.

Follow the road for a few kilometres as it twists through vineyards and olive groves, offering spectacular views of distant peaks. Take the right turn just before the ruined, centuries-old monastery that's now home to a flock of sheep. You can't miss it because the sheep dog often hangs its head out of one of the first-floor windows. Drop down the hill into the valley past the former bordello, taking care not to run over any bee-eaters. A huge flock of the colourful relation of the kingfisher spends part of the year in burrows in the bank halfway down the hill and these beautiful birds have a habit of congregating on the tarmac. It's also not a bad spot to catch a glimpse of golden oriels, hoopoes, kites and even the occasional short-toed or golden eagle.

At about this point you'll cross a stream and get a whiff of that distinctive Mediterranean sewer smell that can make the eyes water. You'll have realised by now that the twisty road is barely wide enough for two vehicles and has nasty gullies on either side. Resist the temptation to enjoy the glorious view of the pine-cloaked mountains. Don't be distracted by the shadow of an eagle overhead – and watch out for old men on tiny two-wheeled tractors towing trailers at a snail's pace, or foot-to-the-floor locals cornering their Renaults or Seats at a precarious angle. At the bottom of the hill the road slices through red rock and then bends sharply right where, on the apex, you run the risk of dislodging a pensioner who is invariably sitting at the corner of his impressively fertile and manicured vegetable plot. When you see a mass of green vegetation ahead of you (a mix of cane, fig and brambles) wind the window up because you are going to cross the stream again. Press on and in time you'll either glimpse the pig farm on your right or hear the howling guard dogs. Slow down. Bang opposite is a track – to Mother's Garden.

Some things are just like our old life in rural Norfolk; the fat rats walking past my traps and gobbling and weeing on our seed potatoes; the occasional scent of pigs; Robin red breast keeping us company in the garden; the gentle pace of life; the watercolour skies. But this is a different world.

Summoned reluctantly to expel a gecko lizard from our

bedroom, I climbed the stairs extolling their harmlessness and virtue as mosquito catchers: 'Now come along, they're our friends and there's absolutely nothing to be—BLOODY NORAH!'

I recoiled at the enormity of the boggy-eyed brute with a head the size of a peach stone and with sucker feet as large as twenty pence pieces. It was glued to the wall just next to the bed and didn't seem the least bit alarmed by us.

'Right, they're harmless, OK?' I said unconvincingly. 'They've had the place to themselves for quite a while and would you like it, Ella, if someone moved into your house?'

'It's horrible.'

'No, it isn't.'

'Yes, it is! It's like a little crocodile. I don't like it. Do something, Dad.'

I tried shooing it like you would a cat, but it just manoeuvred to get a better view of my antics. So I nudged it with a ruler until it got the message and it lumbered away eventually, shaking its head.

On Thursdays and Sundays during the autumn and winter season the guns of the wild boar hunters echo through the forest along the mountain ridge just half a mile from the farm. We've found old cartridges on our land and face the prospect one day of advising men armed to the teeth that they're not welcome here, but so far they've kept their distance. We heard one that first spring, letting rip in a neighbouring almond grove at a pigeon that seemed to appreciate he was a useless shot, and was flying backwards and forwards above him. I watched and waited for the hunter to drift our way, but he never did.

The dogs guarding the pig farm across the road have a habit of occasionally howling for a few minutes in the middle of the night when (we've laid in bed and speculated) a boar, a fox or another dog has disturbed them. It took some getting used to, and in the early months, if these choruses coincided with little Joe Joe waking to be fed, the dire consequences of sleep deprivation – fractiousness, uncertainty and anxiety – circled us like sharks. At least our springer spaniels, Charlie and Megan, never feel inclined to join the choir.

So, you see, those early morning compost bin deliberations were strangely vital, a chance during the heady first weeks and months to assimilate all that was happening to us. Breathing deeply I pondered a great deal about what our friends and family must be saying. I wondered too how inclined other people might be to veer off at such a tangent and give vent to idle dreams of selling up and drastically changing the way they work and live. And it was there, beside the vegetable patch, that I realised I should convert my daily notes (an old habit) into a candid and unavoidably comical chronicle of our experiences, both sweet and bitter, to offer not so much a guide on how to do it – the reverse if anything – but rather an honest account of one typical family's metamorphosis from middle England to another country, culture and way of looking at life.

That morning, after I'd liberally applied some compost

activator, I turned and smiled at the house which was being warmed by the first rays of sun. We'd been in Catalonia on our little farm from January to April 2001. The closed bedroom shutters told me that Maggie and Ella were still asleep, while Joe Joe, who I could see through the kitchen window, was in his high chair ploughing happily through a bowl of Rice Krispies and listening to the BBC World Service. It was unusual for Maggie to stay in bed. Her active mind wouldn't normally allow it, but occasionally exhaustion would overwhelm her. Once in a while we would all be up this early, making the most of the time, Maggie and I would eat and try to decide which of the host of jobs we should tackle next, while Ella swept in and out of the house between her fig tree swing and her breakfast. On other mornings, if the children were out for the count and we'd had an uninterrupted night's sleep, Maggie and I would tiptoe out and tackle some job or other before things got too hot, like gathering old hazel for winter fires or tugging at the wild oats and assorted weeds clogging the little vineyard which runs away from the house towards the mountain.

I'd repeatedly remind myself where I was a year before. In our Norfolk cottage, I reflected, at that time probably dragging myself out of bed after five hours' sleep looking like a stunt double for the Monster from the Blue Lagoon; hoping to spend a few precious minutes with four-year-old Ella, helping to get her dressed and fed and off to nursery before the dogs dragged me round a muddy field behind the house; sifting through the junk mail; maybe, if the sun broke through,

11

strolling instead of jogging to the village shop to get bread and bacon; phoning the office to check that the newspaper, the one I had put to bed in the early hours, had been printed and delivered on time; wishing for a few uninterrupted moments to sit with Maggie over a very late, lazy breakfast when I would scan the *Eastern Daily Press* for my blunders before preparing to leave for work in Norwich. The old and, in many ways, comfortable routine.

We would also have been looking forward to being parents again in just a few months' time. I would have been planning my trip to Mozambique to report on how donations to the newspaper were being used to help victims of the African flood disaster. Maggie and I would both have been coping in our own ways with the concept of another working day and night when I would be away for more than twelve hours. And we would have tried to find time to talk through new and old ideas on how we could change things.

We both knew something had to give.

At the beginning of 2000, after years of growing unease, both of us sensed the time had come to stop talking about changing our lives and to get on and do it. For more than a year we'd been seriously challenging our values, sitting up all hours questioning our priorities and looking for an answer to the realisation that we wanted more – more time with each other, more time with our children, more experiences, more sleep, more from life. If that meant less money and letting go of the structure and security of our organised lives then so be it. Ella was almost five and was about to start full-time school.

Maggie was expecting our second child in June. My work as deputy editor of the local daily paper, much as I enjoyed it, was taking its toll both on my health and the level of support I could give Maggie at home. There was only so long I was going to be able to keep working from 3 p.m. to 1 a.m. or occasionally 2 a.m., while the thought of Maggie coping at home alone with soon-to-be two youngsters every evening, instead of sharing the pleasures and pains with me, was proving intolerable for both of us.

I could have changed jobs. We could have bought a more modest home, but in the end we decided we didn't want to. It would have been a compromise. We'd painted a mental picture of a life of near self-sufficiency on a small farm and we weren't going to let go of it, only it was impossible to see where to start.

During that February and March I spent any spare moment I could find trawling the internet property websites for farms in France where, unlike much of England, we thought we could afford a modest property with a few acres. Going abroad wasn't a certainty by any means at that time, but we were fast abandoning hopes of following our dream in our home county of Norfolk where prices were growing like topsy as families from London, the Home Counties and Midlands descended in their droves looking for weekend retreats. It was hard to blame them. North Norfolk's charms are many, but like others who had grown up in the area we were anxious for the future of the rural communities that were losing shops and services at an alarming rate. The local property boom meant we were likely to get a good price for our home overlooking the cricket green in the award-winning village of Aldborough, but we were reluctant to sell Barley Cottage as a second home.

We'd come within a whisker of selling in the summer and autumn of 1999, but had to pull out of the deal as soon as we discovered Maggie was expecting our second child. It was a relief. At that time we had this vague plan to stay in north Norfolk and to try and find somewhere with a little land. We'd talked of moving abroad and opting for a very different life, but instead of grasping the nettle then we'd drifted on with the stupid notion that we could find somewhere at the right price close to home, somewhere with enough space to somehow, sometime, maybe never, change the way we lived.

It all seemed to be going so well for a while. The first people who saw Barley Cottage after we'd put in on the market in June 1999 said they wanted it but were in no hurry. Perfect. We could stay put until the autumn and in the meantime look for our dream Norfolk smallholding. The sale was likely to leave us with about £75,000, nowhere near enough to let us buy somewhere outright. So we considered various ways we could muster an income, either by me freelancing, or us developing the market research work Maggie had done for an old friend now living and working in Holland and looking to develop an organic dairy business in the UK. In hindsight our plans were all very sketchy and ill-conceived, but we were so desperate to find some way to get off the merry-go-round that we never really got down to brass tacks.

We started to look around at what we could afford in the

area, most of which was totally or nearly derelict. I rapidly started to lose focus on what we would cope with in terms of restoration, talking confidently of dealing swiftly with small matters such as septic tanks, re-roofing and rotten floor-boards, but we soon became alarmed and then depressed. Friends and family kept their eyes and ears open for us, but every time something came up people descended like locusts to look at it. Viewing invariably turned into a feeding frenzy with couples whispering in dusty corners or, in a bizarrely British way, carrying on as if no one else was there when in fact the rickety staircase was at risk of collapse from the number of people on it. Everyone would be on edge, except the bushy-tailed estate agent dusting off his pinstripe suit after brushing against a flaking wall and smiling to himself as he watched the pantomime unfold. The touted price was invari-ably never the selling price, with either sealed bids or those immortal words 'offers in excess of . . .' ratcheting up the stress and the final figure. We grew more and more frightened that we would lose out all round, having to leave our home and then being left with nowhere to go. If we didn't get it right we knew we would deeply regret uprooting Ella from her good school and ourselves from a village with so many qual-ities and so many people we liked.

Crazily we were drawn into a bidding battle for a beauti-fully restored house with a little land that we could neither resist nor afford. We saw it only days after it came on to the market and plunged in, desperately trying to raise the capital while conveniently overlooking the facts we risked bankruptcy

15

if the mortgage rate rose half a per cent, and that all our other plans for a less stressful more family-orientated life would disintegrate with me having to battle on at work 'for a few more years at least'. Four days after seeing the house we were told our offer, £15,000 over the asking price, had been matched by a cash buyer and we'd lost.

We considered countless other places. The last straw was a wreck of a small farm near our village in north Norfolk.

Maggie was expecting baby Joe by then. Although we'd pulled out of our sale we continued to hope that somehow, somewhere, there was a place with a little land with our names on it. Then, early in 2000, we heard through friends in the village that a nearby derelict farm might be up for sale soon. The location was wonderful – spitting distance from Ella's school and close to all our friends – and it had about four acres. The elderly woman owner who'd gone into a home had only just decided to sell but hadn't put it with an agent yet. We sensed we might have a chance, but by this time we were desperate and stupid. I approached the family and naively outlined our aspirations, praying that would work. Our idea was they would have it valued and we would buy it without it being put on the market. They kindly let us see it and we continued to dream about what we could do there despite a friendly surveyor's warning of extreme decay which turned out to be dry rot, wet rot, death watch beetle and structurally unsound walls. Thinking we were being realistic, we recognised that it was too big a project for us to cope with on our own, so we hatched a plot, joined forces with a good friend who shared our ambitions, and who was prepared to pool resources and approach the owner with an offer. Quite how we would have coped with the massive task of restoring the unsafe building and then living cheek by jowl with another family we'll never know. I suspect that sharing the farm with our friend and her three young daughters would have been fine, but the workload and unknown costs would have creased us. And, as with the other houses we'd pitched for, I'd have had to keep working in Norwich and that wasn't supposed to be part of the plan.

Things dragged on and on and we became more and more downhearted as the word got out that the farm would be up for sale soon. The vendor was sensibly advised to auction it and it became clear long before the sale that we were out of the ball game. Months later, after we had turned our minds to moving away, our friend went along to the auction and watched agog as the bidding rocketed past £300,000. She came back ashen faced and broke the news. We said: 'That's it. No more. We can't stay here. We're never going to be able to afford to live here and do what we want.'

In a way our failure to find somewhere local had all been a necessary evil, a series of crushing defeats to expel any doubts about leaving the area and the country. No one could say we didn't try.

There was not, I should add, any serious talk of moving up country or west to Wales, the only areas where we could possibly have afforded to realise our dream, because by the time our Norfolk hopes had been shattered the spell of the foreign adventure had been cast. Our families understood. We laugh about it now but it's true that, with the mass of holiday flights to the Spanish resorts, our nearest and dearest can get to us as quickly here as if we'd retreated to Scotland or Snowdonia, and they don't have to pack so many clothes.

We kept the whole plan secret for a long time, but when we bought the farm and I handed in my notice at work news travelled fast. People wanted to know where, when, how, but not many asked why. I suppose that on an idle thought level it seemed to make perfect sense, especially following the onset of the autumn gales and then the rigours of winter. Why not step off the hamster wheel in search of space, time and sunshine? People congratulated us without digging too deeply.

But some, especially our families, needed to know more, which presupposed that we knew ourselves exactly what we were getting into, which of course we couldn't. What drives us, we told them at the time, is a determination to change things, to heed our instincts and challenge the routine which allows only fleeting moments for family life.

We wanted to see if we could make it work. And the time felt right. Ella was at the best age to adapt and learn. Naturally, the children's wellbeing and happiness remain key issues, but they are gregarious, adventurous and full of fun. Thankfully Ella settled well into her school, community and life on a farm. (After three months she was speaking Catalan confidently. After six months she was fluent.)

Some people, no doubt, thought we were completely nuts and a few may have muttered 'mid-life crisis'. Others may have been inspired to consider upturning the applecart and set about planning a new life. Who knows?

Looking back, April and May 2000 were the defining months. We finally got off our bums and actually did something about trying to find a suitable farm in southwest France which, despite our laughable planning and wishful thinking, proved to be the first step along the path to Mother's Garden. It was then, too, that I went on an eleven-thousand-mile excursion for a timely kick up the pants.

April 2000

Long-haul night flights give me time to think. I've never been able to sleep on aeroplanes and gave up trying years ago, so as the KLM jumbo flew the length of Africa and most people throughout the darkened cabin draped themselves with blankets and tried to drift off, I sat forward and gazed out of the window beyond the winking light at the end of the wing. It was 2 a.m. Flight 594 was on schedule and we were crossing Zaire and the equator. The blackness that seemed eternal was suddenly broken by light. The blanket of cloud beneath us was alive with electricity, highlighted for split seconds as if by the flash of distant guns. It brought me back to what I was doing, where I was going. I'd been going over in my mind again and again what it would be like living on a small farm in France, growing organic crops and selling them on a market stall in the nearby town every Monday morning. Everyone knew I was going to Mozambique, but only our families knew that five days after I returned from Africa I was booked on another flight to visit a farm for sale in southern France.

We'd seen it advertised in the *Willing Workers on Organic Farms* newsletter and, having spoken to the vendors on the telephone, I'd spent two weeks trying to picture it and dreaming naively that we'd solved the puzzle of where our search for a new life would lead us. The speculating was over. Now we were hunting for property and this little farm, in the foothills of the Pyrenees, with an established market stall business, sounded perfect. At less than £50,000 we could afford it outright. Maggie and I could work together as we'd always imagined we would one day. The children would grow up on a farm. They would be at home in the great outdoors, learning about wildlife, speaking another language. It would be amazing.

The scene outside the cabin window interrupted my daydream. For all my travels and hours gazing out of aircraft I'd never seen anything like it. Thunderstorms, yes, but nothing so vast, so compelling and, on reflection, so relevant. Mozambique was only supposed to be a few days of my life but it was then that I started to sense the personal significance of my journey. Now, recounting it all, I know the experience had a profound effect on me, helping me deal with my doubts about letting go of routine and security and pressing on with my life and what we wanted to do – and that what I saw there will stay with me for my lifetime.

Up until the moment I noticed the storm crackling beneath me, my mind had been so full of our plans for a new life that I hadn't really got my head round what I, a rural British hack more accustomed to reporting on life in Norfolk, was letting myself in for.

It started when I was contacted by a local family living in Mozambique. Their story about the suffering in the wake of the appalling floods sparked an appeal that brought £40,000 in donations from *Eastern Daily Press* readers in a matter of weeks. It was then I knew I had to go. It would be an adventure, a great experience, but like the jumbo I'd been on autopilot. Then, that night seven miles high above Africa looking down on the lightning, it suddenly struck me what a troubled continent it was, a frightening place of seemingly endless insurrection, civil strife, shocking atrocities and natural calamities that flared like fires. One minute Mozambique could not have been further from my mind. The next it was crowding my senses and filling my shoes with sand.

John Randell, a customs officer from Caister near Yarmouth, met me at bullet-ridden Maputo airport. He was full of apologies.

'If I'd known you were booked on Smoky Joe I'd have tried to get you switched to another flight.'

Like a lemming I'd trooped onto the Mozambican flight at Johannesburg airport without thinking. It was only when the man sitting next to me couldn't get his seat out of the recline position that the age of the plane started to dawn on me.

'It's the world's oldest 737. Sorry,' said John, taking my holdall and ushering me out to his car.

John had been in Mozambique for two years working for the Crown Agents, trying to bring order and apply the local rule of law in a country crippled first by a prolonged and bloody civil war, then bankruptcy and finally flood. He told me to brace myself as we drove into the city, picking our way along the shattered tarmac and dirt tracks and weaving between people wandering in all directions. I wasn't sure if he meant the potholes or the culture shock.

The next day, after a fitful sleep under a mosquito net in John and Karen's guarded home – alarm buttons in all the rooms and bars at the window – they introduced me to Joe and Lorraine Williams who run a charity called Imagine. Then they all escorted me on a trip deep into the slums to meet young children with Aids who had nothing save a mat to sleep on and no prospect of reaching adulthood. On past travels I'd seen the poverty in Asia and reported on the illegal immigrants flooding from Mexico into America. I'd seen enough, I thought, to prepare me. But now I was getting a guided tour of reality in one of the poorest countries in the world and it thumped into my conscience like a sledgehammer.

Seven days later I was at thirty-five thousand feet again, rolling a cool can of orange juice between my hot palms and feeling as if my brain would pop. I looked a wreck and didn't smell too sweet, but KLM had kindly bounced me up to business class all the same and given me a vast seat and my own video entertainment system – two days after I'd ridden through the bush standing on the back of a sagging pick-up with ten refugees who'd woven me into their arms as we pitched along the track. I couldn't stomach the contrasts or the in-flight three-course meal and claret.

Amsterdam airport was where I came unstuck. I made it to the boarding gate for the Air UK flight to Norwich and then blanked out. My eyes were open, apparently, and I must have watched the rest of the people file through the door to the airport bus. They went, I didn't. I sat there like a plum pudding, listing slightly and with my gob open, staring inanely at the wall. By the time someone had nudged me and I'd managed to fire up what few brain cells were willing to spark after a week of virtually no sleep, and a serious overload of truth about our warped world, it was too late. I trudged off for another injection of caffeine, to try and get on to the next flight and to ring Maggie.

We've got to do this, I told her. Life is too short.

France Here We Come

mother's garden

May 2000

Carcassonne seemed hotter than Maputo. It was just six days since I'd returned from Africa. I'd dived straight back into the old routine, doing my usual night editor shifts at the office from Sunday to Thursday, getting home at 12.30 a.m. on the Friday morning, snatching a few hours in bed (but hardly sleeping) before rolling out at dawn to drive to Stansted airport and catching the flight to southern France. Everyone at work thought I was enjoying a quiet, long weekend at home with the family recuperating from my travels.

The inside of the French hire car was like an oven, and my knuckles were the only part of my anatomy that wasn't flame red as I steamed out of Carcassonne airport car park and proceeded to push the little Citroën to its limit along the motorway towards Toulouse and our dream home. I was running on adrenaline, chocolate and bottled water and talking to myself. But I had it all mapped out. It was midday on Friday 12 May, and there was the rest of that day, plus all of Saturday and Sunday morning, to check out the farm and organic vegetables business we'd seen advertised – and there would still be ample time to cruise around the local villages and towns weighing up schools, shops, and so on.

The shortest way from the airport to the farm, according to the map, was to head southwest into the lower folds of the Pyrenees, but the web of wiggly minor roads looked like a recipe for disaster and I risked getting hopelessly lost and having a nervous breakdown. I'd pored over the map during the flight and then (trying to kid myself I had the whole situation under control) had attempted to close my eyes and do some deep breathing while trying to block out all thoughts of taking the cross-country option. I knew only too well that no sooner had I got behind the wheel I would veer off into the maze and give it a whirl in one of those over-tired, hyperventilated acts of spontaneity that always lands me in the poo. 'Don't even think about it,' I kept saying as the jet started to descend and my heart rate began to rise. 'It'll all go horribly wrong if you do. Think logically. Think, you idiot, THINK.'

I figured the sensible but longer motorway route that looped north via Toulouse would, with a following wind and my foot to the floor, get me to the farm in the shortest possible time. The baking heat in the car was a help. I had to open the doors and windows and wait a few minutes before I could bear to get in and so used the time to walk to the car park exit where I spied a road sign for Toulouse.

'Right,' I said out loud, jogging back to the car, 'Let's burn rubber.'

As I flew along I was gripped by an extraordinary feeling of secrecy and euphoria. Very few people knew where I was, what I was doing and what we were planning. Then, as the sun-bleached countryside and tree-lined Canal du Midi – scene of a previous men-behaving-abominably boating trip – whizzed by, I remembered a 1989 holiday of wine and wind with old friends Kenwyn, Nick, Richard, Martin and long-suffering solo female Hilary which had been such light relief at a bleak time in my life. They invited me to join their trip just after my first marriage had disintegrated and I was sorely in need of humour. We'd chugged along the canal, zigzagging between the vine-yards, doing our damnedest to prop up the local economy. It was glorious, and my memories of the pastel shades and pas-toral pace of life in that area were easily revived when we saw the brief details for the farm in the *Willing Workers on Organic Farms* newsletter. The other crew members are fond of reminding me how, about halfway through the holiday, I was dispatched from some bar or other to check out the local railway service so we could visit the castle at Carcassonne, only to find the station bricked up. Apparently I'd burst back into the bar and much to the bewilderment of the locals had bellowed, '*La guerre est fini, donnez moi quelque chose à boire!*' (I'd meant to say, 'The station's shut, give me a drink,' but out came, 'The war's over, give me a drink!)

With the Citroën rattling along the fast lane I reckoned I could make the farm in about two hours – leaving a big lump of daylight for me to walk the seven acres, get a feel for the place and plan the best spots to tether the goats.

We'd talked endlessly about starting a new life in France, but were clueless. We'd borrowed an alarming book on the dos and don'ts of buying property, read articles about the bargains waiting to be snaffled up (for second homes mostly), and spent numbing hour upon hour surfing agents' sites on the internet. We'd printed off a mountain of details and dug out the battered old holiday maps in a bid to pinpoint where the seemingly more attractive properties within our vague £60,000 price limit were located. The basic and horribly vague plan was to find somewhere habitable with two or more acres and to have a few thousand pounds in reserve to keep us alive until we got established.

Once, about six months earlier, we'd been forced to share our secret with strangers at a dinner party thrown by close friends in whom we'd confided and who gleefully spilled the beans during dessert. 'Martin and Maggie are going to live in France!' I nearly choked, and then we had to sit there and be bombarded with questions we couldn't answer. I blushed and bullshitted and heard my mouth say something like, 'Oh yes, we know exactly what we want to do, it's just a case of finding the right place,' while my brain asked Where? When? How? The truth was we were going nowhere, save round in circles. We desperately needed a shove.

Then, at the end of March 2000, we'd waved off Maggie's

sister Sally, her partner Terry and their children Rosa, eight, and Leila, ten, as they headed for France and Spain to spend five months working on organic farms. They wanted a family adventure before Leila started senior school and so just went for it. They arranged to meet up with a friend in Paris for a few days before spending a couple of months helping on a farm near Bordeaux. They were then due to head to Spain to stay with friends who lived somewhere near Barcelona, and the last leg of their tour would take them to another organic farm in Galicia on Spain's Atlantic coast. It was agreed that all their mail would be redirected to us and that we'd sift out anything that looked important and ring them if necessary.

We watched enviously as they pulled their rucksacks out of the back of our car, waved and then trooped into Norwich railway station. Their trip wasn't exactly what we were ever likely to do, but there was no denying the twinge of envy. They were getting on with it, not just talking about it. We went home and talked some more.

Sally and Terry's *Willing Workers on Organic Farms* newsletter sat unopened on our kitchen table for several days, sticking out from beneath their ever-increasing pile of mail. We weren't planning to open it at all, but one day we decided they wouldn't mind if we had a browse while we downed our customary mid-morning coffee. We wanted to know more about how the organisation ticked and we were curious about the opportunity for free labour on our farm, wherever that turned out to be. We dipped in and out of a few articles and agreed that possibly, maybe, we'd subscribe. I'd moved on to that morning's newspaper and was wincing over a ghastly literal that I'd missed at work the night before when Maggie handed me the newsletter again. 'Look at that,' she said, tapping the page. It was the classified adverts section. I sat bolt upright. 'Gordon Bennett!'

I read out the details of the advertisement – an organic farm close to the Pyrenees with established weekly market stall in nearby town. Seven acres with stream. Owners looking to retire. £48,000.

'I'm going to ring. I've got to!' We grinned excitedly at each other and then I started to jump about, punching the air and yelling like someone who'd got his John Thomas caught in his flies. 'This could be it, Maggie, this could be exactly what we've been waiting for!'

Belting along the motorway towards Toulouse I felt so chuffed. It was four weeks since we'd seen the advert. I'd called and quizzed the owners immediately. They'd invited me to stay and I booked my flight to the south of France for the weekend after I got back from Mozambique. Despite falling down the steps of the plane when I got home from Africa, I'd managed, remarkably, to avoid fouling things up at work. The thing about newspapers is that if, at best, you make an arse of yourself, or, at worst, you let something through which could cost a packet in a libel action or your liberty, everyone sees it and it lives on forever in black and white. Alertness, dove-tailed with mild paranoia, is essential; a foggy head distracted with dreams of a new life is a calamity waiting to happen. I survived thanks in no small part to my colleagues on the night staff. I was determined not to do anything that could destabilise the situation in the office, or give the company any reason to doubt my commitment until we were much further down the road. Thinking back it was a truly freaky time for someone so set in his ways, so wedded to his work, so cautious about financial security, so suitable for the office tag of resident Norfolk fart who'd never leave.

With our second child due in four weeks there was no way Maggie could come with me to France, so I kept a wobbly video diary of my weekend, complete with a breathless and predominantly pointless commentary.

I could hardly contain myself when, after a trouble-free drive from Carcassonne, I found the small side road winding up the valley to the farm. I pulled over beside a narrow bridge that crossed a roaring mountain river complete with rock hopper birds and clear, inviting pools, and my video eulogy about the beauty of the place reached fever pitch. It must have been strange for Maggie when, three days later, she watched my film and heard me rattling on completely beside myself with excitement. She'd seen my face when I got home on the Sunday and told her the sorry tale. She already knew what came after the bridge.

The Citroën turned and twisted up the valley and, finally, ran out of road. The track was thick with mud after recent rain and the hire car slithered round several bends before I reached what I realised must be the drive to the farm. The owner had warned me that the steep drive wasn't suitable for cars. He wasn't kidding. It looked impossible. I pushed on round the next bend and found a place to pull off the track beside a path that seemed to lead in the direction of the unseen house masked by vegetation and high on the side of the valley above me.

The next twenty-four hours were incredibly tough, starting with the gasping climb up the path to the house with my overnight bag and rucksack and then having to mask my utter despair from the welcoming owners. I'd blown a couple of hundred quid we could ill afford on a pointless, stupid exercise which (had I shown an ounce of sense and asked them to send us some photographs after we'd seen their advert) could have been avoided. I felt so stupid.

Oh, it was a pretty place, a sort of half-timbered Alpine design, quite small with an outside staircase leading to the bedrooms and bathroom and with lovely views across the valley. But I knew before I reached the door it was impossible – it was far too remote and too extreme, and it was a world away from the spacious French stone farmhouse in my mind's eye. After months of scrolling through internet adverts I'd convinced myself what it would look like, how it would be. On reflection the owners had been utterly truthful about the practicalities, but I'd failed to absorb them or to press them to be more specific, preferring instead to enthuse with Maggie about the combination of so much land, a house and an established organic veg market stall – all for just under £50,000.

I suppose I should have made my apologies there and then and turned tail. But I'd nothing else lined up. I stiffened the upper lip and became a one-day willing worker on an organic farm, trying to salvage what I could by learning something about growing crops in a different climate and running a market stall. I also needed to complete my video diary for Maggie. Having got her blessing to leave her again just weeks before the baby was due and hare off to France to buy a farm, I now had to show why I hadn't. By this time the commentary had dropped to a miserable whisper.

The recent rain had turned the paths into mudslides and getting anywhere on the steep hillside was tough going. The rolling pasture on the far side of the valley had a lush *Sound of Music* quality about it, but the farm was mostly cloaked by thick undergrowth. There was a gorge to the left of the house and the land behind it continued to rise at an alarming rate. Even the best field was at a challenging angle and however hard I tried I couldn't see us coping in the same way the owners seemed to. I daren't think about the scrapes Ella would get into. I lay awake that Friday night listening to something gnawing on wood above my head and trying to come to terms with their wholly different way of living, which included a chicken nesting in the laundry basket outside the bathroom and a procession of 'willing workers' for whom the owners happily gave up their beds and provided food and wine in return for free labour. This open-house style made up for the remoteness, bringing a variety of people to the farm, but I just couldn't see us doing it. Not there. Not like that.

By the Saturday lunchtime the owners had twigged me and took pity rather than umbrage. They very kindly called the agent who had their farm on her books and arranged for me to see her at her office some sixty kilometres northeast so I could check out other smallholdings for sale in the wider area.

With a jar of their knockout chutney in my bag I skidded off back down the track and gave the Citroën another good thrashing, thinking I was still in with a half-chance of finding somewhere. That afternoon I sat in the agent's office leafing through her files and picked out two farms in the £50,000–60,000 price bracket that were more in keeping with my mental picture of how it should be. They were both big, traditional French farmhouses with a few acres, set in a far gentler landscape further north from the mountains. The buildings needed serious work, but I was assured they were dry and had electricity. Then, just as I was about to leave, I also pulled out the details of a very small derelict farmhouse with an acre and a half which, I noted, was not too far from one of the properties I'd already opted to look at. The price – circa £27,000 – leapt out at me and although we'd agreed we needed somewhere habitable I decided I'd drive by and take a gander, if I could get round before the sun went down.

I was persisting with the camcorder and by this time my commentary was becoming increasingly manic.

'Don't worry, gal – I've still some time,' I gabbled as I panned the camera across the uninviting facade of the first farm that was in the middle of nowhere. 'Who knows, I might strike lucky. The money's not wasted. At very least I'm getting a feel for the area and know a bit more now about how the market works. Right – the clock's ticking – must keep moving.'

In reality I knew virtually nothing and in my panic I was gleaning precious little. I was, by anyone's judgement, giving an award-winning masterclass in how not to buy a property abroad. Before I left England I'd broken a golden rule and failed to research or to arrange to see a selection of properties. I was only charging about the Garonne like a man possessed because it happened to be close to the farm I'd flown out on impulse to view. I knew bugger all about the area or its qualifications as a suitable place to set down roots. And I was still clinging to the daft notion that I had to come up with something before I went home.

After getting lost I eventually found the second farm, only to stand and stare and struggle in vain to picture us living there. I couldn't. It was right on a crossroads and close to a strangely menacing wood.

That's it, I thought. I've blown it. By this time it was Saturday evening and the light was fading. All the property agents would have shut up shop until Monday. Slumped against the mud-splattered hire car I took several deep breaths and looked out across the rolling, peaceful countryside, then reached through the open window and pulled out the details of the little derelict farmhouse. I checked the route again on the map the agent had given me. It was only about five kilometres away.

'Might as well have a look, Kirbs,' I urged myself. 'Damn all else to do.'

I reached the village easily enough but couldn't find the house at first and was on the point of giving up when a lovely elderly couple drinking coffee in their garden kindly untangled my French and pointed me back the way I'd come. The entrance was narrow and cut into an embankment and I couldn't see the building from the road. It was not until I was unravelling the barbed wire weaved across the top of the gate that my pulse started to up the tempo again.

The setting was stunning – within the sound of the village church bells and with incredible hilltop vistas east and west across the patchwork of fields and trees. The house was dinky and long deserted but, boy, it had colossal potential (I kept thinking as I patted the fat walls and timbers). It had only five rooms in all – four on the ground level and one above reached by a rickety ladder – but there was space to build out on the south end. The floor in the main room was rotting away, the chimney breast looked as if it was about to collapse, and there was no evidence of a kitchen or bathroom. But at £27,000 I figured we could afford to transform it.

There were other attributes. The building and garden were surrounded by a springer spaniel-proof, shoulder high, wire mesh fence with concrete posts. It was on the edge of a village, not in the back of beyond, and all that overlooked it was the church steeple that jutted out from a cloud of green oaks. There was a vegetable patch beside which a wooden gate led to a magical one-acre meadow with a lone apple tree on the brow of the hill. I sat and leant against the tree, watched the sun go down and listened to the bells chime through an hour. Having walked around it again and again, shooting it from every angle with both the video and 35mm cameras, my gut told me I might well have tripped over the jackpot. I tried to make myself work calmly through the things we would have to do – septic tank, damp-proof course, timber treatment, rewiring, plumbing, not to mention new floors, stairs, kitchen and bathroom. It would need to be taken back to bare walls and earth floors, but at £27,000 we would have £30,000ish to spend on making it a home. We'd have to live in a caravan in the garden while the house was transformed, which would mean we could oversee the work and get stuck in to keep costs down. The unpalatable alternative was to buy it but plough on in Norfolk until it was restored. That would mean a further delay, more stress. There were rows of hurdles to clear, but, sitting in a stupor under the apple tree, I still came to the conclusion it was worth chasing, just so long as Maggie agreed there was enough land for her vegetable and livestock plans and that the school and community pieces of the jigsaw fitted into place.

Before crawling off in search of a hotel shower and bed, I wandered back across the road to the elderly couple and managed, eventually, to make them understand that the francs I was offering them were to use their phone to call my wife. 'Do you like the little house?' they asked with smiling eyes. Yes, I said, very much. They wanted to know if we had children. They told me there were several families with youngsters Ella's age. I asked about schools and they told me the bus stopped opposite the drive to the house. The school was four kilometres away in a nearby town which had everything anyone could need. I was exhausted, relieved and near to tears. And there was by now a rosy tint to the sunset.

June 2000

Ever since I'd returned from Mozambique it was in my mind to suggest the name Joseph if we had a baby boy, after Joe Williams the charity worker I'd met there. When I discussed it with Maggie we remembered another Joe we loved and admired – Joe Cliffe, a dear friend's father, a gentle Yorkshireman from Huddersfield who died in 1998. We agreed. If we had a boy he would be Joseph David Thomas. David was Maggie's father's name, Thomas was grandfather Kirby. Funnily we never got to grips with girl's names.

The month of June has been good to us. Ella was due on the nineteenth, but arrived on the eleventh. Joe Joe was expected on the seventeenth and made his appearance on the eighteenth – Father's Day (and both births suspiciously nine months after my September birthday). As we waited those last weeks, retrieving the cot from the garage and feathering the nest, I mounted a montage of my photographs of the derelict French farm on a board which we propped up on the kitchen table. We talked endlessly about the baby, about the little house on the hill and about how Ella and her new brother or sister would find life in rural France. We tried to learn from our earlier mistake and took advantage of this quiet time to do a bit more homework, looking on the internet for other properties we could check out in the area on the next visit go give us options. We researched the Garonne region and discovered it was indeed an affordable, attractive target area which, appealingly, was five hours or less away from the mountains, Spain and either the Atlantic or Mediterranean. We even checked out flights for a July sortie, assuming all turned out fine and the new baby and Maggie were fit and well enough to travel.

And we had Barley Cottage valued ready for sale. Thinking back it might seem crazy to discuss uprooting the family at a time like that, but we both felt it was the right time. We were adamant that we didn't want to continue in the same vein, with me trawling off to work after lunch every day leaving Maggie to cope with two young children every night, and each of us having to settle for goodnight kisses over the phone – and we were both fired by the notion of not fudging the issue by just changing jobs, but grasping the nettle and trying to find exactly what we wanted. In those first three weeks of June the atmosphere in the cottage was charged with quiet optimism, and family and friends who called in during those buoyant days before the birth were shocked and intrigued to see evidence that we might actually be serious about leaving.

Little Joe's arrival proved as eventful as Ella's, but, as is often the way, for completely different reasons.

In 1995 Ella took a whole week to make an appearance from start to finish. A planned home birth on the Monday (when we got as far as towels, hot water and warmed-up midwives with their sleeves rolled up) turned into a Saturday night sprint to the Norfolk and Norwich Hospital and an emergency Caesarean on the Sunday morning. Ella was blessed with my broad skull and, basically, got stuck. By the end of a week of clock-watching, sleepless nights, hot baths and bumpy car rides (someone had suggested this might get things moving) Maggie was so exhausted she was barely able to stay awake. Thankfully, a colleague, Dick Watts, a proud father of twins, had told me that if push came to shove and the medics insisted it would have to be a Caesarean we should opt for local rather than general anaesthetic. We owe Dick a great deal. After such a traumatic time it would have been easy to say 'general' to give Maggie some respite. Instead she was conscious and elated as Ella was handed to me and I laid her by her mother's beaming face. We figured it had to be close to the record for a start-stop-start labour.

Second time around I was ready. So was Maggie. The experience with Ella had all the doctors twitchy about any talk of a home birth, and we conceded (finally) that we'd have to go to hospital so they could standby with all the bells and whistles should there be a repeat performance. But Maggie conceded nothing else. She was determined to take control.

I reached for my old stopwatch at just after 6 a.m. on Sunday, 11 June, when Maggie called through from the bathroom that her waters had broken. 'No worries,' I called back, having a stab at sounding calm and collected while pulling on my clothes. 'Tell me when you get a contraction.'

It came three minutes later. An aberration, I told myself. The next one will be longer. Three minutes. I've never dialled a number so quickly in my life. The nurse at the Norfolk and Norwich was relaxed but not very comforting. 'How frequently? Waters broken you say? Right – get her here now.

You should make it.' Should? I checked the timing of the next contraction. By this time Maggie was crying out like we wouldn't make it to the back door. I rang Anne, a neighbour, and she tore round a couple of minutes later to look after Ella just as I was about to guide Maggie out to the car.

'How are you feeling?' I stupidly asked as I crashed the gears. I wanted Maggie, who had reclined the passenger seat and was panting, to reassure me everything was under control down there.

'Just hurry up! HURRY! Can't youooo . . . go any faster?'

I wound our old Mercedes up along the deserted Aylsham bypass and prayed that with 190,000 miles on the clock it wouldn't decide today was the day to retaliate for neglect. 'It's Sunday morning, Maggie. Don't worry, the roads will be clear – we will have a clear run. It should take half an hour tops.'

The cows were ten deep across the road. They must have been like that for ages because there was a long queue of cars waiting for them to clear. Maggie bellowed, 'Overtake them! Overtake them! Go to the front of the queue for God's sake!' I did as she demanded, pointing frantically at the huge stomach which was all that was visible to the other motorists, and mouthing BAY-BEE repeatedly while trying to slow down before I ploughed into the herd. The cowman didn't seem to be getting the message and when finally the last animal had sauntered off the highway Maggie broke her concentration for a second to pull herself up on to her elbows and question his parenthood.

I confess to breaking the speed limit through the city to the hospital and I hopped one red light. We screeched to a halt in the car park beside the high-rise maternity block only to see nurses rushing to another car that had just pulled in. We could hear the cry of a newborn baby.

'Now everything's going to be fine, Margaret,' we heard a nurse tell the woman who had just given birth (on the Dereham bypass we later discovered). 'Your last delivery was by Caesarean wasn't it?'

'No,' replied the woman.

I stood in the lobby propping up Maggie and calling for a wheelchair. When one of the two lifts finally came more medical staff piled out of the lift and ran past us saying we couldn't use it, as they needed it for a woman who had just had a baby in a car. I got as far as 'Yes, only—' but they were gone. After we finally made it to the delivery room on the sixth floor I scuttled back to the car to get our portable CD player and the soothing birthing music we had bought on Cromer market, along with an enormous picture of a blooming dahlia. The music worked. The tempo dropped briefly then Maggie moved into overdrive and little Joe Joe was born a couple of hours later. Maggie's mum Beryl, a retired nurse and health visitor, was there too, just as she'd been in the operating theatre for Ella's dramatic birth. But this time there was no medical emergency, no intervention, no pain relief, nothing save Maggie's iron will to do it all herself, including delivering the placenta unaided. Wow. It is hard to think of a better advertisement for yoga.

Maggie fed Joe Joe, had a drink, was stitched, rested for a

while, tried to get up and promptly fainted. The first serious contribution I made since we reached the hospital was to catch her. Her iron will had seriously sapped the iron levels in her blood. They kept her in overnight, which didn't please her, but the protests were short. She had achieved her goal and we three were now four.

Spanish Destiny

mother's garden

July 2000

'I'm very sorry about the delay,' said the pilot, 'but I'm afraid the aircraft thinks it's in Stansted.'

We'd been sitting on the tarmac at Norwich airport for nearly an hour and mumblings among the passengers were developing rapidly into loud grumbles. Then the pilot attempted to explain our predicament.

'We've been talking to our engineers and we'll be on our way as soon as we possibly can – once the navigation system registers that we are flying to Gerona from Norwich and not Stansted. Rest assured we are doing all we can to get this problem sorted out. Please bear with us.'

There were scores of families with children on the crowded jet and noise and temperature levels were rising. The stewardesses were exchanging furtive 'oh-eck' glances. Maggie and I looked at each other and blew out our cheeks. Four-week-old Joe Joe was nuzzled to Maggie's breast and Ella was drawing pictures and humming to herself. She was coping far better with the inertia than her parents who kept thinking about the late-night drive they faced at the other end – if we ever got there. The last-minute, dirt-cheap tickets to northern Spain on the holiday charter flight had seemed too good to be true. I'd seen it advertised in the newspaper and once Joe Joe had popped into our world and we'd satisfied ourselves as far as we could that both he and Maggie were well enough to travel, we'd bagged almost the last seats.

We intended to spend the week trawling round the south-west of France visiting the derelict farm I'd found and checking out other properties for sale, with excursions to swimming pools and beaches to keep Ella happy. But once we discovered we could fly from Norwich to Gerona in northeast Spain we changed our plans. The flight would deposit us just an hour from the French border but also not a million miles from where Maggie's sister Sally and her family were staying in southern Catalonia during their five months away. Once we'd fathomed out exactly where they were and that it was within striking distance, we agreed we would head south first, spend a couple of nights with them and then drive north over the Pyrenees into France. The detour would take valuable time out of our schedule, but it was irresistible. We were missing Sally, Terry, Leila and Rosa and it would be good to see their close friends Mac and

Conxita (pronounced Conchita) who had called to see us in Norfolk two years before.

The fact that we were flying from Norwich – just thirty minutes from home – would, we'd figured, save us from a huge slice of stress and made the concept of carting a newborn baby and a livewire five-year-old on such a testing journey a little more tolerable for us all – and the concerned grandparents. Maggie was a beacon of calm assurance, but it was also highly questionable that she should put herself through it (and I should let her) just days after she had given birth. Her iron levels were back on an even keel, but by rights she should have been at home being fussed over by her mum as she physiologically, psychologically and emotionally came to terms with our newborn.

But that was the whole point. Maggie was determined to act on her instincts and find a way to change our lives as soon as humanly possible. The last thing she wanted to do was to wave me off to work then sit at home and contemplate months, possibly years, of surviving most evenings on her own with two young children. In those first four weeks of Joe Joe's life we learned what we had long suspected – that neither of us would cope well with the pattern of life as we'd known it. The consequences of dithering any longer or putting the whole idea on ice could have been hugely damaging while the journey, the act of doing something, seemed imperative. And there was something else, something which is difficult to explain. We both had a strong sense that it was profoundly *the right thing to do* and that something amazing was happening to us. There was a powerful accord – a shared, overwhelming sensation of change, and that we would eventually find what we were looking for if we remained optimistic and open-minded and pressed on. Someone described it later as an extraordinary leap of faith.

The longer the jet sat on the tarmac and the longer we all sat like stuffed turkeys, the more the nerves of the assembled started to fray. We knew that as soon as our kids had had enough, things would rapidly turn pear-shaped. And we had a sinking feeling they were going to have to unload our pushchair and assorted paraphernalia and we would end up with a harrowing, time-consuming coach trip to Stansted airport with our plans in tatters.

Then the pilot came on again, still unruffled but now with a smile in his voice. 'We've been advised by our computer experts to try switching the power off and on again.' There was a cry of 'Hurray!' from one passenger and nervous laughter. 'This means we'll have to shut down all the systems on the aircraft and the lights will go out for a moment.'

Minutes later, after the disconcerting experience of sitting on a crowded, darkened jet and trying to reassure Ella there was nothing whatsoever to worry about, we were bowling down the runway, an hour-and-a-half behind schedule and praying that the Boeing 757 had indeed got a grip on itself. From there on everything was as smooth as Joe Joe's bottom. Both he and Ella were exemplary travellers, and the evening warmth and mellow twilight that greeted us at Gerona airport were dream-like. Loaded to the gunnels with a knee-buckling and embarrassing amount of hand luggage, we were the last down the aircraft steps. We took Ella's photograph in front of the plane, I gave the pilot a grateful wave and we went in search of our luggage and hire car hoping it had a big enough boot.

While I was suffering heart palpitations at the hire car desk (they wouldn't accept my credit card at first) Maggie went to find a telephone to let Sally know we were off schedule but had made it to Spain. She also double-checked our route with Mac and he told us to give them a ring when we got to their mountain village. By this time it was about 8.30 p.m. He reckoned we wouldn't be with them before midnight at the very earliest once we'd followed the motorway past Barcelona then wound our way up the valley from the coast.

The children slept as we spun south. The journey went well. We made excellent time and turned into the quaint village square at 11.25 p.m. after being lost briefly in the maze of narrow streets. The air was still and hot, and small children were charging about in the open space under the magnolia lamplight. The adults who were sitting on the wall watching over them stopped chatting to look at the strangers pulling up beside the telephone box. Feeling mightily conspicuous we stood and stretched, trying to get the circulation back into our legs and bums before jamming ourselves into the box to make the call. Ella stirred, clambered out of the back of the car and wandered to the edge of the square to stare like a statue at the other children who, unbeknown to us all, would soon become her classmates.

Fifteen minutes later we were hanging on for dear life in Mac's old Land Rover as it pushed past bamboo and brambles and pitched up the mile-long track up to his house. We'd left the hire car in the village and in the blackness we didn't have a clue where we were being taken. Nieces Rosa and Leila had come with Mac to pick us up and to meet their new cousin Joe Joe who, bundled up on his mother's lap, seemed unperturbed by the very bumpy final leg of that day's journey. There were hugs all round at the house and, after he'd met everyone, Joe Joe was fed again and put to bed on a pillow in a large wicker basket lined with a soft cotton blanket, while Ella settled on a mattress alongside Leila and Rosa in their room. Mac and Conxita insisted we have their bed and, after our protests fell on deaf ears, we collapsed on to it and pulled the sheet over us.

Joe Joe sounded the reveille at about 6 a.m. We quickly cuddled him to stop him waking the house, then opened the shutters and stared out in awe. We'd sensed from the rocky Land Rover ride that we must be high up, but now we knew. We could see forever. Mountain ranges rose one behind the other, each softened a little more by distance until they merged with the pastel sky. In front of them the higgledy piggledy roofs of the village huddled round the church bell tower, all in the lee of a conical crag dressed in forest firs except for three elegant Cyprus trees beside a house built on a step just beneath the summit. The folds of sun-baked land below us were crisscrossed with terraces and patterned with the stone walls, winding tracks and the greens of what we later discovered were vines, olives, hazels and almonds. It was breathtaking.

I looked out onto Mac and Conxita's solar panels and contemplated their life so far off the beaten track. Is this what we want, I asked myself. It was only five hours' drive away from where we were looking in France, but it was completely different, far more extreme. We hadn't really discussed Spain as an option. A few weeks earlier Sally had sent us a couple of pictures of a ten-acre farm for sale just across the valley. She and Terry thought we might be interested and said we should view it, but from the pictures it looked arid and remote, crowded by forest and in no way as appealing as your average rural French property. Besides, it was £40,000 beyond our budget. We'd dismissed it. But what if we could find somewhere like Mac and Conxita's? Don't even get started, I told myself. France was the target. This was just a detour to see the family. That's all, just a couple of days break before the serious business north of the Pyrenees.

Over breakfast Mac told us to go steady with the water as there'd been no rain for months and the situation was getting desperate. I thought about admitting to flushing the loo twice already that morning, but decided against it. Sally and Terry mentioned again the farm that was for sale. They'd looked at it and had arranged for the owners to show us around that morning. Mac was keen on it too – 'It has two major attributes, loads of shade and water' – and we agreed it would at least be interesting to compare prices with France. They'd set up viewings at two other smaller farms as well.

First port of call was an old and quite pretty two-up, two-down house surrounded by tall hazel bushes at the bottom of the valley. It was close to the dried-up riverbed, and overshadowed by the tree-lined mountain ridge. In the corner of the kitchen there was an open well complete with frightening black hole, bucket and rope. A thick coat of dust on the windows cut the amount of light, but we could see enough to know it had been deserted for years. Several lizards bolted for cover when we opened the shutters in the main upstairs room and the walls and doors were patterned with flaking paint. It was for sale for about £25,000, along with a couple of acres of land.

Interesting, but we dismissed it as too small, too hemmed in and too much for us to get our heads round. Terry liked it, but we said the derelict French farm by comparison seemed better value and was in a much better setting.

Next stop the ten-acre farm.

We trundled back up the track to the road and turned right. The road started to rise gently and passed through a cut in the red soil and rock where small clumps of wild rosemary and other plants clung tenaciously to the vertical sides. When we emerged at the far end Terry pointed across a parched meadow to a derelict building that looked worse than the one we'd just left. But we knew from the photograph they'd sent us that this wasn't it. 'That's part of the farm – this bit of meadow too – but the main house is just behind it. See?'

Jutting out from above a bunch of billowing fig and walnut trees we could just make out the rise and fall of the roof and catch glimpses of sandy-coloured walls through the green leaves. The hire car bumped off the road again, brushed past some olive trees and scraped across a seam of rock that bulged in the track just before the final rise to the house. The sun was high and the air was still as we pulled up in the dappled shade of one of the trees and got out.

Mother's Garden blew us away.

The whole setting – the house with attached red stone barn, the overgrown terraces, the vistas and the lush vines running away beyond the fig trees – was unbelievably beautiful. There were holes and cracks in the rendering, small patches of dull, grey cement slapped on here and there and evidence enough that it was in need of love. But despite the blemishes it was enchanting. It had symmetrical three-storey towers at either end, mottled walls the colour of the bleached earth, and a sundial at the centre above two balconies which the vine above the front door was straining to reach. I remember thinking, 'Come on concentrate, boy. This is amazing, yes, but look for problems, look for problems. Anyway, you can't afford it. It's nearly £100,000. YOU CAN'T AFFORD IT.'

I repeated this mantra countless times as the elderly owners, Enric and Nuria, spent an hour and a half showing us round the house, walking the land and telling us it was derelict when they bought it twelve years before. For all their love and care the place still looked battered and bruised. Inside, some of the walls were scarred and flaking, floor bricks were broken and wiring sockets were hanging out of the wall. The older window frames carried the scars of woodworm and rot.

But it's habitable, said my heart. It's got four bedrooms, a shower room, an open fire and two wood burners, water pumped from a well, electricity, and a bloody great barn. Part of the roof has been replaced. There is a huge water reservoir, a cottage you can rebuild, not to mention healthy vines and almonds and olives. How many olives did he say? A hundred and thirty? How many vines? More than seven hundred? And what about the space round the house – the barbecue, the bread oven? Come on! COME ON!

That afternoon, evening and most of the night we talked about Mother's Garden, trying to imagine what it would be like if – a big if – we found ourselves living somewhere as incredible as that. We played with the idea of how we might survive, what our budget would be, where Ella would go to school, what the pattern of our lives would become, dreaming as we had done so often before after seeing farms and cottages in Norfolk which in truth were beyond our reach but which for a heady few days so fired the imagination that the dark realities were forgotten.

After leaving the farm we went on to another dilapidated *finca* that was half the size and half the price and had none of the same charm or outlook.

Sally had taken the children to the village swimming pool while we went to the bar before we all met up again to have lunch in the restaurant overlooking the square. By this time Maggie and I were soaking up every detail of the place, checking out the school, the grocers, the bakery and the swings and seesaws shaded by eight plane trees beside the ages-old and now peaceful spring-fed washing pools that resembled a Roman bath, and where it wasn't difficult to imagine the chatter and the clothes being slapped onto stone.

Just up the hill we couldn't help but notice graffiti on the white wall beside the school entrance proclaiming in huge blue letters: UNILAND CEMENTERA NO PEDRERA BURGUERA! As fate would have it there was nobody about to offer a translation and we quickly forgot all about it. It was only after we'd been living in Catalonia for a couple of months that I fathomed it out and had a panic, tearing about seeking reassurance from anyone in authority that our new life wasn't about to fall apart. It seems a quarry company wanted to carve into the side of our beautiful valley, near enough to the farm to ensure a constant din, a procession of lorries and a disgusting film of dust on everything. It didn't bear thinking about. But I was told the plan had caused a furore in the area and been thrown out some months before we signed on the dotted line. To say we were relieved is a gross understatement. We were also told it was never likely to surface again because a major wine producer had subsequently bought a huge swathe of land across the valley and planted tens of thousands of vines. I say fate played a part because, had I grasped or been told the meaning of the graffiti and its potentially enormous implications for our new lives during that first wide-eyed wander through the village in July 2000, it's quite likely we'd have dithered and missed our chance or been too scared to even think about buying Mother's Garden.

In the restaurant we gabbled away about what a complete community the hilltop village appeared to be. As well as the newly built junior school (where Leila and Rosa had joined the twenty-four pupils for a couple of weeks) and the pool, bar and restaurant, the village also had a football pitch, a hairdressers, a hardware store and a bakery, all sprinkled among the narrow streets and watched over by the church tower whose bell rang out every quarter of the hour.

If it feels right you should go for it, Sally and Terry said. Yes, it felt right, we said, quaffing the local wine and feeling giddy. But could we dare to think it was possible? That evening, when teacher Pere and his wife Nuria joined us all for supper, Mac and Conxita kept up the pressure, stressing how they as locals could sense the magic and see the possibilities of Mother's Garden, adding they would do all they could to help us. Pere and Nuria, who lived next door to Mother's Garden, nodded in agreement.

We were due to leave for France early the next day, but we stalled until lunchtime. After breakfast we left the children and grabbed the chance to go back and have another look at Mother's Garden. Sally came with us. The farmhouse was all bolted up, of course, but we had time to wander quietly at our own pace through the trees and lower vineyard and to sit beside the *balsa* and look for flaws in the walls and in our daydream. More than half the land was overgrown and the paths were lost in undergrowth that scratched our shins and ankles. It looked as if great lumps of rendering were about to fall off the back wall, but we could see where the roof had been replaced. All in all it seemed the perfect place – fundamentally sound with heaps of character and potential in a breathtaking setting. Furthermore, it was close to a seemingly strong community and to people we knew. Sitting there we found the colours, the scenery and the peace intoxicating.

But how the hell could we seriously consider it when the price would almost break us? How badly were we being bewitched by romantic notions?

The next four days were spent in France as planned. We headed due north through the middle of the Pyrenees, staying the first night near the border in a cheap and cheerful and decidedly quiet hotel with quaint shutters and wooden walls that was clearly just ticking over until the skiing hordes descended again in December. After seeing the unsmiling man behind the counter stroll out of the kitchen with a fag in his mouth we skipped breakfast and stopped for coffee and doughnuts in a village a few miles into France before setting course for the Garonne region and the little derelict farm I'd enthused so much about at the end of my May video diary.

We walked gingerly over the rotten floor, risked a rickety ladder to peruse the roof space where our bedroom might be, slapped the beams and soaked up the panoramic views of rolling green meadows and clouds of woodland, worked out where our caravan home could be parked while the wholesale restoration of the house was underway and then picnicked in the garden. Maggie could understand why I'd been so keen for her to see it. The vistas alone made it appealing and plausible. The house was very small, but could be extended. It could be charming. The one and a half acres was probably not enough in the long run, but neighbouring meadows seemed abandoned and maybe we could acquire them in the future after we'd got the house and existing vegetable patch up and running.

Compared to Mother's Garden it was a wholly different kettle of fish save one thing, the location. Both were in idyllic settings, but now we were looking at somewhere far more modest and (crucially) affordable if we could keep the rebuilding under £30,000. We could develop it as we wanted, but with it came the unchartered waters of prolonged life in a caravan and the stresses of trying to organise and negotiate with local craftsmen and the mayor's office. My French could hold up to run-of-the-mill chatter but was likely to come a cropper in the quicksand of Gallic bureaucracy. We couldn't be sure how much or how long the work on the house would be or would take, what restrictions might be placed on development or what extra land we could acquire, and as we talked about the various imponderables we kept thinking about Mother's Garden and how right it had felt.

But we still had three days in France, and we agreed we should press on and see the property agents, check out the area and basically wise up. I'd taken into my confidence two colleagues who'd bought a house in France and they'd lent me a sobering book on the dos, don'ts and daunting challenges before my insane three-day farm-hunting trip to the south of

France two months before. All the same, our knowledge of the market was ridiculously sparse and we didn't feel we could make an informed judgement until we had some miles under our belt and a wad of discarded property details scattered through the hire car. We both sensed that it was going to take a remarkable farm to dislodge the Mother's Garden seed that was growing like crazy in our heads, but at the very least we needed something to measure it against.

After leaving the dilapidated French farm we drove through the tiny village that appeared to have a community centre of sorts but no shops, and then headed off to the agents. By the time we emerged from the office we had been fazed by a pile of files featuring scores of houses and farms for sale, had picked out a handful to see and had been told about a good place to stay where small children were welcome.

We spent the next two days getting a feel for the area, driving past several properties but not bothering to see inside, and enjoying a very colourful, noisy and boozy festival in the town where Ella would go to school if we bought the hilltop farm. The gloriously raucous, ragged yet tuneful town band was good value, and it was all very relaxed with the scent of barbecued food wafting over the crowded bar tables and chairs that spilled into the street.

A very good-humoured couple watched in amazement as Ella drifted up to their table thinking it was ours and, eyes still glued on the band who were now trying to march and play, proceeded to eat their chips. People were warm, the community spirit was obvious as the evening light cast a rosy wash over the sandstone buildings. But it didn't click. The truth was we were distracted, unfocused and rapidly running out of steam. The children, bless their cotton socks, were wonderful but there was a limit to what we felt we could put them through. We ended up seeing very little by way of property and told ourselves that the area didn't feel right. Not compared to Mother's Garden.

Flagging and in need of succour we rang a friend's brother who lived in Paris but also had a country home about forty miles north of us near Auch. He and his French wife were there with her parents for a summer break and immediately insisted we went, too. They were so welcoming and were such a mine of information on the local property market that we felt our awareness took a quantum leap forward. Their rural retreat was everything I'd dreamed about – a rambling picture postcard French country home with heaps of character and space, but the likes of which was way out of our price league. Two other concerns were confirmed. The region, which we'd naively targeted for its low prices and peaceful contrast with the hugely popular Provence and Brittany, was charging up the foreign-buyer popularity stakes, and wherever we went in the area we were likely to be rubbing shoulders with English, Dutch, German and Irish owners. No offence, but if there was one imperative it was to avoid ex-pat communities. No doubt we could have found a French farm and community that were perfect for our needs, if we'd had the resolve and stamina, but when and where that would have been we hadn't a clue. Maybe by that time we were looking for excuses to give up before we had barely got started. And our attention span wasn't helped by the fact that our heads had already been turned.

Incredibly, six days after leaving England full of thoughts of settling in France we were drawing a line through that dream and turning our minds to Catalonia.

Down to the Wire

mother's garden

*F*rom falling in love with the Catalan farm on that beautiful summer's day, 19 July 2000, the next three months proved to be the most nerve-jangling, frantic and utterly draining time of our lives.

It all started so well.

On our return to Norfolk from our foray into northeastern Spain and southern France, and with Mother's Garden dominating all our waking and sleeping thoughts, we sat at the kitchen table and had one of those 'Could we? Should we? Oooo . . . Dare we?' lip-biting, heart-fluttering conversations reminiscent of puppy love phone calls. For all our chunterings about the need to change our lives this was it – the crunch, time to decide. With our stomachs doing somersaults we weighed in with an offer for the farm. Then we asked Mac and Conxita to help us find someone they trusted who could handle the legals and do all the necessary checks for us at their end, and also someone to carry out a structural survey of the house. Last but not least, we rang a Norfolk estate agent and put Barley Cottage on the market.

Our offer for Mother's Garden, five thousand pounds short of the asking price, was rejected immediately so we capitulated and agreed to pay the full amount of 25 million pesetas which was, we reckoned, almost bang on £95,000. If we got the £195,000 guide price for the cottage it would leave us (after Spanish taxes, fairly steep moving costs, legal fees and paying off our mortgage) with only about £10,000 to survive on until we found our feet. We tried not to think about it.

The for sale sign had barely gone up outside Barley Cottage when a family in a spanking new Mercedes estate pulled up and asked to look around. They were from Cambridgeshire and were scouting for a second home. We winced, tried to sustain our smiles and welcomed them in. They went through the rooms whispering, said thank you, adding it was all very delightful, and then went on their way. That's really encouraging, we said. 'At this rate we will have a buyer within a week.' Minutes later they were back, offering the full guide price, drinking coffee in our kitchen and readily agreeing to be flexible on the completion date, even to the point of stalling until December while I worked out my notice at work. Rock 'n' Roll.

Meanwhile we confirmed in writing (with Mac and Conxita's endless help) our full-price pledge to Enric and

Nuria and we were told to expect a draft contract to be faxed back.

Easy-peasy lemon squeezy. The ducks were lining up in a tidy row ready to fly south. This is actually going to happen, we told ourselves tingling with excitement, and straightaway started sharing the exciting news with close friends despite our feeble pledge to keep the whole thing under our hats and in the family until it was all sorted, signed and sealed.

Then the ducks scattered.

We held off accepting the offer for Barley Cottage for a week to see if any bids came in higher than the guide price. We thought we had learned a harsh lesson when bidding for the £200,000 guide price house the year before, when we offered £215,000 and still didn't get it. Our chocolate-box cottage was obviously going to be snapped up and any extra money would leave us with more vital pesetas in the bank. But to our amazement nobody else came to view and when I rang on the Monday morning to confirm that we would accept the Cambridgeshire couple's offer the agent dropped the bomb. 'I'm afraid they rang this morning and pulled out,' he said.

'What?'

'They've changed their minds.'

'They can't!'

'Yes, they can.'

They had carried on looking at property while waiting for our answer and had found something else that was available immediately.

A few days later, by now early August, the contract arrived

from Spain. Terry, who was back in Norfolk with Sally and their daughters after their French and Spanish adventure, pored over it for us. He'd studied Spanish and had taught English in Madrid and Zaragoza, but the contract was in Catalan which made it more tortuous. Slowly it all became alarmingly clear. It was an 'agreement to buy' contract detailing the extent of the farm and properties for sale but also stipulating that an equivalent of £2000 deposit had to be dispatched immediately and which would be forfeited if the purchase was not completed by 31 August. In a panic, we rang Mac and Conxita, who confirmed it was standard procedure. We hadn't the remotest chance in hell of making 31 August because we'd just lost a potential buyer. We felt our dream was already disintegrating.

It's not over, they told us calmly. They advised us to try asking for an extension on the completion date because there was a fair chance it was negotiable. Terry got on the phone and it was agreed. We had until Friday 29 September to come up with the full sum if we sent the deposit straightaway. We had no ready cash but Sally and Terry stumped up a loan and we sent it off sighing with relief and telling ourselves not to panic. It all seemed very relaxed, and the Spanish way was obviously not the English way. We still had the best part of August and all of September to find a buyer for Barley Cottage, and even then we might be able to negotiate a little more time. Meanwhile we again took Mac and Conxita's advice and opened a Spanish bank account, and let them press on with instructing both a local legal beagle and an architect to run their rules and eyes over the documents and basic structure of the farmhouse.

The days and weeks ticked by. A few people came to view the cottage but nobody pitched in with even an offer so, bewildered and increasingly anxious, we decided to switch agents. As September arrived and we could see our (or rather Sally's and Terry's) £2000 disappearing down the plughole, we reinstated the first agent as well and prayed that between them the two firms, one with a huge nationwide network and the other small and local, might crack it. I paid a visit to the building society and negotiated as big a mortgage extension as my salary would allow, but this still meant we were £30,000 short.

It was during this giddy time that we took another seemingly daft gamble. We'd seen a television production company's advert placed in the *Willing Workers on Organic Farms* magazine for people who were planning a life change and who were prepared to have their story filmed for a Channel Four documentary. Then, in a twist of fate at work, a letter from the production company also touting for volunteers found its way into the pile of letters to the editor I ploughed through every day in the hunt for some that were publishable.

I took the letter home and showed it to Maggie. We talked. A documentary could provide family and friends with a very clear and positive account of our adventure (and earn us a few bob, although 'few' turned out to be the operative word), so we rang Ricochet Films. The answer to what possessed us to take the further risk of public humiliation and trial by television lay with me. It was a classic case of in for a penny in for a pound – a painfully cautious man letting his brain off its lead like a normally abstemious and thrifty person under the influence of a bottle of bubbly seeing no harm in ordering the waiter to bring another one. After years of being static I was finally rolling and gathering speed at a fairly alarming rate. Maggie went along with it, bless her, buying my argument that it could be fun and fruitful. Of course we hadn't the slightest idea of how demanding or damning it may prove to be.

Although (we later discovered) the production company had more than a thousand replies to the advert, the producers liked the sound of our plans enough to dispatch a researcher to north Norfolk. They said there was no fee but we could claim expenses. A week or so later they were back again in force and the die was cast. We were one of five stories to be filmed through the year and to be broadcast at the end of 2001 or beginning of 2002 – if our wing-and-a-prayer plans to buy the farm and to move early in 2001 didn't fall apart. The way things were going the chances were they would.

One day, to escape the telephone and cloud of worry that had descended on Barley Cottage, we left the children with relatives and took ourselves off along the coast to Blakeney to see the sun go down and to talk softly about what we were doing with our lives and to dream of how it might be. It was a beautiful evening and we looked up at the vast, darkening sky as gulls, wildfowl and a sound like goats' bells filled the salt air. There is nothing quite like a north Norfolk sunset when the marshes are crowned with crimson to the music of a stiffening breeze slapping the halyards against the metal dinghy masts. These were sights, sounds and smells I'd known all my life and it was weird to think I was prepared to leave them. But all the same I didn't doubt what we were trying to do.

Back home we pressed on with our checks in Spain, drawing up the necessary papers, receiving a reassuring architect's report on the house and keeping in as close contact as possible with Enric and Nuria, forever emphasising our firm intention to buy but not admitting we still had our cottage to sell.

Our naivety was about to plumb new depths. We thought that as Enric and Nuria had been so at ease about extending the completion date they would be happy to wait a few weeks longer, certain in the knowledge that we would go through with the deal. They had our deposit in their pockets and there was ample evidence of our determination. The contract, we thought, was a necessary formality. Given all that we were doing, surely the vendors would give us a little more time. We planned to ring in the next couple of days to keep them in the picture.

Thursday 21 September 2000 – my forty-second birthday – dawned happily enough with the children helping me unwrap presents on the bed before Ella went off to school. It was a day to try and forget the pressures. Breakfast had barely begun when the phone rang. It was Mac.

'I've some bad news, I'm afraid,' he said as gently as he

could. 'It seems that a Dutch agency is also after the farm and has offered more money. Enric can't switch, of course, because he's under contract to you. But that runs out in eight days' time and he says that if you're not here and the deal is not done next Friday, it's off.'

I went cold.

Bottom line was we had to decide there and then – call it a day and wave goodbye to Terry and Sally's £2000 or crazily have a tilt at raising £30,000 at the drop of a hat as well as getting the whole 25 million pesetas (plus a little extra to cover assorted fees and bills) transferred to our account in Spain in time. We'd also have to get ourselves over there by the Wednesday to make sure all the papers were in order and then draw the cheque and do the deal with the notary on the Friday. Mac had tried not to sound downhearted, but he felt the game was over. We felt gutted. We made some more coffee and, finding strength from somewhere, decided that having come so far and with £2000 at stake, we might as well at least have a bash. If we made a few phone calls we'd know soon enough if we were in with a chance.

The huge challenge was finding £30,000 in ready cash and getting it into our Spanish account in six days – or rather four working days as the weekend was looming. We couldn't ask anyone to give us a loan by drawing money from building societies or writing us a cheque, because it would not clear fast enough for us to send it to Spain on the Monday. That ruled my mum out as her few funds, which she had offered to loan before, were all tied up. We could only ask people with cash in instant access accounts. Then the only way we were going to do it was to have any money we could beg or borrow transferred electronically to our English bank account by the Monday, and for Lloyds to do an express transfer of the full £95,000 (including the £65,000 mortgage extension I'd already banked) to our Spanish bank account to clear no later than the following Thursday, the day before the deadline. Try saying that without taking a breath and you'll get an inkling of how we felt.

But who to turn to? Who on earth do you ring and ask for a lorry load of loot and have to fudge the fact that you couldn't be sure when you'd be able to pay them back? The obvious first stop was Maggie's sister Liz and brother-in-law Gary in Enfield. Gary ran a musical instrument business and might just have the means if I had the courage to ring him. Employing the old work tactic regarding difficult calls of 'dial first, think later', I picked up the phone. Liz answered and I blurted out the bones of the crisis. 'I may be able to find £5000,' she said immediately. Thanking her, I asked if Gary was around and she put me through to his office on the top floor of the house. Again I explained mission impossible, loading every sentence with profuse apologies, blushing at my impudence and then pinching my eyes shut waiting for his answer. He had every right to tell me to go forth and attempt something physically impossible.

Maybe I can, he said. 'You could? You might be able to find £20,000?' I replied in amazement, prompting a fire in Maggie's eyes which were darting about as she immediately set about working out who to ask for the last £5000. It just so happened that Gary had been saving up to replace their two cars, both of which were getting long in the tooth. He was prepared to stall on the cars until the end of January when he'd need the money back. I explained the huge hurdle of getting the money to Spain in four working days and he said he'd mull it over.

'Holy smoke, we're still in the hunt!' we told each other. With Maggie's mother unflinchingly agreeing to loan us the last £5000 we spent the next two days on the telephone, transferring money, advising our bank managers in Britain and Spain what they had to do and planning our week ahead.

Ray, the bank manager in Sheringham, checked the exchange rate and told us on the Friday that at the time of his call it was extremely good – 279 pesetas to the pound for a large transfer. Wow. He said it would take two days to get the money into our Spanish account if we paid for a priority service, but warned that the rate was changing every minute. We told him we would be in on the Monday to action it, by which time we should have all the loans from the family logged into our account.

That Friday we made our plans. We would fly out on the Wednesday, go to our Spanish bank on the Thursday morning and draw out the money, then do the deal at the notary's office on the Friday morning before flying home on the Saturday. We decided that, given all the stress and legal and linguistic hoops we would have to go through, Ella would find the whole thing extremely tedious and we might be distracted. So we asked Sally and Terry to look after her while we were away. We explained the situation to Ella as simply as possible, laying on as thickly as we could the amount of time we were likely to spend in banks and offices and she readily agreed to stay with her cousins Leila and Rosa in Norfolk.

During one of our many frantic phone calls Liz made a suggestion – why not take the mothers with you? Both said 'yes' and I set about finding the cheapest air tickets for four adults and a three-month old baby and then booked a hire car. Mac and Conxita continued to beaver away on our behalf, booking us some rooms in a guesthouse in the village and making final checks to ensure we had all the papers, information and fees we needed for the notary.

Pumping up the blood pressure yet further was the fact that I had to carry on at work as if nothing out of the ordinary was happening in my life, that I was as cool as a cucumber and as wide awake as the job of night editor on a daily newspaper demanded. The truth was my veins were coursing with caffeine and adrenaline and my left eyelid had started to twitch with stress. I was concentrating incredibly hard because the last thing I wanted to do after eight years in the job was to make an arse of myself. But I was a pressure cooker waiting to pop and was quite likely to forsake all diplomacy with anyone pressing for an honest opinion. There was also the ticklish matter of negotiating a few days off for 'family reasons' which thankfully went smoothly without any testing questions. I had confided in a couple of friends on the paper who kindly kept

quiet about my out-of-office labours and I noticed with gratitude one of them double-checking some of my work.

We realised too we had to let Ricochet Films know about
the crises and they said they wanted to come up to Norfolk
before we left and then travel with us.

I worked on the Sunday afternoon and evening, then on the
Monday morning after a fitful sleep I rang Ray at the bank to
see if any of the cash transfers had turned up. Two had but we
were still £5000 short. He said he'd also checked the exchange
rate and it had nose-dived to 265 pesetas to the pound
because traders had moved to bolster the flagging euro. We
faced losing thousands of pounds. Later that morning we carried Joe Joe into the bank, our fingers crossed. All the money
was there. We couldn't wait any longer. He dialled to check
the exchange rate. It was back to 274.82.

'Buy! Buy now!' we cried and the 26 million pesetas express
international transfer started winging its way to Catalonia.

On the Tuesday I did a double shift, working from 9.30
a.m. to 12.30 a.m. the following morning trying desperately to
get ahead before being away for three days. Still nobody
seemed to twig that I was by now only firing on three cylin-
ders and spending an inordinately long time repeatedly
thrusting coins into the coffee machine.

While I was at the office treble-checking everything I did,
Ricochet Films director Billy and Australian cameraman Craig
turned up at the cottage, booked into a local pub and told
Maggie they'd be back first thing in the morning to film
breakfast and Ella going to school.

I don't think either of us got any sleep that night and it's the most uncomfortable feeling welcoming a camera crew into your home when you are wrecked, anxious and unable to shake off the thought that it is all going to end in disaster and ignominy. It was like the one and only time I've been on a fairground big dipper, when there's no way you can get off and the long, slow haul to the top gives you time to doubt the sanity of being talked into climbing aboard in the first place.

A Walk in Our Garden

mother's garden

*W*ednesday 27 September 2000 dawned still and cloudless. There was a heavy dew and, as I pulled on my old sailing jacket and leaky wellies lined with carrier bags in readiness to walk the dogs, Billy and Craig arrived and piped up that they wanted to tag along.

Looking like a scarecrow (the plastic bags were protruding from the tops of my boots beneath my torn jeans) I let Charlie and Megan pull me into the field behind the house where Charlie immediately broke the cord on his extendable lead. I froze. We were just a few yards from the home of the wildfowl collector where, three months earlier, Charlie had run amok to the tune of £250. With the camera recording my every move, I uttered a pathetic high-pitched 'Ch-Ch-Ch-Charlie? Goood boy, there's a goood boy. Stay . . . Stay . . .' as I edged towards him like a butterfly collector. For the first time in his countless escapes and jaunts around the countryside he stood still. Time will tell how effective the microphone inside my coat was, but I breathed some foul utterances and farted with relief as I grabbed his collar. Had he charged off into the sunrise the world would have witnessed a broken man. As it was I was shaking and the day had only just begun.

When I got back to the house Ella was ready. It was harvest festival at school and we both wanted to go. We also felt very strange at the thought of leaving her behind and wanted to keep reassuring her.

'We'll film you walking to school,' said Billy, which was a reasonable suggestion given the clear skies and fact that it was not very far.

'But we never walk,' we said. We usually left it far too late to think about walking and I'd fallen into the routine of driving on to Sheringham woods to give the dogs a really long outing.

But walk we did that morning, getting our first flavour of the 'Would you just do that one more time please?' life in front of the camera, when the most natural and seemingly spontaneous events can be anything but.

We were late and ended up running up the hill to the school where we were put through the emotional ringer yet again, watching a tear-jerking performance by the children who showed off the jam they had made and then sang the giant turnip song while Ella and classmate Oonagh made up the percussion section. Afterwards we stood chatting with other proud parents in the bustling playground as Ella scampered about with her friends. Out of the corner of my eye I could see Billy looking around for the best shots but at the same time seemingly wearing an expression of disbelief that anyone would be so daft as to trade all this in for a new life. My assumption of his doubt fuelled my own.

Back at the house Billy predictably pressed us into some 'Do you know what you're doing?' interviews that seemed to take forever. Our Norfolk life, apparently, was the sort of escape many people in London and other cities dreamed of. My mum Pat turned up and we packed our bags and the car in a panic before heading off to pick up Maggie's mum Beryl at her little farm near Dereham. Running through a verbal checklist that (a) Sally would pick Ella up from school and (b) friend Dave knew where the key was to look after the dogs, we were relieved that the car appeared to have shaken off the worrying smell of fuel that had persisted for weeks and was now running smoothly. Beryl squeezed into the back alongside Pat and Joe Joe and we made up time, arriving on schedule at the airport where we'd arranged to meet up with the film crew again. This time Angani, the researcher who had come to Norfolk several weeks before to check us out, was with Billy and Craig and the mums got their first flavour of what it's like to be stalked by a television production team.

The flight was nearly an hour late. The film crew sat in front of us on the plane and as Joe Joe dozed we snacked on Pat's sausage rolls and Beryl's sandwiches. Our spirits were lifted by our mothers' support and obvious excitement. They were still buoyant three hours later as the hire car spun through the motorway tunnels on our way south from Barcelona, but it all went quiet as we left the lights behind and the road narrowed and started to twist up hairpin mountain bends.

We rolled into the village just after midnight. This time it was deserted. We'd left the film crew at the airport, agreeing to meet the next day at the bank, and for the first time during that crazy day we felt alone. We could understand why the mothers found the lifeless empty streets so strange and uninviting. We tried to sound upbeat, but failed miserably. A good night's sleep was the answer, we said, adding it will all look different in daylight. We rang Mac who turned up in his Land Rover and took us to the guesthouse where we were greeted by tired and relieved owner Enriqueta and her husband Joan Salvador who was sporting an alarming bruise on his forehead. Mac ascertained he had acquired it from a policeman while taking part in a farmers' protest march in Tarragona earlier in the day. The news prompted further worried glances between the mothers who then did their best to put on brave faces before sloping off to bed.

No sooner had our heads hit the pillows than Joe decided to wake up and work shifts with the church clock to help us remain conscious and lie there worrying that the money hadn't arrived in our Spanish bank account.

We were not due at the bank until mid morning so we bumbled about the guesthouse for a while half asleep, eating a light breakfast, sorting Joe Joe and looking out of the kitchen window across the roof tiles in the general direction of the farm. Conxita had volunteered to accompany us to the bank to overcome any language problems and we followed her little red Citroën back down the twisty road to the large town where the film crew was waiting. Now there only appeared to be two of them. Billy relayed the sorry tale of how Angani – who held a Commonwealth rather than standard British passport – had been locked up in a cell all night before being put on a flight back to the UK. This was despite the fact that she had worked in Spain before without anyone batting an eyelid at passport control.

To our enormous relief Jaume in the bank said the cash – 26 million pesetas – had plopped into our account that morning. For the first time we dared to hope we were going to make it. With a fat cheque for Enric and Nuria and a reasonably plump one for the notary, we celebrated with glasses of orange juice in a chic café in the main square and told our mums and the film crew that we had decided to keep them in suspense for another day. The plan was to stay away from the farm until we owned it and that meant kicking our heels until the deal was done at the notary's office at noon the next day. Only then would we drive up the bumpy track to Mother's Garden.

Back in the village we ordered food and wine at the bar. We had planned to treat the mums to a slap up meal at the restaurant where we'd eaten with Sally and Terry back in July, but it was closed for a holiday break so we were relieved when the bar owner said she would rustle something up. She duly arrived at our table with slices of bread smeared in tomato and dribbled with olive oil and slabs of cheese and assorted meats, together with a carafe of cloudy wine that looked and tasted like rough cider. By mid afternoon the sky was clouding over and Maggie retreated to the guesthouse for a nap while I, Joe Joe and the mums, shadowed by the film crew, went to have a look at Ella's new school. It had been built on the site of the old football pitch and Beryl and Pat sat on the redundant concrete terraces recounting their first impressions for the benefit of the camera. I wandered about at a respectable distance with Joe Joe in my arms, trying but failing to tune in to what they were saying. The interview seemed to take an exceptionally long time.

The dried leaves of the plane trees round the swings and slides were being blown about the playground and the temperature was dropping. Maggie surfaced at about six o'clock and we went to the phone box and called Mac to agree a time when he would come and collect us to take us to his house for supper. Then we rang to speak to Ella expecting tears and retribution. She was glued to the box watching 'Buffy the Vampire Slayer' and giggling with her cousins and definitely wasn't going to haul herself off the sofa to come to the phone. She eventually shouted a cheery 'HELLO!' and didn't seem the least bit bothered by our absence which was good on the one hand but a little disconcerting on the other.

We could hear the crash of distant thunder as we emerged from the village store with fruit and milk for breakfast the next day and, by the time we left the guesthouse an hour later for our rendezvous with Mac, the first spots of rain were falling and it was almost dark. He found us huddled under the awning of the bar bracing ourselves for the next clap of thunder. No sooner had we helped the mums into the back seat of his old Land Rover than the heavens opened. The windows steamed up before we left the road and started up the long, bumpy climb to the house, pushing through undergrowth and pitching over rocks. Rain was dripping in through the roof lights and the wipers were struggling to cope. The mums fell silent again. They were hanging on to each other. I opened a window slightly in an effort to clear the condensation, only for the Land Rover to tilt and a bucketload of water to pour off the roof onto my legs.

'All good fun, eh?' I offered, while Mac, hunched over the wheel, nose to the screen, joined in with a timely, 'Don't worry now – nearly there.' But it was wasted. The mothers were clearly alarmed both by the ride and the seemingly incomprehensible route along which Maggie and I had opted to steer our lives. It wasn't hard to work out what they were thinking.

The comfortable living room and kitchen were warmed by candlelight and we were greeted by Conxita and two of their friends from Barcelona, Kim and Maria, who were staying for the week. Mac had disconnected the solar power batteries because of the storm, but with the shutters closed and the wood burner radiating heat the drama outside rapidly faded away and the mums started to relax. We ate pasta and fish and talked until midnight while Joe Joe slept on the sofa, and it was a huge relief to see Beryl and Pat begin to appreciate what wonderful people Mac and Conxita were and to recognise that we were not devoid of friends or support. Despite its thunderous beginnings, that evening was the turning point in what up until then had been an increasingly stressful trip, and that homely feeling helped to settle the nerves a little on the eve of our big day.

Friday 29 September. Mum's seventy-sixth birthday. Time to buy our farm.

The skies had cleared by the morning and we'd managed a few hours' sleep despite the church bells.

First stop was the office of Manel the accountant who had acted as our legal beagle. His wife Neus double-checked all our paperwork and then we followed her car to the notary in the town two miles away. We piled into the office mob-handed – me, Maggie, Joe Joe, Beryl and Pat, Mac and Conxita, the cameraman Craig, director Billy, and Neus.

Enric and Nuria were waiting with their daughter and his face lit up when he saw us, probably out of sheer relief. We were a few minutes late and he was, no doubt, concerned that the English couple he'd only met once would actually be true to their word and burst through the door waving a cheque for twenty-four-and-a-half million pesetas.

We all moved around the small waiting room as if pulled by a current and Mac worked overtime trying to keep various conversations between foreigners going. Pat and Beryl took up station on a sofa, handbags on their laps, hands on bags and smiling and blushing every time anyone looked at them. Craig was zigzagging between the assembled with his camera as

Billy dived in and out of the doorway issuing instructions while desperately trying to stay out of shot. Goodness only knows what the office staff thought was going on. It wouldn't have been out of place if Brian Rix, devoid of trousers and sporting spotted underpants, had burst out of a cupboard.

Finally Maggie and I were called through to have our passports and papers checked by a serious, methodical young woman who I figured must be a secretary. Mac, ever relaxed, came with us to interpret. He told us this was just the preamble before the deal was struck.

Then we were back in the melee where the camera had started to jangle nerves and Enric and Nuria's faces were again creased with anxiety. I must have looked the same. Maggie and I were being given time to think that in a few minutes, all debts considered, we would be about £170,000 in the red.

I'd a mental picture of the notary being an opulent man with greying temples and a sash across his chest and I tried to fend off thoughts of bankruptcy by trying to work out which was the door to his office. Up until that point I'd seen no one who remotely resembled the man and figured he was behind his vast desk beneath a picture of King Juan Carlos, busily dusting his shoulders and aligning his fringe in readiness for television stardom.

The secretary appeared at the door again and said something to Mac.

'This is it,' he told us. 'But no cameras.'

We followed along the corridor into a windowless room and were invited to sit at a round table. Enric immediately fished in his pocket and put an enormous key on the table along with an assortment of others.

'Where's the notary?' I whispered to Mac who was standing at our shoulders.

'That's her,' he replied and nodded at the 'secretary' who had sat down opposite me and all but disappeared behind a large pile of paperwork.

'Are you sure?'

'Yep. Now sshhh.'

With all the sobriety of a judge, although appearing to be struggling to suppress a smile, the notary started to read through the formal agreement. It was painfully slow and although I didn't have a clue what she was saying everyone else seemed to be hanging on her every word. She seemed to be itemising the assets of the farm, but I couldn't be sure. Then all of a sudden the tone changed. She stuttered and stalled and then started asking questions, prompting Enric and Nuria's daughter, who had been standing against the wall, to shoot forward and whisper in her father's ear. I thought her mother was going to have kittens. Mac pitched in with questions of his own while whispering 'don't panic', but given the hand-wringing that was going on opposite us it was impossible not to.

The stumbling block was our certificate from the bank (which was needed to show that we were good for the money) stating we had brought twenty-six million pesetas into Spain. If that was the price we were paying for the farm then the legal papers which stated twenty-five million were wrong. No, said Mac, we had merely transferred enough money to pay for the farm, to pay the notary and to cover various other expenses.

Enric must have thought we were taking the pee. He could have sold the farm for twenty-six million to the Dutch agency who had tried to wrestle it from our grasp, but Enric had signed a contract with us and his hands were tied for a few more hours at least.

There followed a painful pause when most of us held our breath. The notary pondered for a few moments then finally, to our enormous relief, said, 'OK,' and carried on reading. Finally the time came for her to hand Enric our cheque. He folded it neatly in half, fished out his wallet and then put it in his back pocket. The paperwork was passed round the table for us all to sign and then Enric pushed the farm keys across the table until they touched my hand, lifted his head to peer at me through his thick glasses and then beamed. We stood up. In a fluster I shook Enric's hand so vigorously that his glasses slid further down his nose. Then I attempted to lean across and kiss Nuria. My feet were paddling for grip on the marble floor and the notary recoiled as I sprawled across the table.

Outside in the midday heat we offered to buy everyone a drink and agreed to meet at the hotel in the high street where we planned to sit outside and down a couple of bottles of Cava. To our surprise Enric and Nuria and their daughter agreed to come. Maggie borrowed a mobile phone from somewhere and rang to give Ella, Sally and Terry and their girls our good news, while everyone settled around a table and the pantomime continued. My efforts to order a fruit drink for our mums brought forth a plate of sliced lemon. Beryl and Pat chatted to each other, Enric passed the time by ploughing through a plate of olives in silence, Nuria read the newspaper and Billy and Craig ducked and dived around us while Mac kept filling my glass.

'You've done it! You've blummin' well done it!' he kept saying, which was considerably wide of the mark since he and Conxita had done a vast amount of the work. Any elation on our part was crowded by a mass of other feelings, not least bewilderment, doubt, trepidation and exhaustion. I wasn't sure what to think and with every glass I was rapidly losing the ability to think.

Everyone grinned and raised a glass when we toasted the moment, but only Maggie, Conxita and Enric's daughter were making any headway in crossing the cultural divide. When all the olives had gone Enric rose to leave and explained to Mac that they would meet us at the farm to show us around and explain among other things the gummings of the plumbing and electrics.

We polished off the sparkling wine and followed. This was it. Time for the mothers and the film crew to see what all the fuss was about. Time for us to see the farm for just the third time.

As the car dropped down the road past the village and into our valley I remember saying a quiet thank you for the sunshine that now cast a golden hue across the landscape which less than twenty-four hours before was being shaken and soaked by the thunderstorm. Showing everyone round the farm in the middle of a downpour didn't bear thinking about. Both Maggie and I were also praying that everyone would be swept away by the charm and beauty of our future home and, most important of all, that we would still love it. In the back of both our minds was the chance that the magic would be gone, that a host of problems and faults previously unseen through rose-tinted spectacles, would now reveal themselves and that the day and our dream would fall apart.

We needn't have worried. Mother's Garden stood peacefully among the fig and walnut trees waiting for us, more beautiful than I remembered. No one could help but fall in love with it.

The house slowly filled with light as we drifted through the rooms opening shutters and doors. While Maggie took the mums on a tour I tried to take stock of what appeared to be a huge amount of furniture and possessions Enric still had to clear. Most rooms looked as if someone was still living there. In the kitchen there were paella pans hanging on the wall, a fridge, a gas hob, china and chairs. There was a table and more chairs in the living room along with board games, pictures and candlesticks, and upstairs we found five single beds, a double mattress and a huge wardrobe. They couldn't possibly be thinking of leaving it all, there was just too much. I felt slightly annoyed that the house hadn't been cleared yet, but wasn't sure how to broach it with Enric or Nuria who were proudly opening doors and pointing.

Next Mac, Enric and I made our way to the barn. I couldn't

believe it. Inside there was a mass of tools and farming implements, a pile of wood, shelves, pipes, four olive nets, pruning saws, several pairs of wellies, cupboards full of pots of paint and even a chainsaw.

In a daze I dared to ask: 'Is . . . er . . . Could . . . er . . . Does he want all this stuff?'

'Apparently not, you lucky bugger. The stuff in the house too.' said Mac. 'And—' Enric was saying something in Spanish and tugging at my arm. 'There's something else he wants to show you.'

We went back outside and, coaxing one of the keys from the bunch in my hand, Enric unlocked the door to the storeroom. The shelves were lined with empty jars, as well as unopened beer bottles, liqueurs and lime cordial. For the life of me I couldn't fathom out why he wasn't at least taking the alcohol with him. At the far end of the store there was a large round tank which, I remembered from our tour two months earlier, held the household water after it had been pumped from the well. Mac double-checked with Enric how the system worked and then told me we'd go over it again later once things were quieter and we had more time. But that wasn't why Enric had taken us in there. He pulled open the bottom draw of a pine dresser, fished out some plastic cups and pointed to three small wine barrels on which were chalked 'NEGRE', 'BLANC' and 'RANCI'. I made a snap decision to opt for the 'RANCI'. He proudly half-filled the cup and handed it to me, waiting for my verdict. I gulped instead of sipped. Big mistake. Instant heartburn and vocal chord failure.

A Walk in Our Garden

My nervous system had already conveyed its crisis to my stomach which was equally in no mood for further stimulation of any sort. I tried to convert my wince into a smile but my eyes were watering. Next he hit me with the 'BLANC' which was a little better, but I'd still not fully recovered the power of speech to ask him to go steady on the measures. I looked down into the cup of 'NEGRE' and felt decidedly queasy but knew that to decline was impossible, particularly after Enric had just told me he was leaving all his farming kit and half the household furniture, not to mention the booze. But this time Enric didn't wait to see my reaction and turned for the door. I confess that the moment his back was turned I hid the cup on the floor behind a bag of walnuts.

For the next half an hour Maggie joined the three of us to walk the ten acres as Enric pointed out parts of the irrigation system including the well, various valves, the spring and *balsa*. The explanation was vague (which we would regret later) but the whole system was obviously far more comprehensive than we'd ever imagined.

Then we sat down outside the back door and Enric pulled out pictures showing how the buildings were derelict when they had bought them just over a decade before. They had re-roofed it, rewired it, re-plumbed it – and plans had been drawn up to extend out towards the *balsa*. The footings for the extension were already in. Although the house still looked tatty inside and out and many of the features and services were very basic, so much of the essential work had been done. We couldn't believe it. It wasn't a case of them selling up because the place was worn out and major work would be needed in the not too distant future. There were no horrific revelations.

By now Nuria was proudly showing the mums the outside bread oven and they were clearly enjoying the tour. They'd given the place a thorough going-over and were liberally offering opinions on what changes we could make. But it was all positive, all of it parcelled up with words of appreciation for what an enchanting place it was. Beyond their concerns of us taking such a giant step away from them and the families, there was no denying we had found a special place.

Enric, Nuria and their daughter took their leave. Conxita arrived with baskets of food and we carried the table and chairs to under the fig trees where we picnicked, shaded from the hot afternoon sun by the canopy of broad leaves. Joe Joe, who had slept for much of the time, was at Maggie's breast.

When the time came to lock up and leave we found our steps weighed down by rotting figs that had welded to our shoes like dog poo.

There were other reminders of our day. My fingers were stained by the green walnut I'd picked up and clawed away at as we'd walked the land, and my legs were scarred and sore from wading through the sea of coarse grasses between the derelict hazel bushes. All that and the abiding thought of how deeply in debt we now were.

A day later we were back in Blighty. We flew home on the Saturday afternoon and by the time we were driving north from Stansted airport to Norfolk on the M11 it was dark and

Joe Joe had had enough. He bellowed with all his might so in an effort to pacify him we burst into song with the mums opening up with assorted hits by Vera Lynn and Perry Como.

I plunged back into work on the Sunday night where I bit my lip about our adventure. Revolution in Serbia meant a particularly hectic shift and very late night, but I was glad to be busy.

I was woken on the Monday morning by a strange sound coming from the front garden and looked out to see Maggie vacuuming the lawn. The biggest challenge both in the village and at work was to carry on as if nothing unusual was happening in our lives, but there were ample clues we were on the edge. It turned out Ella and little Izzy, a cute three-year-old from round the corner, had managed to puncture a bean bag and distribute the little white balls all over the garden while playing on the Sunday afternoon.

So our dream-like existence persisted through the week, with no signs of a buyer for our house and the fear of financial ruin weighing heavier every day. Just when I felt I couldn't get any more round-shouldered, a thumping great Spanish tax bill arrived – £6500 all bar the shouting – bringing fresh concerns about the exchange rate.

There were other hurdles too.

Mac told us we needed to get our heads round the impending olive harvest. We had 130-odd trees and needed to plan to be back in Catalonia at the end of November with some willing labourers. The headache was that we needed to book flights as early as possible to keep the cost down, but had no way of knowing exactly when the olive harvest would be. We took a deep breath, hazarded a guess and booked for 22 to 27 November, while also roping in Maggie's sister Liz and husband Gary, plus brother Philip and Maggie's best friend Deanna. There was a ticket for Ella too – we couldn't bear to leave her behind again.

The following Sunday we somehow broke out of the gloom for a few hours. I didn't have to work and it was a bright and clear weekend when I enjoyed some quality time with Ella and felt I was getting a foretaste of what might be to come. The two of us walked the dogs in Felbrigg woods, talked, giggled and mimed to T Rex in the car, Ella turning her balloon sword into a Fender guitar, me singing with gusto. The house sale worries were put to the back of our minds as Maggie cooked a wonderful lunch and we were joined by Deanna and her American friend Susan from Chicago who was celebrating her birthday. And it helped to know someone – the first person in weeks – was coming to look at the house on the Monday morning.

It never rains but it pours.

We were really taken by the woman from London who came to see Barley Cottage. She, it seemed, liked the house too – enough to make it clear there and then she wanted it! There was no chain and she had the funds to buy. The plan was she would carry on working and living in London for a few more years and rent the cottage out in the meantime. She said she would instruct a surveyor as soon as possible and left us hugging each other with relief.

Then on the Tuesday the other joint agent rang to say he had a lady who was interested. Remembering both agents' advice not to turn anyone away even if we thought we had a buyer, we agreed for her to come. She was at the door within the hour and subsequently declared she loved it too. We warned her that another woman was keen enough to instruct a surveyor and she said immediately that she would do likewise. Before we knew it there was a contract race. One minute not a nibble, the next all hell was let loose.

Meanwhile Joe Joe was up two or three times a night giving Maggie the runaround while I was plonked in front of the television until nearly daybreak for two nights viewing videotapes of news broadcasts and mini-documentaries. I'd been invited to be one of the judges of the regional Royal Television Society awards but had left the pile of videotapes untouched until it was almost too late. Collectively the tapes lasted hours and the only time I could sit down and watch them was after I got home in the small hours. The deadline was Thursday when all the judges were due to sit round a table and decide on the winners. In my befuddled state it later transpired I'd managed to swap a potentially award-winning promotional video for Addenbrooke's Hospital with Ella's recording of the Tweenies.

I also let my defences slip. One of the other judges, a film maker called Terry, mentioned Spain out of the blue and how he wanted to buy a small farm and set up a painting school. I couldn't believe what I was hearing. He said he and his wife (an exhausted teacher) aimed to head south in January to scout for property. After the meeting we walked together through Norwich and unable to help myself I spilled the beans to someone I barely knew. His eyes popped and naturally he wanted to know the whole story. I then spent the next few minutes backtracking, begging him to keep mum. I'm grateful he did.

The surveyors came and went at the house. They were both nice guys and one, Nigel, veered off the subject of house values onto life values once he gleaned our plans. He made some telling remarks.

'The English,' he said, 'can be such worriers and so wrapped up in organising a secure life that they don't get on with living. Everything has to be watertight, wrapped up, planned for – careers, pensions, etc. They tend to be suspicious too of change, which is understandable given the preoccupation with status and working towards retirement. But time flies when you are doing things habitually.'

He and his wife had just moved. They'd had a lovely house that family and friends adored and envied and everything seemed perfect. 'What more could one ask for?' was a common remark. But eating away at them was always the thought, Well, this is it then, this is our last home. It proved unbearable.

We certainly empathised with his feeling of being trapped, of having our lives so well organised and planned out. People would tell us that we were 'set'. Set for what? Where was the time for ourselves and our children? The conversation with the surveyor, albeit relatively brief and devoid of negatives, was a timely dose of reassurance. We'd been wobbling and had lost focus a little amid the stresses of being between two lives emotionally and well and truly in a pickle financially.

When I came home from work that night Maggie was still awake and fired up. They say adrenaline can be good for you, but in what measure I'm not sure. She was all for a ritual burning of one of my work suits. I, on the other hand, was worried.

It was normal in the office to check 'Sky News' at midnight. That night another journalist was doing it, but I glanced up from scanning first edition page proofs to see a car drowning in mud.

'Where's that?' I asked casually.

'Spain.'

'What? Where?'

'Northern Spain. Flooding. Some people have drowned.'

'Wh-what d'you mean northern Spain. WHERE?'

'Tarragona province.'

Another sleepless night. We rang Mac and Conxita at the crack of sparrow fart and Mac said there was news of villages being cut off and general mayhem. They were all right but their drive had been washed away so there was no chance of them going to check on Mother's Garden. He assured us that someone, probably our neighbour Pere, would walk across and have a look. I paced about until Mac rang back an hour later to say everything appeared to be OK, but that our cash transfer for the tax bill hadn't arrived and the notary was getting twitchy.

Meanwhile both our potential buyers were keen to agree a completion date so we settled on 16 January, a Tuesday. I was still on a year's notice at work (a legacy from a three-year stint as editor of a series of free weekly newspapers) but aimed to talk it down to two months. There was no way of knowing how the company would react, but after twenty-two years' service I figured they owed me a little leeway. I had always found them fair. I also had no doubts that my editor would back me, but it might require some ticklish negotiating to settle on an exact date. The fact that I was going to propose January should make things easier as nobody was likely to be on holiday, but I also agreed with Maggie that I would offer to do the late shift on Christmas Day and New Year's Eve to soften the blow. I wanted to leave work on 4 January which would afford us time to treble-check everything and to pack and clear the cottage while also lengthening the odds that we would have nervous breakdowns. I was, of course, forever rehearsing how I would tell my boss and my colleagues, gabbling away at the traffic lights driving to and from work, or walking the dogs, or in the empty lift on my way up to my desk or sitting on the loo – anywhere I was alone.

Friday 27 October 2000. Miserable, wet and a solid one-tone grey from horizon to horizon. We were all leaden-headed too, stricken with colds. I trudged off round the field with the dogs worrying about how hefty a surcharge the notary would levy for our late payment of taxes. The cheque should have arrived several days ago and all we could do was wait and hope. I got back to find Maggie standing in the conservatory hugging a bottle of champagne.

'WE'VE EXCHANGED!'

What a sense of relief. The floodgates opened. We danced for joy. It was one thing to get the farm, but to find a buyer for our house, to exchange contracts in just twelve days and know, for certain, we could clear our debts and were on our way was such an extraordinary feeling. It was the day the course of our lives changed. We uttered more than a few thank yous. Amid the euphoria there was also gratitude stemming from our abiding sense throughout the year that someone was looking after us.

We rang all the family and close friends and then I told Maggie I had to get into the office immediately and see Barry the managing director who was due to be away all the next week. I was on a day off and my editor Peter was away for a long weekend, but I couldn't wait. I would tell Peter and then my colleagues on the Tuesday when everyone was back.

The biggest fear was I wouldn't get the words out in any sensible order, but I did and Barry listened with an expression of bewilderment. He hadn't been with the company for long, but I'm sure that in one of his earliest briefings he'd have been advised that Kirby was the resident Norfolk peasant who'd never leave.

The next day I felt a bit of a fraud. I'd been invited to unveil the village sign at High Kelling where I lived until I was seven. I was introduced to the small gathering who had braved the cold and rain as 'the deputy editor of the *Eastern Daily*

Press'. Not for much longer I thought. Evelyn, who used to lead Sunday school at All Saints', stepped boldly out of my dim and distant memory. Tributes were paid to my mum for helping to raise money for the social centre, and to my dad who returned to the centre about five years ago to give an organ recital. Our house had been one of the first as the woodland community sprouted in the fifties and sixties. I remember a few things from our time there – running wild, sledging, fishing, exploring with friends – but most of all the shouting and shock as our family fell apart when I was seven. I vividly recall sitting on the stairs clutching my knees to my chest, listening to my parents in their war of words and saying to myself, 'It's 1965 and you will never, ever forget this.'

Dad stood proudly at my side beneath the covered sign as I rattled off a few words, and then invited local children to pull the chord. The little event was over. I took Dad home and went on to see Mum who'd said she didn't want to go. I could understand her not wanting to revisit a place with one overriding memory, but she seemed distressed on the phone and wasn't making a great deal of sense. She was still like that when we sat on her sofa and talked. My stepfather Horace said she was just tired, but something seemed fundamentally wrong. It wasn't the first time. Later my sister Jackie and I shared our thoughts on the phone about her health, how for several years there had been moments like this and that she seemed to be weakening mentally, not gradually but in sudden steps. She was seventy-six and had been diabetic for about ten years.

We'd feared she may be suffering mini strokes and tried

several times to get her to see her doctor, but both she and Horace always implied it was not our business. A former nurse, she would always say she knew what was best, but we were never sure she was keeping to her medication. Jackie and I decided that during the next week one of us would ring her doctor.

On the Sunday Maggie and I got as many of the family together as possible and walked across the village green to have a pub lunch at the Red Lion. Mum seemed fine again. Liz had turned up at the house with an apple pie and Mum was cradling a huge trifle, so we agreed we'd dodge dessert at the pub and head back home to continue our meal. After the first course the publican proudly reeled off his list of desserts, but we all lied that we were full, settled the bill and prepared to leave. Ella beat us all to the door where the publican was standing to say goodbye.

'Thank you very much,' she said, very politely, then added, 'We're going home now for our pudding.'

That evening two pictures and a poster dropped off the walls.

When everyone had gone and we'd cleared up we switched off the lights and left the wood burner to cast its glow in the cosy kitchen. We stood in the doorway for a few moments looking at the scene and saying thank you to our cottage. You know how some houses have a cold feeling while others are bright and friendly? Well, Barley Cottage was one of those optimistic, warm places, a very happy home brimming with so many memories. I'd been there fifteen years, Maggie eight.

We'd loved it and felt it wanted our attention one more time. Upstairs we found Ella fast asleep covered by the large poster of the Owl and Pussy Cat verse that normally looked down on her.

Monday 30 October. N-Day minus one. Terrible storms overnight with 90 m.p.h. winds. Southern England has ground to a halt. Snow in Manchester. 'I'm giving in my notice tomorrow after twenty-two years!' I said repeatedly to nobody as I was blown across the field with the dogs. The village stream was just an inch from flooding. The oak trees outside Ella's school were creaking and shedding twigs. Over a late breakfast Maggie and I started to plan our strategy. We agreed we'd keep Ella in school until 16 January, the day we were due to leave, so as to sustain as much normality as possible for her and give us space to crack on with the packing.

Tuesday 31 October. Time to tell. I wasn't due into work until after lunch so I spent the morning ringing round removal companies making appointments for quotes on the cost of shipping our bulky furniture and considerable paraphernalia across Europe, while Maggie ironed feverishly in a bold bid to put a dent in the mountain of washing. I felt strangely at ease as I packed a map and photographs into my bag and drove to work. I didn't dither, strolling straight into the editor's office and handing Peter my letter of resignation. He was taken aback for a second, but said he'd sensed something was afoot over recent weeks and was keen to know what path my career was taking. We'd talked often enough in the past year about the strain of the night shift and my need to ring the changes somehow. He'd been concerned about my health and had done all he could to lighten the load and find a fitting challenge for me on the day shift, but it came to nothing, because there was nothing else that appealed to me. He knew better than anyone that I was a prime candidate to jump ship.

Then, as I pulled out the map and photographs and remarkably calmly told him where we were going, what we'd bought, what we'd be doing and that the whole thing was being filmed for Channel Four, his eyebrows went into orbit.

Olives, then Tragedy

mother's garden

*W*ith the cat well and truly out of the bag about our impending emigration and television notoriety, a steady stream of people made their way to our door and my desk at work to find out if it was all true. The expressions on the faces of a few of my colleagues had to be seen to be believed. I was a piece of the furniture, bolted to the floor. 'Someone said you're leaving – they're having me on. Right?' By the end of the first week I was growing tired of explaining but there seemed no let up. People I rarely spoke to were sidling up for a natter and to ask to see the photographs. My work was suffering, the time was ticking by and we'd made painfully little progress with either planning or packing.

Maggie was at a very low ebb as well. Both she and Joe Joe had dreadful colds and his rasping cough meant we were all starved of sleep. His cot was at the end of our bed so when we eventually managed to get him settled Maggie and I would take ourselves off to the spare room to try and rest and talk through the things we had to do without running the risk of waking him. But instead we lay looking at the depressing piles of paperwork and clutter piled high around the bed – a pot-pourri of my reference books and work files, cardboard boxes crammed with Maggie's paperwork from her years as a classical concerts promoter, and a mountain of clothes we never wore but couldn't bring ourselves to throw out. We'd joked that the move would be the time for a long overdue cathartic clearout, but now that it was staring us in the face it was far from funny.

There was another reason why that time sticks in the memory. It was the week when thousands of British homes were flooded as rivers burst their banks and everyone talked about how global warming was seriously screwing up the weather. It dominated the front page of the *Eastern Daily Press* for several days, including a story that parts of Spain would turn into deserts before long.

Slowly we managed to galvanise ourselves. We applied our minds to getting the dogs ready for their new lives. We could take Charlie and Megan out of the country, no problem, but there was no guarantee Spain would accept them without written confirmation from a vet that they were fine – and we wanted to have the option of bringing them back to the UK in an emergency. That meant they needed pet passports, assorted jabs including one against rabies, and have microchips put in their necks, all of which was going to cost £300 – if we could fathom out the various forms we had to fill in.

We weighed up what we could sell to offset the bill. Our garage, which had never been home to a car, was stacked to the gunnels with my tools and an ever-growing mass of 'may be useful one day' or 'perfect for a car boot' odds and sods. There were also boxes of garden toys, broken garden furniture, bicycles, old window frames, several hundred Norfolk red bricks salvaged from a lean-to I'd demolished ten years before, some roof tiles, half-used pots of paint – and a load of old doors and small oak beams I'd bought for no good reason save to fill the last remaining space in the garage.

One of the best press pictures I've ever seen was taken after storms in the mid-nineties had torn across Britain wreaking havoc. It spoke volumes about the way most of us live. It was an aerial shot of a block of eight garages and the roof had been torn off in the gale. One garage was completely empty, another had a bicycle in it, and the rest were jam packed with tat, just like ours.

The old bricks and tiles were our first sale. It felt good. A builder friend said he'd give us £130, and in clearing a path through the debris to get to them we managed to bring ourselves to throw a few things out. We also agreed to have a sale just after the New Year that would include a fair amount of clothes from our wardrobes and cupboards, some of which hadn't seen the light of day for a decade.

While America was deciding on the eve of Thanksgiving which turkey to vote for, Bush or Gore, several removal firms came to weigh up what it would cost to move us. Then the estimates started to pop through the letterbox and our daft notion that we could try and keep pace with our costs by flogging things fell apart. We were forced to face the fact we were going to have to part with at least £4000, about double what we'd expected. We knew the move would be expensive, but in the flurry of excitement and stress we hadn't got down to brass tacks. What with that and the growing realisation that we'd have to change our car too it looked as if we'd have virtually nothing in reserve once we arrived at Mother's Garden.

We eased the pain by selling my old oak writing desk (which doubled as a dining table) for £300, not a bad return on a £15 purchase fifteen years before, but we were still way off the pace.

Then my colleague Pete Kelley – who in my league of good eggs is a splendid soufflé – gently asked if we'd considered moving ourselves.

'You kidding?' I replied.

'It's possible – I'll drive if I can get the time off work,' he said.

'But we'd need a fleet of Transits.'

'No, you won't. You don't need an HGV for one of the smaller lorries and you can pack a hell of a lot in. Check out what it costs.'

That night at work a few of us on the graveyard shift stayed at our posts until 3.45 a.m. watching the Florida election debacle in disbelief while frantically trying to write and then rewrite the front page. A few hours earlier, though, blissfully unaware of the impending American soap opera, I'd grabbed

103

a moment during a lull in proceedings to sidle away to a corner of the office where I'd trawled around on the internet looking at vehicle hire websites. I did some sums. Pete was right. We could do the trip for a third of the cost if we could muster a few volunteers to help pack and load the lorry and then, all for love rather than money, give up a week of their time to make the trip with us. If.

But there was still a serious doubt whether the lorry would be big enough. As luck would have it, the next day our old friend Rob Stuart got in touch and without batting an eyelid volunteered himself and his Transit van. Remarkably within the week we had a crew – and the crackpot idea of leading our own convoy halfway across Europe didn't seem remotely potty. Maggie's brother Philip said he was game on and that he'd drive the truck with his friend Lawrie. My eighteen-year-old nephew Yan signed up too and we tracked down a good deal with Barford Truck Hire. In the meantime I'd negotiated to write an article for the *Daily Mail* that would take a sizeable bite out of the remaining cost.

We were still afloat and paddling like crazy.

While all this was going on we'd also been coming to terms with the fact that Henry, our much-loved but aged Mercedes estate, was never going to make it. He was liable to peg out halfway there and, even if he did keep going, the rocky track up to the farm would finish him off in a matter of weeks. It was a painful decision, but we knew we had to find another vehicle. We talked about what we needed and what we could afford and then, with a budget of £3000, I started searching for a cheap, reliable, comfortable, left-hand drive, diesel 4x4. Needless to say, they are thin on the ground. Ex-army Land Rovers were an option, but given how desperately basic, slow and noisy they are we soon abandoned that idea. We were looking for the proverbial needle in a haystack. I put an ad in the paper but no one called, so I started ploughing through the classified advertisements in every appropriate publication I could think of.

Finally, over a pint in a Norwich pub, I found one in a magazine. It was a 1989 Range Rover 2.5 diesel. It seemed to meet all our needs with the bonus of air conditioning, and was just £2750. I rang immediately. The car, which was in Lancashire, had been in Africa most of its life, hence the left-hand drive and air con. The owner seemed genuine enough and readily agreed for it to be checked over by an engineer. Bingo.

Meanwhile we continued our old habit of writing lists, only now they contained thumping great issues like finding out whether we could claim for child benefit, how to apply for Spanish residency, notifying all the authorities about when we were leaving, nailing a date with my boss when I could go, booking ferries and doing last-minute checks before we flew out to pick our olives.

All of a sudden the week of the harvest had arrived. I sat in bed on the Tuesday morning drinking tea, looking out across the cricket green and trying to get my head together. We were due to fly out the next day and the work gloves, hot water bottles, kettle, coffee and tea were packed. I had arranged to do the day shift to ease the trauma of the early morning flight on the Wednesday. There was still no news from the engineer about the Range Rover and it seemed increasingly likely I'd have to ring him from Spain. This time tomorrow, I thought, we'll be somewhere over France and heading for our olive grove. *Our olive grove.* I leant over to put my empty mug on the floor and noticed that the three books beside my bed were about health, downsizing and natural history.

Wednesday 22 November. Out of the house by 3.30 a.m. and at Mother's Garden by 2 p.m., along with harvest helpers Deanna, Philip, Liz and Gary. We just made it to the local wine cooperative to stock up before it closed for the afternoon and then to our delight we found the farmhouse full of treasures – food in the kitchen and flowers in many of the rooms. Then, as we opened the shutters to let in the autumn sun, Mac and Conxita chugged up the track in their old Land Rover with bedding and wellies. We felt overwhelmed by their kindness.

The discoveries continued. While the sleeping arrangements were being sorted out I attempted to light the wood burner in the main downstairs room. It was a lot more impressive than I remembered and eventually, as the house warmed and after I kept declaring my disbelief at our good luck, Mac gently admitted he'd replaced the old one with a more effective burner they had stored at their house. He'd replaced all the flue too.

Anything else you want to tell me? I asked.

Well, he said meekly, there's a new saw horse in the wood store, but that's all, honest.

But in the next four days we discovered a great deal more.

Ella trotted off to school for a day and a major worry dissolved when she said she'd be happy to go again. While she was in the village and Joe Joe slept, we went to work. Gary rigged up a fig tree swing for Ella, we sifted through the contents of the barn and, in between spreading the nets and gathering what few olives there were to be had on our neglected trees, we explored the land and bashed our way into the derelict house beside the track. Inside we found old wooden caskets for carrying grapes, thousands of unused wall tiles – and a yellow 1960s Seat. The car looked complete, but the tyres were flat, the upholstery was rotting, the screen and paintwork were covered in bird poo and the bonnet was up, suggesting it had long since gasped its last.

Then, two days into our trip, we realised we owned more land than we thought. Two terraces of almond trees that we'd dismissed as belonging to a neighbour were (a check on the map over a boozy lunch in the village restaurant proved) in fact ours. We'd lost our bearings during the one and only guided tour of the boundary back in July, and wrongly assumed that because the terraces at the top of the track were relatively neat and tidy they couldn't be part of the farm, much of which was all but abandoned.

The whole harvest trip went remarkably well and there was plenty of time to relax and socialise over the five days. Marta, Mac and Conxita helped us gather our olives then we went on to their farms to return the favour, but generally the crop was poor and we had plenty of time to chat about what we faced when we moved.

I rang the motor engineer I'd paid to check the Range Rover and he seemed satisfied, so I picked up the phone again straightaway and agreed to buy a car I'd never seen. We flew home on the Monday morning happy but tired and at Stansted airport Maggie and the children headed back to Norfolk while I worked out how best to get to Lancashire. By the end of the day I'd travelled by Spanish hire car, jet, taxi, London tube, bus and Range Rover.

The taxi and tube got me to Victoria bus station which was bursting at the seams on account of the rail safety chaos that followed a series of autumn track disasters. I had two hours to burn. London was in the grip of a pre-Christmas bomb alert and all my big city anxieties bubbled to the surface.

I jammed into the waiting area with the crush of people, found a seat and watched as a drunk checked the rank of pay phones for forgotten change. The place was noisy and dirty and the air was foul. Two pigeons were flying just above our heads and amid the melee two Japanese girls sat slumped together like ragdolls fast asleep.

My plan was to try and find a late-night bus to Oldham and then ring Tony, the man who was selling the car, and ask if he'd pick me up. I needn't have worried.

He was waiting for me at Manchester bus station.

Back at his house he and wife Jenny tried to persuade me to stay the night, but I made my apologies, said I wanted to get home, downed a coffee and roared off at midnight across the moors towards Holmfirth and the A1.

The next day we saw our new car in the daylight, found a

copy of the *Ghana Highway Code* inside, had a little drive and then settled on the name Robbie, Robbie the Range Rover. The number plate ended in CVR, the initials of a famously erudite theatre reviewer and likeable colleague called Charles Roberts, but our dog was called Charlie so the Christian name was out of the question. Anyway, it didn't go with Range Rover.

The run up to Christmas was understandably chaotic, but we pressed on and I finally brought myself to sell my most valuable books, some of them more than two hundred years old. That brought in a few hundred pounds and, seeing little point in lugging them halfway across Europe, I sold some more to friends at knockdown prices. Most of the old books were too frail to be read which to my mind rather defeated the object of owning them (I kept telling myself) and, anyway, we had to find a way to cut back on the volume and weight of our clutter. As it was we faced taking hundreds of books with us.

We had some cheery news too – P&O Stena was interested in our story and their staff were very helpful in organising our unusual convoy's ferry hop to France. We settled on the 4 a.m. ferry on Wednesday 17 January. Within a few hours we discovered that because of my national insurance contributions over the years we qualified for an A106 certificate giving us free health cover in Spain for up to eighteen months. I also found a sturdy second-hand road trailer for Robbie, and Liz and Gary said we could use their roof box. Things were coming together.

*

Then tragedy struck.

Mum started to find it difficult to express herself. She muddled words, started dropping things. She'd always been strong and fit and with an unerring vitality, but now she seemed so frail. Yet despite her deterioration she remained defiant, steadfastly insisting nothing was wrong. My stepfather, ever supportive of her, did not argue. They said she was tired, that was all. There was nothing we could do. Our anxiety grew and grew in the week leading up to Christmas and finally, on 23 December, she admitted to me she sensed something may be wrong. My sister Jackie and I went round immediately and persuaded Mum to let us call a doctor. He was there within an hour. By this time she couldn't finish a sentence. He examined her and said she may have had a stroke. But she refused to leave her home, so the doctor said he would arrange for her to see a specialist and have a brain scan immediately after Christmas. He left and we all burst into tears.

For several years Jackie and I had discussed what were, on reflection, obvious steps in Mum's decline, moments when something seemed to have happened to weaken her. In the past eighteen months she had grown increasingly irrational. There were days when something had occurred but it was impossible to define. Maybe there had been other strokes. Now, aged seventy-six it seemed as if her diabetes may have overpowered her.

She spent Christmas Day in bed, saying nothing more than 'yes' or shaking her head, unable to walk unaided and needing to be lifted onto the loo.

The doctor came back on Boxing Day and immediately called for an ambulance. The last remnants of dignity went and, watching them carry her down the stairs wrapped in a blanket and strapped into a chair, I sensed she would never return.

After an hour in casualty I followed her through to the medical assessment ward where she lay on a bed near the main door, shielded only by a curtain from all the comings and goings. She gripped my finger with her left hand. Her right arm was now paralysed. I watched her trying to rest as people coughed and cried out beyond the curtain and I thought about her flowing handwriting and wave at the gate, always with her right hand. A machine kept bleating and she seemed to mutter 'bloody hell' and then repeatedly pointed for me to go.

The next morning and for two weeks after that she was on Filby Ward in the Norfolk and Norwich Hospital as the staff ran tests and we all sat around her bed in a daze. They told us she had cerebral vascular disease. The consultant said she had suffered brain damage and there was little chance of even partial recovery. Dear Lord. We refused to believe it, clinging to the hope that, like so many stroke victims, she may one day recover some faculties. We spent hours on the ward, where other patients seemed to be in various stages of dementia, looking for signs of understanding in Mum's face. She seemed to recognise us. We believed she was aware of what was happening but couldn't tell us directly. It was all very surreal. The sweet woman in the next bed tried to take Mum's slippers off her feet, claiming they were hers. Staff seemed to be thin on the ground so I tried to help another patient with her food. 'Oh, you shouldn't touch that,' she scolded me. 'It belongs to London Transport. Now be a dear and fetch a telephone would you. I want to call the police.'

I would visit Mum during the day when she might be awake for a few moments and she would fix me with a stare as if she was desperately trying to communicate. Then I would go again and sit alone at her bedside in the early hours after work. It was a peaceful time, a chance to tell her how much I loved her and to sit in the dimmed ward and try and work out what we should do. Everything was set for us to emigrate in three weeks' time. 'What is the right thing to do, Mum?' I'd ask as she slept.

On New Year's Eve I was able to finish work and be at her bedside before midnight. I stayed until long after the New Year had chimed, and by the time I rose to leave I was reconciled. Suddenly, somehow, the guilt and uncertainty lifted. I can't explain exactly why but in the end it was not a difficult decision to continue on our journey to Mother's Garden, however distressing my mother's illness was.

From that moment I have applied a simple rule regarding all decisions concerning Mum – I would do what she would do. An indomitable spirit who spoke frankly and sparkled in company, she always lived her life to the full, and pushed hard to fulfil her dreams. She would want us to carry on.

Journey to Mother's Garden

mother's garden

As people toasted the arrival of 2001 there was a myriad of emotions in my head and heart that many people may recognise.

During more than twenty-two years at Eastern Counties Newspapers I'd waved off countless colleagues who were either bolting for pastures new or simply being (or volunteering to be) put out to grass. Listening to the farewell speeches I always wondered what it must be like to suddenly stop doing something that so dominated your existence, to leave familiar surroundings, routines and, most importantly, friends. The goodbyes, particularly the ones for staff who were retiring after decades at the coalface, were usually quite poignant and I would try and imagine how it would feel for them two weeks or two months later when the reality kicked in, even for those who couldn't wait to get out of the door.

My work also brought me into regular contact with people

who had hopped around the country from company to company and had, in my eyes, earned gold braid for bravery. They didn't seem to need security or continuity. I, on the other hand, had worked for the same company in the same county for more than half my life and they were both a huge part of me. I was proud of it in a way, and felt a strong sense of loyalty to the newspaper and a kinship with my colleagues many of whom had clocked up a similar innings. Despite all that, though, I'd sensed for some time for reasons of my family and health that I should sign off and try something new. But leaving was not going to be easy.

3 January was my last time in the night editor hot seat. It was uneventful, thank goodness. The next day I moved to the day shift, cleared my desk and found out what it felt like to walk away.

Billy and Will from Ricochet Films followed me around the office with their camera and understandably added a little tension, but actually I felt remarkably calm. I suppose it was the huge sense of relief that, despite all the physical and emotional stresses of the past months, I'd managed to reach the finishing line without the egg falling off the spoon.

So, having put the paper to bed for the last time, I squandered my final day on the payroll chatting to friends, obliging the camera crew, finding long-lost notes in the mountain of dust behind my computer and under my desk and rereading my last piece for the paper. It was a feature about Tusha, a tiny Mozambican waif who'd sidled up to me and sat on my knee during my African trip ten months before. She had Aids

114

and had died just before Christmas. I have a treasured photograph of her above my desk as I write – she's sitting bewildered on the ground among other sick and dying children at Father André's mission, her charity jumper with its lines of little hearts reflecting the love she found in the last months of her short life. I hoped some words and a picture of her might generate a few more pounds for Father André. It seemed my most worthwhile parting shot.

Then it was time for the formal send-off and I was facing a crowd of colleagues in the newsroom as the editor comically ran through my years at the company, from the time when I scraped through the recruitment aptitude test way back in 1977 despite deciding that 'affluent' meant 'proud' and 'harangue' was a 'vessel'.

I did my best to respond, swallowed hard when it was revealed that the office whip round had raised half the cost of a rotovator for the farm, and then was presented with a stunning photograph of a sunrise over Norfolk marshes. The final acts were to hand in my mobile phone, security pass and the keys to the editor's office, then it was over to the social club for the customary final jar or two.

There were just eleven days left before we emigrated.

I slept a lot over the next two days, Friday and Saturday, and in the waking hours we fretted about what needed to be done but achieved precious little. On the Sunday, after buying a second-hand road trailer which at least felt like a significant step in the right direction, Ella and I visited Mum in her hospital ward on the seventh floor, taking some oil to massage her feet. She drifted in and out of consciousness and we stayed a long time, somehow ending up leading most of the patients in a chorus of nursery rhymes. One woman complained about the draught from the window and when it became clear it was rotten beyond repair we blocked the cracks with piles of the New Testament.

On the Monday we began packing in earnest and the house and garage started to feel different as we set about building mountains of cardboard boxes. That night I sat in the conservatory looking into the kitchen at the familiar, cosy scene and said a few thank yous for so many happy times over fifteen years. We'd wanted to say a big thank you to the village, too, so had booked the community centre next door for a party on the Saturday night, two days before we completed on the sale and were due to begin our journey. It was another thing to organise but everyone seemed to appreciate the notion, while our nearest and dearest gamely volunteered to help with the catering. We'd no idea how many people would turn up, but optimistically put in an order for enough sangria to satisfy about a hundred people.

In those disorientating days it turned out that the government agency dealing with our dogs' passports had lost the forms, while the DVLC declared it couldn't issue an export licence for Robbie the Range Rover because the chassis number didn't match their files. Both shocks took valuable hours to sort out and we also had to fork out £447 for a major service for the car which revealed a variety of little problems.

But we kept plugging away, urging each other on and staying up late into the night emptying the loft and agonising over the fate of every possession.

Some weeks earlier Maggie had hit on the idea of a table-top sale to raise cash so our clobber was put into four heaps – Spain, sale, waste tip and 'can't take with us but can't bear to part with' pile. The last assortment, which included things like my beer mat collection and our hefty boxes of vinyl albums that hadn't been played for years, was destined to gather dust in Maggie's mother's barn to await export at a later, extremely vague, date.

The table-top sale was also set for the Saturday just before the party. It proved to be an exceptionally weird and wonderful day. During the day in the community centre, scene of so many lovely occasions including Ella's fourth birthday bash and fleeting glories in the village vegetable show, a great lump of our lives was laid out for all to see and hopefully buy. A steady stream of local folk sauntered in and (probably out of charity) wandered out again with a variety of unnecessary plastic objects, tatty books, out-dated fashions and daft *objets d'art*. We raised about £100, folded up the tables and with just over an hour to go set about blowing up balloons, laying out glasses and praying someone would turn up to say goodbye.

By midnight we were elated, inebriated, and incredibly appreciative of our friends and families who turned out in force to help and to send us on our way. The sangria was gone in a flash. It was probably the first and last time, too, that a barbershop quartet (a brilliant bunch from the village), a

Spanish guitarist duo (including Steve Holmes who'd played at our wedding reception eight years before) and flamenco dancer have successfully shared a bill. Looking back it would have been unthinkable not to do it, to be able to say goodbye in such a positive, loving atmosphere, even if it risked stressing us out or filling us with doubts. In fact it did the opposite. It soothed us, made us enormously grateful and in a strange way made it easier to leave. We'd tied a ribbon around that chapter of our lives.

On the Sunday we pressed on with the packing. By the evening, with so many people helping, we felt we had almost broken the back of it. First thing on the Monday I went to pick up the hire truck, roared back to the cottage, rammed it into reverse and promptly knocked over one of the brick gate posts I'd built ten years before.

'How on earth am I going to tell the buyer that?' I cried, slapping my forehead, but builder friend Dave said immediately he'd fix it after we'd hit the road.

Rob arrived with his Transit and, along with Dave, my nephew Yan, my stepsister Veronica and her partner Steve, Maggie's sister Liz, went through the house like a dose of salts.

The cottage had a different resonance as it emptied. I found pictures from the time I'd bought it in 1986 and before I'd put my handprint on it. I wandered about remembering the milestones – like when I discovered the bath overflow went nowhere except down through the kitchen ceiling; my years alone there when I was broke and mildly reclusive; the day

Maggie came to stay and never left; her leaning against the landing wall, larger than life with Ella due to burst into our world. So many memories.

Ella went to school on both the Monday and Tuesday to keep things as seam-free and stress-free as possible for her, then at 3.30 p.m. on the Tuesday we were done.

Maggie's brother Philip and his old pal Lawrie were driving the truck and were joined by Yan. Ricochet film researcher Angani, armed with a camera, kept Rob company in his Transit. We'd agreed to meet up in Dover.

Every last square inch of the truck, Transit, trailer and roof box was used and, after an emotional hug with neighbours Arthur and Audrey, we waved off the other vehicles, handed over the house keys, loaded up baby Joe Joe, fired up the car and headed for the village primary school. I didn't look back.

I suppose she had no idea what was happening to her, but five-year-old Ella clambered eagerly aboard and waved happily to her friends as we began our journey to Mother's Garden.

The P&O Stena ferry was booked for 4 a.m. on the Wednesday morning. We gathered at Maggie's Mum's farm for supper and to pick up the dogs who'd been there for a couple of days while we cleared the cottage. Then Maggie and I borrowed Beryl's car and went to the Norfolk and Norwich Hospital to say goodbye to my mother. I couldn't be sure I'd see her again and the tears flowed.

Back at the farm we tried to rest but before we knew it the

time had come to carry the sleepy children out into the cold night and to hit the road. One of the biggest concerns was that Charlie, our loveable springer spaniel who is a bit of a blouse, would be freaked by the yellow trailer and break through the dog guard. When he was a puppy he'd jumped a mile the first time he farted. We'd made a very comfortable bed for him and his younger sister Megan in the back of the Range Rover and they had more room than the rest of us. But no. Three yards out of the farm drive and Charlie had propelled himself through the barricade and was sitting shaking on top of baby Joe Joe. I lost count of how many times during the two-day journey our nutty hound was suddenly gripped by the notion the trailer was out to get him and ended up on Maggie's lap for reassurance.

Dover docks leave a lot to be desired at 3 a.m. on a freezing winter morning. Not surprisingly there were no other emigrants or tourists queuing to get on. We left the engine running to keep us warm, walked the dogs in the empty car park and watched the lorry and ferry traffic coming and going. Our truck weighed in at 7.4 tonnes. The limit was 7.5.

Ella was just starting to question what on earth we were doing, while the rigours and emotions of it all were beginning to weigh on both of us when, thankfully, we were waved aboard. The ferry company knew we were being filmed and I, looking like nothing on earth, suddenly found myself shaking hands with the captain. We were shown to a posh lounge, offered drinks, and then our troupe crashed out on the bench seats.

I wedged myself into a bar chair with Joe Joe asleep on my chest and started to reflect that we were dangerously wrong to attempt a house move and a self-drive emigration all on the same day. If proof was needed that we were foggy headed we managed to loose £300 in francs somewhere between Dover and Calais.

It may have only been 7 a.m. but the French roads were madness. It was still dark as we left the French port. Maggie was behind the wheel as, hearts thumping, we plunged into the stream of traffic and panicked about keeping the truck and van in view. We also found out how remarkably fast a fully laden truck can go.

The skies began to lighten as we passed Abbeville and then, feeling we were doing really well, we stopped for a late breakfast just beyond Rouen. The concerns about the convoy getting split up were discussed and Lawrie lent us his mobile phone so we then had one in each vehicle.

The dogs had a walk again then we rattled south heading for Le Mans, but now the decision to save a little more money by avoiding toll roads suddenly didn't seem such a good idea. There was a roundabout virtually every kilometre along one stretch and poor Ella first went a funny colour and then threw up. It was a first for her on a car journey, but instead of blubbering she immediately wanted us to ring her friend Kate to tell her.

The aroma and our anxiety for Ella did something to Charlie, too, and he promptly decided he'd had enough of the trailer again. We stopped, cleared up the mess, put Charlie back and then Ella came in the front with me to try and avoid a repeat performance. Maggie went in the back to try and sleep and to dissuade Charlie from sitting on seven-month-old Joe Joe who, like Ella, was being an absolute trouper.

Charlie was having none of it, of course, so Maggie tried to sleep with a four-stone dog on her lap. Ella, poor thing, was gripped by nausea and at one point I was driving one handed at 70 m.p.h. on a dual carriageway where it was impossible to stop with my other cupped hand full of, er . . . yes.

Matters deteriorated further when, during a disastrous pit stop at a greasy spoon café in a town just north of Le Mans, Ella was violently ill over the table and several plates of food, all over Maggie and, just for good measure, in Joe's change bag. I went in search of a chemist and bought some travel sickness pills which eased her ordeal a little but she had a dreadful day.

Our destination was the farmhouse of Philip's friends Kath and Martin about thirty miles inland from La Rochelle. They had converted the outbuildings into gîtes and had kindly invited us to use them as a pit stop.

We arrived just after 8 p.m. The inside of our car was a scheme of utter chaos with bags, clothes and rubbish everywhere and it was a hugely depressing thought that we were only halfway through our journey. Everyone else went off for a meal in a restaurant, but we couldn't even think about it. We got the kids to bed and then set about reorganising the car and washing our clothes. Within minutes Kath's beautiful kitchen was filled with our clobber and stank to high heaven. We just prayed they didn't come back early.

Luckily, the children slept well and seemed fine the next morning. We managed to sleep too, albeit fitfully, and were keen to press on. I walked the dogs before breakfast and saw men with guns skirting the woods across the field. Kath told how boar hunters had once chased a wounded animal into their yard and killed it. The last thing we need, I said, is for Charlie (who loves to go walkabout and so has to be kept on a lead) to escape. 'But Dad—' said Ella, 'Charlie just went past the window.' He'd found a way out of the car and was heading for the horizon.

I bounded after him cursing and manically waving my fists at the heavens like Basil Fawlty. Given the likelihood that it would be several hours before he came crawling back covered in mud, I figured our plans were in ruins. Worse still the daft dog would probably get shot.

But for once the fact that he's scared of his own shadow paid off. One distant gunshot and he was back eager for a cuddle. From that point on he made his peace with the trailer and stayed put with Megan in the back of the car.

From Kath and Martin's we headed down the Atlantic coast towards Biarritz. Although Mother's Garden is in north-eastern Spain near the Mediterranean coast, we'd decided to cross the Pyrenees at the western end. It seemed to make sense given that we were in western France and the roads heading due south looked very good. We also opted to pay motorway tolls in an effort to speed things up and limit the chances of travel sickness.

Going over the middle of the mountains in the depths of

winter was not an option and the only other way was to cross southern France and skirt the mountains at the eastern end but, given where we had broken our journey, that looked more complicated. So we belted past Bordeaux and finally reached the border by 4 p.m. when the sun came out to greet us.

'Not long now!' we cried. If only we knew.

It took another ten, painfully long hours (including a debacle in Zaragoza when we managed to get the truck wedged in a one-way back street) before we finally skidded up the muddy drive to Mother's Garden. In the last four hours the convoy fell apart, we got lost and then fog followed by torrential rain made driving and navigating a nightmare. At least one thing was certain. Mac and Conxita had said they would be waiting whatever the hour with the fires lit and food on the table.

But the farmhouse was in darkness. A film crew emerged from behind a tree, told us to ignore them and then recorded our struggle to find the key and get it in the lock. The house was damp and cold. We stumbled about in a daze, sat our wonderful children on a chair wrapped in a blanket, and then tried to light the wood burner.

The van and truck rolled up and while I brought the dogs into the house Maggie went to the back of the van to try and find their bedding. She heard a rustling in the bushes. Thinking it was wild boar, she was about to beat a hasty retreat when Mac and Conxita popped up their heads and asked if it would be OK to come out. It turned out the film crew had told them they couldn't go into the house as it would be far better for the documentary if the house was cold and empty when we arrived. They'd been forced to wait for hours in their Land Rover which was hidden further up the track.

With the wood burner roaring, our exhaustion and stress gave way to relief and laughter as we slapped backs and toasted our achievement. Somehow we'd made it without any major disasters or cock-ups.

We popped the children into bed and then popped the cork of a magnum of sparkling wine given to us by ex-neighbours Tim and Claire. Then we talked and talked and talked until someone said it was 5.30 a.m.

First Days

mother's garden

*O*n that first full day at Mother's Garden, as we unloaded the vehicles and stumbled around our new home in a fog of tiredness (and hangover) trying to remember what was in which box, I suddenly noticed an enormous television aerial on the roof. How the hell I'd missed it before I'll never know. I commented that it made the farmhouse look like a defunct Soviet listening station.

'Where's your television set?' Yan asked hopefully as the barn slowly filled with a mountain of extraneous belongings.

'We haven't got one, ' I replied. 'Not sure it would work here and, anyway, we needed to cut right back to just the essentials. We didn't feel a TV was essential.'

'Another question then,' Rob piped up from under a rolled rug he was carrying on his head.

'Yep?'

'What on earth', he dropped the rug and staggered back to his van, 'is this doing here?' He re-emerged holding my ancient Imperial typewriter. 'It doesn't work – I've tried it – and it weighs a ton.'

'Ah, um.'

'And these!' said Yan, pointing to two boxes full of empty jam jars, under a split carrier bag full of metal coat hangers.

'Now those I can explain. Maggie's going to be making a lot of jam.'

'And clothes too?' Then their eyes flitted backwards and forwards between me and the typewriter seeking an explanation for that.

'And as for that,' I obliged, 'I've . . . I've had it, well, for yonks – it was my first typewriter. My first. I've got rid of two others, but this one is . . . is . . .'

'Buggered.'

'I like to look at it.'

'A typewriter?'

'We kept it in the bedroom at the cottage, in front of the fireplace on my side of the bed. It's lovely don't you think?'

My question, it seemed, didn't merit a reply. Yan changed tack.

'You could have brought the old TV and just tried it and thrown it if it hadn't worked.'

'Yes, I suppose so, but we wanted to try living without one for a change, so we gave it away.'

Forsaking the box wasn't intended to be a great crusade, just a trial to see if we could kick the habit. We used to kid ourselves that we weren't great TV watchers and felt that we were discerning viewers who dodged the garbage, but in truth we could be lulled into a trance as easily as anyone.

Remarkably in the following weeks and months as we started to settle at Mother's Garden we only once or twice toyed briefly with the idea of getting a set. The plausible arguments were that it would have been a huge fillip to our flagging linguistic development – and there were those classic parental moments when it would have been bliss to wish the kids sweet dreams, to curl up on the sofa with a bottle of wine and blot out the big picture in favour of the small one, even if we couldn't understand all the dialogue. Getting a television might also have been propelled up the order of merit if Ella had squealed, but there was barely a peep from her. Her small selection of videos gathered dust on a shelf. As for Maggie and me, in those first weeks we rarely had either the time or the inclination to even think about it.

Six months after arriving we were taking time out under the fig trees watching Ella and her visiting cousins Caleb and Savanna run races round the house in the twilight. Little Joe Joe was charging about on all fours and throwing up a trail of dust. His sagging nappy was covered in bits of grass and the mucky chap resembled a mudlark from the Victorian slums. But he was glowing with fun – they all were – and none of them used the T word.

My sister Jackie did, though, under the heading 'things we missed and things we didn't' (a regular question from visitors) and having again pooh-poohed the idea of television there were a few titters at the thought that our metamorphosis from middle England to Mother's Garden was to be the subject of a TV documentary.

But we hadn't been completely cut off from the outside world since our move. Yan's comment about a television set on that first day did set me foraging for my new Roberts radio. Once a journalist, always a news addict. I denied it, of course, declaring that a clean break would be edifying, but I thank the stars that I weakened and splashed out £30 on the dinky radio just days before we left. I traced it to one of the boxes in the barn, upturning countless others in the process, and every day since then the BBC World Service has kick-started my day.

But one thing was different. My perspective. Listening to the radio there was no more of the Norfolk and British news focus I was accustomed to – just a sobering view of events as if from the pale blue balloon we call the moon, tied to a world which indeed often resembled a bear with very little brain. In a way the morning radio ritual rapidly became an essential part of my new life as I detached myself from old thoughts and widened my horizons.

Maggie was less attached to it – except for the day I picked up that the BBC was going to devote nearly an hour to the Wigmore Hall classical concert venue in London where she worked in the eighties.

'That's William! And Paula! Damn, the signal's gone again.'

It didn't help that the programme coincided with an essential (but I've forgotten why) frantic dash down the twisty mountain road to Tarragona. Turning it up to full volume and hanging out of the car window with the radio pressed to her ear and aerial extended seemed to help, but every time we zigged we lost contact and Maggie issued a few expletives until we zagged again.

As for television, I wasn't, I confess, entirely abstemious. Not long after we settled in Pere sidled up to me after he'd unlocked the school gate and the kids had poured out.

'Come round tomorrow night if you want. Barcelona are playin'. Half past eight, I think.'

By the time I rolled up he'd carried his television and an extension lead onto the patio where, much to the amusement of his artist wife Nuria, we drank beer and were bitten by mosquitoes while cheering on Barca as darkness fell. In the course of the first year I ended up in front of his set about six times, always for football.

Maggie and I knew the computer had a DVD player but we didn't have a clue how to work it until a more technically minded visitor from England showed us. Then, excited at the prospect of flopping on a sofa, we joined the local library and borrowed a few films and wildlife documentaries, but most of them for whatever reason elected to grind to a halt halfway through, causing consternation and tantrums. Even the children got upset.

In those first days the January weather was kind to us as we tried to organise ourselves, but even though it was dry and bright it was toe-curlingly cold at night. The old doors and windows leaked like sieves and the stone floors were like ice.

Before going to bed on the Friday, our second night at the farm, we had a stab at blocking a few of the draughts, and in a stroke of luck managed to track down the hot water bottles among the luggage. But it was still bitter and Joe Joe was put to bed in a hat and mittens, a routine that was to continue for weeks. We'd pitched camp with the kids on a couple of mattresses in the large open space at the top of the stairs where the wind whistled from several directions. The wood burner just couldn't cope all night, and lying awake shivering we endured our first wee small hours recital by the howling guard dogs at the pig farm across the road.

'If this is how it's going to be I vote we get a gun!' said Maggie burying her head under the pillow.

The next morning we found that the water pipes to the kitchen and shower room – which had been rather crudely laid from the tank in the storeroom in a groove cut along the outside of the back wall – didn't (surprisingly) need a lot of encouragement to freeze.

The old wooden beams supporting the first floor had clearly had a serious attack of worm and we couldn't be sure when they were treated, if at all, so that would need addressing before long. And the ceiling in the kitchen, directly below the bed in the spare room, was cracked and shedding the occasional piece of plaster, so I laid a large piece of wood on the floor upstairs to spread the weight, while pondering on how best to explain to friends that came to stay that it was in their interests to avoid getting frisky during the night.

It also became abundantly clear that the general state of the electrics could, at best, be described as wobbly. If we plugged in the kettle or the little oven with the dodgy door (which we later discovered had a hole at the back) all the lights lost about a third of their power. And when we tried to unplug an appliance the socket invariably came out of the wall as well. This was helpful, in a way, because I learned very early on that one of the challenges that lay ahead was working out which was live and which was neutral – every wire in the house seemed to be blue. There was no sign of an earth.

But, we said, looking on the bright side, the house was generally dry and we had the little Calor gas hob which, although it sported as much rust as the knackered Seat I'd owned in the late seventies, worked remarkably well. If we dragged old hazel wood from the abandoned terraces, chopped it up and loaded the wood burner and fireplace we could be cosy. A bath would have been bliss, but when the water was running the shower worked well. If you flushed the loo everything disappeared to a relatively new twin pit septic tank. It could have been far worse. The house could wait while we got our heads round some more pressing matters on the farm.

On the Saturday our volunteer truck drivers Philip and Laurie, who intended to head back to England the next morning, put a smile on the woman's face at the local wine cooperative when they loaded up with fifty litres of red wine. Then, that evening, we formed another convoy and followed Mac and Conxita's Land Rover into the town two miles away for the festival of St Antoni.

'You might find it fun,' they said. 'And, befitting the occasion, we should see our friend Antonio on his horse.'

'Oh good,' said Maggie with a broad grin.

We'd met local farmer Antonio during an earlier visit and he'd created quite an impression – friendly, helpful and gorgeous.

'Where're we off to?' asked Philip.

'Oh, some sort of local street parade,' I replied. 'I know everybody's knackered and we don't need to stay long, but we might as well go and have a look. We could mingle a bit.'

'Mingle?' asked Maggie.

'You know, get our bearings, meet people, that sort of stuff.'

We couldn't believe it. It was dark and very cold, but the streets were jam-packed with people waiting for the parade to begin. Somehow we managed to push our way through and meet up with neighbour Marta and her daughters Helia and Paula, and had just guided Ella and Paula to the front to get a good view of whatever was about to happen when all hell broke loose.

A number of men dressed as devils suddenly made their presence felt by swirling deafening firecrackers in the air that spat into the crowd like huge sparklers. People around us cheered and laughed but for the uninitiated with a nervous disposition it must have seemed like a masochistic pyromaniacs convention. We ducked for cover as they passed, praying Ella was OK and that Joe Joe, who was in a carrier on my back, wasn't on fire or irrecoverably traumatised. The racket all but drowned out the small band of musicians walking dangerously close behind the devils.

'Is that normal?' I asked. Mac nodded with a grin.

Then, squeezing through the crush, came a seemingly endless procession of pony and donkey carts, beautifully decorated with paper flowers and laden with children in traditional Catalan dress throwing copious quantities of hard sweets, one of which nearly took my eye out. It was quite a spectacle and the sense of fun was contagious. Then, bringing up the rear, came elegant women and handsome men on prancing horses. Antonio saw us and waved.

'Shall we go to the church?' Conxita asked when the last horse and rider had passed. It was agreed and we cut through the back streets to get there before them. We pressed on through the crowds and up the hill to the old part of town where we stationed ourselves on a street corner overlooking the square in front of the church.

The carts trundled by along the old brick street and then came the frisky horses again, just inches from us and looking as if they may bolt at any second. They turned and clattered their hooves impatiently as the procession stopped and started, but the riders were serene and you sensed the crowd's trust.

Then, suddenly, Antonio was there on his white stallion, reaching down to pluck Ella out of the sea of people. We watched open-mouthed as our beaming daughter was swept off her feet and then she and Antonio rode off down towards the square.

'That should have been me!' yelled Maggie.

'I'll borrow a mule,' I said.

Then, as the crowd stood and listened to the speeches we could see Ella in the middle of it all, now alone atop the horse and looking for the world as if she belonged. The other horsemen and women had dismounted so for a moment she was the centre of attention, riding straight-backed as Antonio held the reins and let the horse move in a circle.

We went home with horse poo on our shoes, pockets full of sweets and with a tingle of excitement about our new world.

On the Sunday we waved off Philip and Laurie and turned our attention to the vines which, we'd been warned, would need pruning immediately. Rob, with his raft of experience from working in French vineyards, was ready to get stuck in, but he wanted to check on the local way of doing things before wielding the secateurs.

Marta asked an English-speaking friend Alex, a horticulturist from the village, to give us a masterclass. He obligingly turned up early that morning and, having wrapped ourselves in scarves, and armed with old pairs of secateurs from among the tools in the barn, we eagerly followed him and Rob into the little vineyard beside the house.

Each vine had six to ten bare shoots from the previous year, splaying out from the swollen, older growth with its three or four twisting stems and flaking bark. It was a cold scene, far removed from when we'd first been enchanted by Mother's Garden in the previous July, when the stems were a

135

beautiful mass of green leaf arching over with the increasing weight of ripening grapes.

These were *garnacha* vines, Alex told us – very strong and usually not trained along wires like other varieties. He knelt in front of the first one. 'Now to begin,' he said. But it was impossible for us to see where. It seemed to be sprouting at all angles. I glanced at the next vine, which appeared even more complicated.

'You must choose three shoots that are growing upwards and which keep the shape of the vine. This one, this one and this one. Then,' snip, snip, snip, 'cut these back to two or three buds. See? These will be the shoots for this year. Now,' snip, snip, snip 'cut away all the other shoots you don't want back to the old vine. Be sure you don't leave any extra buds, OK?' It took him about as long as it took you to read about it. 'Now you.'

We moved along to the next one, blew out our cheeks, threw a knowing smile at each other like two people about to be let loose on a potter's wheel for the first time, and rubbed our chins. It was fascinating, engrossing – a knowledge we wanted and which, despite the host of challenges we now faced, had been the farm task at the forefront of our minds.

I plunged in. 'How about keeping this one and, er, this one and, maybe this one?'

'Good. Very good. But maybe, because the vine is leaning we keep this one instead,' snip, snip, 'OK? Also, you need to look for the strongest shoot, too, so maybe not that one but this one.' Snip snip. 'Also think to keep the shape, the balance of the vine with an open space in the middle so air can flow, yes? So, where there is no new growth on this piece of old vine we cut it off.' Alex pulled a curved saw, about a foot long, and laid into the vine. None of the three shoots I'd selected survived.

'You have to be quite hard on them then?'

'If you prune carefully the vine is stronger.'

Maggie had already moved on to the next plant. We were on our way. We worked together, as we have loved to do ever since, debating the options and trying to solve the puzzles. Alex watched over us, while Rob went to work on another row. The strongest shoots were about the thickness of a finger and tough to cut, and after several vines our hands were already stiff.

'You need to get some new cutters, I think, yes?'

'The worry,' said Maggie, standing for a second and looking at the rows of unpruned vines, 'is that we won't be able to do this well enough. We have to do this properly. It's an important crop for us.'

'Don't worry. You will learn.'

'Maggie's right, though,' I added. 'We need to get some money from the grape harvest.'

'You will get a little money,' said Alex. There was a slight pause and as he turned his attention to another vine he added, 'In the first years a very little money, I think.'

There were only three hundred vines in the five-year-old lower vineyard, but another five hundred or so far older ones at the top of the land – a rather sad-looking collection of *carinyena* vines which, like the *granacha*, were also freestanding and just as mind-boggling to fathom out.

The immediate problem was that at the rate we were working it would take us weeks to prune the lot. If we managed to avoid doing irreparable damage to the vines we hoped they would bring in the equivalent of several hundred pounds – not a lot, but given our vastly reduced cost of living it was very important to our budget. And, just as crucially, we wanted to prove to ourselves and the locals that we could do it.

Thank heavens for friends, because by this time Rob was working up a head of steam and then the cavalry, Marta, Conxita and Mac, arrived to lend a hand. Slowly the vineyard changed shape, and Alex, seemingly content that we'd grasped the basics, told Maggie he'd come back another day to explain what needed to be done with the sulphur powder and copper sulphate.

'What's that for?' I asked.

'I'm not entirely sure,' said Maggie. 'Mildew is one threat, I know. I'm just concerned to get it right about exactly when to put this stuff on and to keep it to a minimum. It's acceptable to use them on an organic farm, but sparingly. The timing is so important and I'm worried because I don't know enough about them . . .'

'. . . Yet. We've a lot to learn.'

'Mmmm.'

Conxita, Mac and Marta, who had vines of their own, saw the daunted expressions on our faces and urged us not to worry. They would help to guide us too.

So we pressed on, working through the rows, breaking for coffee, then turning our attention to the old vines up the land.

Eventually I looked up and it was all done, and the happy members of the Mother's Garden formation pruning team, us included, then moved on to Marta and Benet's vineyard further up the valley. It all proved to be a baptism of fire and by the end our hands and backs were very sore, but we were mightily chuffed. The learning curve was going up like a sky rocket.

While all this was going on Joe Joe either gurgled happily in his pushchair or snoozed in the baby carrier on my back. Ella, meanwhile, seemed to be relishing the space, sunshine and freedom and was fast cementing a lasting friendship with Paula.

Our five-year-old girl was tearing hither and thither with an ever-increasing wonder at her new home that was lovely to see, but we were worried about the nine-foot deep *balsa* behind the house. She'd still not mastered swimming, so while we turned our attention to the front terrace (where Maggie was determined to establish her first vegetable patch) we asked her to play indoors for a while.

'Right,' she said. 'But it's not fair.' Her protest went further. She unleashed a snowstorm of talcum powder and shaving foam out of a window. When advised to clear up the mess, she retorted, 'Oh, I'm Cinderella now am I?'

'I think she's ready for school,' Maggie whispered.

So off she went, shedding a few tears on the first two days but after that willingly joining the gaggle of other village children at the school gate. She started at ten o'clock, came home for lunch between one and three and then we picked her up again at five. We looked on proudly and gratefully as she trotted off, relieved that one major worry had been allayed. The journeys to and from the school also meant we started to make tentative contact with the locals. A few parents wandered over to say warmly, '*Hola! Bon día!*', and with both them and the women in the grocer's and bakery we ummmed and errrrred our way through a few feeble pleasantries and smiled a lot.

Desperate to explain who we were I pointed down the valley and said slowly, '*L'Hort de la Mare – finca L'Hort de la Mare. Sí?*'

Not everyone twigged what I was trying to say, such was my appalling pronunciation, but those that did usually went, '*Ahhh, Sí, sí, L'Hort de la Mare,*' and then, '*Ooooh,*' and shook their fingers as if to say, 'You haven't half got your work cut out there, mate.'

We knew it.

Despite the daily joy of realising we'd got here, and having to remind ourselves that this beautiful farm was actually ours, there was even then an undeniable niggling indigestion that we may well have bitten off more than we could chew.

The part-derelict farmland threatened to return to complete wilderness if we didn't keep at it. The problem was that even with Rob and Yan on hand we were barely scratching the surface. In those late winter weeks so much of our time seemed to be taken up with scavenging for wood to keep the fires going, and with only three wheelbarrows, a broken chainsaw and an assortment of hand tools we were woefully equipped for coping with even one acre let alone ten.

Mac and Conxita generously said we could borrow what we needed if it wasn't in use at their farm, and they said they would help where they could, but even so, without machinery of our own it was starting to dawn on us that we were at risk of losing the physical and psychological struggle before we'd barely started. An old tractor with some of the bells and whistles was the long-term aim, after we'd sold some farm produce and I'd earned a little cash with my occasional freelance newspaper work, but in the interim we reconciled ourselves that we'd have to eat into our tiny capital reserve to buy a rotovator, strimmer and possibly even a mower.

And I was worried about Maggie. The blend of anxiety and determination on her face was not unusual – she was a perfectionist and a worrier – but even her antithesis (me) was struggling to see the wood for the trees. There was never a doubt in either of our minds that Mother's Garden would be Maggie's farm. We would work it together, share the parenting and the tasks, but it would be in her name and she would call the shots. Farming was in her blood and for years she'd hankered after land of her own to rediscover, and for our children to find, the space and freedom she knew as a child on the family fields at Park Farm between Enfield and Barnet in the green belt of north London. She was, justifiably, fiercely proud of her family and part of her wanted there to be another Whitman farm, one her late father David, the gentlest of men, and her tireless mum Beryl would have been proud of.

Only this was a different country, different climate, different everything to what either of us knew about living off the land.

Mac rolled up one morning on their old Ford Super Dexta tractor and ploughed up the rough grass on the terrace in front of the house in readiness for the vegetable plot. Rob and Yan helped dig it over, then Conxita, herself a farmer's daughter, brought seedlings and guided Maggie in the local way of planting into the side of channels that, once flooded, ensured sufficient water for the plants at the end of a hot day.

Maggie settled into a routine of rising early and spending an hour before breakfast planning and tending her new garden while Ella slept in and I gave Joe Joe his breakfast.

Then, with my son on my back, I tried to reacquaint myself with the plumbing and electrics while sorting out my tools and trying to make some sense of the boxes and furniture we'd dumped in the barn. It was then I made the grisly discovery that rats had been munching their way through the sacks of seed potatoes that Mac and Conxita had got for us. The gnawed debris and tattered sackcloth stank. The question was how many of the swines were there – and what other havoc were they wreaking on our piles of possessions. They certainly looked well on it. I watched a couple of them scaling the walls and charging along the roof beams, plump but understandably perturbed that we'd turned up and interrupted their feast.

'They're strangely more beautiful than I expected,' I told Maggie who wrinkled up her nose. 'No, seriously, they're

142

definitely different to the ones that would leap – do you remember? – from our oil tank onto the bird table outside the kitchen window back in Norfolk. They're slightly smaller with fatter tails, white tummies, a soft brown fur and large ears.'

'Even so, a rat's a rat,' said Maggie. 'Where's the nest?'

'In the roof, I think. I saw one go straight up the wall and in the top corner above the door.'

'So did I. Martin, we've got to do something. I'll see what seed potatoes I can salvage, but if we leave them to their own devices they may break into the store room' – the house and barn are attached, and the storeroom is adjacent to the barn with a wire window between the two for ventilation – 'and if they got in there they'd run amok among our food supplies and possibly contaminate the water tank.'

'I know, I know,' I said. 'It doesn't bear thinking about. I'll get a trap and load it with quality cheese.'

As it was we knew there were mice in the house. The eighteen-inch thick stone walls obviously contained a labyrinth of little tunnels and the mice would chew their way through the thin plaster and leave their calling cards around the broken brick floor in the kitchen. I kept plugging the holes only for another to appear, and we always knew when there had been another break-out because Charlie would freak in the middle of the night and bark for help.

When it looked as if I'd finally caught and dispatched all the rats, the remarkably efficient trap was brought into the house and placed behind the piano where, to our great alarm, we'd discovered that at least one mouse had been making bedding out of the felt. If we'd tickled the ivories occasionally we might have put him or her off, but the idea of downing tools to play the piano couldn't have been further from Maggie's thoughts.

By the end of the first week we were flagging. We'd all been going at it like bulls at gates and were in desperate need of a break. But it was impossible to rest at the farm when there were so many urgent tasks staring at us, so we resolved to head off in the car for a day out on 31 January. The date is etched on my brain.

We headed far south past picturesque hill villages and swathes of manicured vineyards running endlessly across the folds of red land down towards the valley of the Ebro, Spain's largest river. Then we turned east and followed the mighty olive green water to the sea. The deep river swirled swiftly past orange groves and through gorges. It was awesome, spectacular. At its end was the Ebro delta where, after a seafood meal in a restaurant, we looked out across reed beds at flamingos, egrets and marsh harriers. It felt very much like our favourite waterscape of the Norfolk Broads, only instead of a backdrop of ever-changing cloud, there were mountains.

It was a lovely, mellow day. Just what was needed.

Then, when we'd got home and put the kettle on, the phone rang. It was my sister Jackie with dreadful news.

'Martin, H has died.'

Horace, my stepfather, who'd been coping so well following Mum's illness, had just been rushed to hospital and passed away that morning. The conversation was brief and I

144

told Maggie. Then, before I could get my head round that bombshell the phone rang again. It was H's daughter Veronica repeating the message, but to add that my father, Earle, had also been taken to hospital the same day and was on the trauma ward with a life-threatening condition.

Unbelievably, while one was dying on one ward of the hospital block the other was two floors up where staff were trying to save his life. Both men were in their eighties, but had seemed so fit and well just days before. With Rob and Yan agreeing to stay on to help Maggie, I flew back to England the next night, catching a few hours' sleep at a friend's house in London before going straight to my father's bedside. They'd operated on his pancreas and he seemed to be coming through it OK.

Two hours later, together with my sister and stepsister, I was in Mum's and H's kitchen. H, ever hopeful that Mum would return home one day, had changed absolutely nothing and so sitting there with Jackie and Veronica it was as if our parents had got up from the table and simply vanished, abandoning their dogs and cats and worldly possessions.

We organised the funeral and started to come to terms with what we faced. I was to return from Spain to England another five times during that year as we struggled to sift through the puzzle of our parents' lives, to organise Mum's care and finances, to empty and sell the home and to sit with her as she faded away.

A New Rhythm

mother's garden

I returned to the farm shattered and short-fused. It was a huge relief to be with Maggie and the children again and to pick up the thread of our adventure, but I was running on empty. Thank goodness that, despite the trauma of the funeral and sadness at leaving Mum again, the sense of wonder of where we were and what we were doing with our lives flooded back. As I took Charlie and Megan on their walk the next morning the beauty of the farm and valley, now with the almond trees in full bloom, took my breath away all over again, just as it had done the first time I had stood in the top vineyard and tried to take it all in. It was hugely reassuring amid so much uncertainty.

Even so, such was my state of mind that Ella's mildest antics brought barks of unfair rebuke. Maggie, herself stressed from worrying about me and the pressure of coping alone with the children so soon after the move, was equally exhausted. We clashed and for a day or two everything seemed so fragile. It took a while for us to regain our rhythm, strength and senses and we encouraged each other not to be fazed by the tasks we faced. To help we went walk-about whenever we could, sometimes together, sometimes alone. While wandering the land, collecting firewood and picking up stones to heap beneath olive trees, I played around with ideas to bring in a little money and hatched a plan for two of the derelict terraces that were swamped by a mass of undergrowth. Maggie, it turned out, had had much the same idea.

At the back of the meadow, away from the house and road and next to a hilly corner with grass and fir trees – we have dubbed it Holkham which lovers of north Norfolk will under-stand – there are two wide terraces with attractive stone walls mostly obscured by brambles and weeds. The rows of neg-lected hazel trees could be salvaged, we thought, but we were not sure it was worth the effort. Instead we both independ-ently came up with the idea of a campsite for hardy people more interested in scenery, bird watching and walking rather than luxury sites with all the mod cons.

We walked the area with neighbours Pere and Nuria and explained our crude plan. We discussed how we might clear the bottom terrace while still leaving plenty of trees for shade, then how we would run a water supply down from the well at the top of the land. We thought a gentle start would be about six or eight pitches. Phase two would be to extend the site to the second terrace doubling the number of tents, while restoring the derelict cottage that overlooked the meadow to provide loos, showers and washing facilities on the ground floor. Phase three would be to create an apartment for the less hardy on the top floor of the cottage with its knockout view up the valley towards the village. All pie in the sky, of course, but we gained strength from discussing the future and exploring ideas.

Pere shared our excitement and said a campsite was something he'd toyed with on his land for some time, but hadn't got round to it. Then, having driven a coach and horses through our plan for phase one by asking what we had in mind for toilet facilities for our first campers, he said he'd help us – if and when we got our arses into gear. These weren't his exact words, but Pere has a selection of facial expressions that are understandable in any language. He wasn't a cynic but he wasn't blind either – he could see from the general state of the farm that it was going to a long haul.

As for scrubbing out hazels we felt we had enough on our plate with the vines, almonds, fruit trees, olives and assorted vegetable beds to have any energy or interest left for another crop. Plus fierce competition from other countries meant that the days when local hazel nuts commanded a good price were long gone.

The campsite notion, on land sufficiently far from the house to preserve our privacy, made increasing sense the more we thought about it. The children would enjoy having people around and it would also be a mild boost for the village economy. As we worked on the land we talked through other things we could develop, such as offering barbecued meals or bread oven pizzas and home-grown salads on a long table in the shade of the fig trees, all washed down with the local wine. Our customers would need to be the more adventurous travellers. It was obvious to us from the first time we came that the southern Catalonian mountains were little known to outsiders, many of whom found what they needed in the beach bars and bright lights of the resorts.

But there was a conflict of interest. One talking point over supper at Mac's birthday bash was the new road being constructed from the coast into our part of the mountains. When opened it would iron out most of the forty or so twists in the old road up one of the valleys and dramatically cut the journey time from Barcelona. No thank you, everyone agreed. The positive arguments were that the main hospital and city services and shops would be nearer, but there was a real sense that a protective barrier and a feeling of being off the beaten track were slowly being eroded. It wasn't the time to air our plans for a campsite.

We told the assembled company, though, how we'd seen open-topped safari jeeps whizzing up the old road, loaded with excited holidaymakers clutching the rollbars and their camcorders – proof positive that we were indeed living in the wilderness.

There were quite a few nice surprises for me on my return from England. Maggie and the guys had moved our brass bed together with Joe's cot from the draughty space at the top of the stairs to the cosy bedroom with a glorious view down the valley. Rob and Yan had redesigned the wood store, using hazel weave to make neat, strong hurdles that meant we could separate and stack logs by size. They'd also built me a writing desk by the window at the top of the stairs so I could get on with some work I'd been asked to do for the *Daily Mail*. And on top of all that Mac had trundled down on his tractor to harrow the olive grove behind the house.

The fact that Rob and Yan had agreed to stay until I got back greatly reduced my worries about the fistful of disasters which might befall my family and the farm, not least the spring-fed *balsa* overflowing and flooding them out. The vast water store is on higher ground just fifteen feet behind the house and I had visions of a cascade. But I needn't have fretted. Rob was his usual self, utterly reliable and practical. In my absence he'd also mastered the art of firing up the outside bread oven with old vine cuttings and was dishing up yummy-scented pizzas. I also found out that he and Yan had been doing their level best to endear us to the locals by bolstering considerably the revenue at the village bar while taking on all-comers at pool into the early hours (including, we later discovered, the local member of the Guardia Civil).

Then they were gone and we were on our own for the first time since moving to Mother's Garden. Some of the panic about the hundred and one things we should be doing eased and some things then started to come together. With Maggie's mum Beryl due to arrive in a few days, we wanted to show her that we were making serious progress. The rotovator was, we agreed, the most important piece of machinery on our wish list and was needed immediately because the vines were slowly being swamped by weeds. We had nearly £250 to play with, that being the generous parting gift of my former colleagues, but it was not enough. Maggie talked idly of getting a mule instead but I begged her to drop the idea.

'You can't be serious,' I said. 'No, no, no-oh-no. Pleeease, no. I'm beaten up enough as it is, I don't want to be dragged about by a dumb animal. Just think about where we're going to keep the ruddy thing – think of the damage I could do if it took a wrong turning or bolted in your vineyard.'

That seemed to be a winning argument and the subject was dropped. Instead it was agreed over a boozy lunch with Pere and Nuria that we would split the cost of a rotovator and share it. Perfect financially, but risky. It could lead to friction or even neighbourly wars, but they seemed like reasonable people and the arrangement was that we would have the beast during the week when Pere was working at the school and he would have it every weekend. They were being more than generous. They would use it for two days to churn up their modest vegetable patch while I intended to thrash it remorselessly for five days trying to clear our vineyard.

Having settled on a sporty red Honda 5.5 with an impressive array of controls I, not knowing a thing about rotovators or any Catalan technical terminology, nodded sagely as the engineer rattled off what appeared to be the merits of the model and the essential maintenance details.

Thankfully the manual had a section in English so I was able to say to Pere that I'd be responsible for the oil changes given that it would be living with us most of the time. Pere and I then slapped our cash on the table – 133,000 pesetas or just over £500 – and wheeled Katie out of the shop. We agreed it had to have a name and Katie came to Pere from a Blues Brothers lyric, but I've never been able to fathom out which one. It didn't matter. Katie was a lovely name and it felt good to have acquired a half-share in a vital piece of kit. And I still had a couple of days to master it before mum-in-law showed up. Then, as Pere pushed Katie down the street to our car trailer, he revealed that Nuria would have preferred a mule.

Back at the ranch I couldn't wait to get cracking. The newly pruned vines were disappearing in a sea of a prolific and rather pretty white flowering weed that's not unlike shepherd's purse found in England. The weeds were knee-deep, but hey, it would be a piece of cake for our Katie.

'Are you sure you know what you're doing?' asked Maggie who was holding Joe. He seemed to be thinking the same thing.

'No worries, I've read the manual.' I hadn't. 'Now, stand back please, thank you!'

Katie roared into life and shot off at a fair old rate of knots without scratching the surface. 'Oops,' I blushed, picking myself up off the ground. 'Ha Ha! Forgot to lift the front wheel. Obvious now. Right. Here we go again.'

This time she buried herself and I had to wrestle, pull and tug to keep her moving forward. I never got into my stride.

After a few yards the rotating arm was so clogged with the wretched weed that it was hopeless to try and continue.

'Right,' said Maggie, head on one side. 'We're going to have to pull those weeds out by hand before they go to seed.'

'What?'

'Come on, let's get cracking.'

'But—'

'You get to play with that once we've finished.'

Anyone who saw and can remember the first Channel Four 'No Going Back' documentary at the beginning of 2002 will know what a battle that proved to be. We spent days on our knees, and our hands were raw by the end of it. Beryl got stuck in too during her week-long visit, tugging away until the sun went down. But we did it. Maggie just wasn't going to be beaten and despite suffering with pains in her arms and back, she refused to let up. I did my bit too and then followed behind with Katie whom I eventually tamed.

It was at about this time we first met our neighbour on the other side, Baltasar. He lived in the village but farmed the land next to ours where there were also hazels, vines and olives. We suddenly became aware during our war on the weeds that he was chugging up and down the track close to our boundary an inordinate number of times. We were certain he was watching us, but every time I raised my hand in greeting he seemed to avert his gaze.

The heat was rising and as we toiled in the spring sun we shed more and more clothes. Then all of a sudden Baltasar was there again, only this time he'd stopped the tractor and was getting off. He waved for me to come over, shook my hand and then urged me to walk with him. He looked to be in his fifties and, blinking through his large spectacles, had obviously been plucking up courage to say something. We crossed back onto our land and made our way to the little *balsa* close to the spring. I knew why. We had been told that there was a long-standing agreement – he would have the spring water for three days over the weekend and we would have it for four days. The system looked simple enough. There were two plugs at the bottom of the *balsa*. One led to his land, the other fed our large *balsa*. He would come over and pull his plug every Thursday evening. And replace it on the Sunday. I recognised a few of the words he was saying and figured this was what he was explaining.

'No *problema, señor, no problema*,' I gestured and it was then I realised he was looking me up and down with incredulity. I suddenly became conscious that I was wearing precious little – just tatty shorts, wellies and a friendly smile– while he was decked out in cap, jeans, boots, T-shirt, shirt, jumper and body warmer. Word reached us a few days later via the school gate that people in the village had heard the crazy English were farming in the nude. I've never gone that far, but I have to say it was warm enough.

Maggie nose-dived into planning and planting, working out a host of things at the same time as watching over the rest of us. She was pushing herself very hard and in no time transformed the first terrace in front of the house, and also between the trees in the young olive grove, into an amazing pattern of assorted vegetables, while I wrestled with huge lengths of plastic piping, trying (and repeatedly failing) to provide a reliable water feed from the *balsa*.

In truth, I was in a spot of bother.

I was finding it more difficult than I ever imagined to adjust my rhythm from the ordered society of the office to the mind-numbing world of complete self-reliance. For a significant slice of my past life I'd lived at a desk not too far away from a coffee machine and Mars bar dispenser, knew exactly what I had to do, put on my blinkers and worked to crystal clear deadlines, knocking a ready supply of neat bottles off a wall. How refreshing, I thought, to leave that behind and take on a new challenge.

But suddenly I was rudderless, going round in circles not knowing what to do for the best. It was like every day was a Saturday or Sunday – full of expectation as the day dawned and then rapidly crowded with tasks I'd put off from countless weekends before, to the point of me being completely phased and achieving nothing. Only now there was no excuse.

I was also suddenly the permanent man about the house, trying to slot into the system and taking on more responsibilities from Maggie, but displaying a woeful inability to juggle, see things, remember the simplest tasks or do them well enough. That's not meant to be ironic. From Maggie's point of view it must have been (and occasionally it was very apparent) mightily stressful to watch me at my new work, or to have me at her shoulder inquiring what needed to be done next when, in hindsight, it was glaringly obvious.

I needed to get my arse into gear, so reverted to type and, having fixed on one challenge, set myself a target, blocked everything else out of my mind and went for it.

Now it was Maggie's turn to stand and stare as I whizzed about talking to myself, side-stepping without a second glance at things we'd discussed and agreed needing sorting. I became scratchy and monosyllabic, felt increasingly useless and then closed my mind to yet more of our general needs. I think it's what's known as a man retreating into his cave. Maggie took it for so long then brought me down to earth with a bump and, rightly, pointed out we were seriously at risk of missing the point of why we'd headed for the hills. I'm still learning.

The temperature hit eighty in the shade for a few days in March, which turned the ground to iron and had us steeling ourselves for the attrition of a long, sweltering late spring and summer. But it didn't last and in the following weeks we settled into an pattern of sunny blasts punctuated by short rain squalls and thunderstorms which kept the vegetation lush, swelled the young fruit and vegetables, freshened the air and washed the dust off the car.

The front terrace was soon crowded with lettuces, onions, leeks, broad beans, carrots, cabbages and broccoli, while in the large vegetable plot behind the house we set the seed potatoes and Maggie made beds for courgettes, aubergines, melons, water melons, peppers and tomatoes. I beavered away with Pere's strimmer trying to keep the grass at bay, continued to fiddle with my Heath Robinson irrigation system and chugged back and forth with Katie. We set up some old canes and cut some more from the swathe that grows in a gully at the northwestern corner of the land. Then, suddenly, virtually to the day Alex had said, the vines sprang to life. All of them! The thrill was immense and we returned to weeding around them with renewed vigour.

Joe Joe looked on happily from his pushchair or on a blanket surrounded by toys in the shade of a young olive tree, while Ella would come home from school, help a bit, charge about singing and dancing in the soft evening sun and then take great delight in collecting scores of fat snails from under the vegetable leaves. These we popped into a clay pot with a lid and small holes in the side that was obviously designed for the purpose and which we'd found beside the steps to the *balsa*. We gave them to Joaquim, the broad-grinning, curly haired farmer (from the paella/straw bale debacle) whom we paid to keep us supplied with eggs until we got our own chickens. In exchange for the snails he brought us a basket of pears.

We turned a blind eye to the greater part of the farm that was wilderness and concentrated on the vines and vegetables, while trying to keep the ground clear around the olive, almond and fruit trees. Maggie also tended the roses round the *balsa* and we tried to tidy up the approach to the house and to hack away the undergrowth to reveal some of the old walls. The big stone barbecue outside the back door was pressed into service and as we began to spend more and more time outside, the general chaos inside the house – where we didn't have enough drawer or storage space, plus a host of things we kept saying we had to change – just didn't get addressed.

We also started to get our bearings in the village and nearest town and fell into the local routine of shopping in the mornings or evenings. Most places close at about one or two when the shutters come down for the long lunch and afternoon siesta, then they're open for business again from five to eight.

Very occasionally we've splashed out on a lunch at a local restaurant where they asked us to part with eight euros, about five pounds, for a three-course meal, wine and coffee included, which (if we weren't careful) could drift on through into the late afternoon.

'Oh! Maggie – look!' I whispered tactlessly on our first jaunt, after the couple at the next table had got up to leave. I nodded sidewards and rolled my eyes as if Michelle Pfieffer or Sean Connery had just walked in. The departing couple had left half a bottle of exceedingly fine wine. Being British – 'I've paid good money I'm damn well going to drink it' – I had to use all my will-power not to reach across and nab it.

'Hummph. Honestly,' I muttered. 'You wouldn't see that back home would you?'

With undisguised disbelief still etched across my face I then watched open-mouthed as another party got up from their table. This time it was nearly three quarters of a bottle going begging. When we finally finished our meal the restaurant was mostly deserted, save us and about ten partially empty bottles of wine. Some were house wines (part and parcel of the eight euro menu but very good all the same) while others were local vintages at ten to twenty euros a bottle. It was clear from the outset we had a lot to learn about living amid vineyards where the people loved their wine but knew when to stop.

As for the locals, whom we found to be gentle, proud and welcoming (and have never had reason to change that opinion), I was struck by how I was constantly seeing weathered faces, rich in years and alive with smiles, that reminded me so much of characters in the quiet villages of my native Norfolk. People in different countries aren't so different.

But picture in your mind's eye how things were in your community some thirty or forty years ago. I'd hazard a guess that there were no supermarkets in the local town, just a host of small businesses ticking along as if from time immemorial. Some villages still had their craftsmen and women as well as shops and inns to supply a senior generation who saw no need to leave the parish even for a day.

Well, ever since we uprooted ourselves from middle England to set down roots in Mother's Garden it's as if we have travelled back in time. We could see that down the mountains along the coast the twenty-first century was gathering pace, but not here. Our nearest town still had no supermarkets in the modern, aircraft hangar sense of the word, rather five or six grocers about the size of your average shoe shop peddling (it seemed) exactly the same mix of foodstuffs, toiletries and drinks on their crowded shelves and the pavement outside.

Cheek by jowl with them on the main street there were four bars all doing a reasonable trade offering a blur of tobacco smoke, golden beer, espresso coffee and snacks or tapas to a predominantly male clientele. You could dodge the haze by using the pavement tables and chairs, where once in a while we took a breather and sat ourselves down to watch the world go by.

We saw the occasional tourist with bright shirt, baggy shorts, white socks and sandals and bum bag, but it was obvious tourism hadn't taken a hold. There was a high street hotel offering modern comforts, but the hostel opposite has to be seen to be believed. We checked it out as possible low-cost accommodation for friends if the strain got too great at the farm, and we couldn't believe our eyes. Though clean, it didn't look as if it had been altered in any way for at least fifty years – and with its tiled floors, high ceilings, unheated rooms and pre-war bathroom and plumbing, it looked like the setting for a Poirot mystery.

And to reinforce the feeling of a lost world we found that everywhere was shut on Sunday, save the petrol station, a sort of grocers selling wine, crisps and olives where the queue for a roast chicken (or rabbit) tailed out of the door and onto the cobbled street, and a cake shop making long, round, cream-filled desserts unappetisingly known as gypsy's arm.

Some aspects of our new existence could not, reassuringly, have been more up-to-date, like the 24-hour medical centre with full-time paediatrician. But it was obvious that there was something distinct and ingrained about the attitudes and pace of life.

You can't help but wonder how long it will last.

In our village, with a population of about six hundred, there is a carpenter, blacksmith, plumber, electrician, mechanic, hair-dresser, tobacconist, baker, chemist, two grocers, bar owner and restaurant proprietor – all managing to eke out a living. There's a bank, and surgery too, and what makes this self-contained community all the more remarkable is that the village is just two miles from the town where most services can be found.

Going back and forth to the school, we slowly started getting our heads around the jigsaw of the generations, figuring out who was related to who, and from very early on the Latin tradition of large, tight-knit families was clear. More often than not it was the grandparents, men as much as women, who came to the school gate at lunchtime or 5 p.m., then in the summer evenings they'd sit on the low wall and chat while watching over the little ones as they tore about in the square until long after the sun had gone down.

Although we'd observed how everyone else stopped for a long breather at lunchtime and in the early afternoon, we didn't. Like mad dogs we battled on through the hottest part of the day and when it all got too much plunged (naked if Baltasar wasn't about) into the *balsa* to cool off. Alex, meanwhile, came to prune some of the trees for us and for several days we rose at dawn, left Ella to snooze and took Joe Joe up the land in his pushchair where we lit piles of twigs before the sun dried the dew and mid-morning breeze fanned the flames.

Living at altitude – OK it's only a thousand feet but I'm from Norfolk, remember – has only one serious drawback as far as we can see. The scenery and skyscapes here blow your socks off, but so (we soon discovered) do the thunderstorms, the frequency and intensity of which during those first months came as something of a shock. It was good to have the rain to replenish the well, to feed the spring and soften the soil, but we could do without the trauma. We weren't beneath the storm, we were in it. It all got glass-rattlingly, Sound of Musically terrifying. Everyone congregated on our brass bed and we encouraged Ella to remember a few of her favourite things, but such calming tactics don't work on a demented dog who has burst through the bedroom door and buried his head under the duvet. There we all sat at about 3 a.m. during our first storm with Charlie scrabbling to get into the bed and then parking his rear on me and shaking like a leaf. Fear also fosters his wind problem which rather takes any Julie Andrews charm out of the drama.

With that first crash of thunder another Mother's Garden idiosyncrasy came to the fore. Off went the power. Nothing unusual about that, of course. It's a fact of life and in most households all you have to do is pop your head into the cupboard under the stairs and flip the trip switch on again once the storm as passed. Here things have proved a little more tricky.

Our trip switch, along with the meter, is in a box stuck to a pole protruding from the undergrowth at the top corner of the land, the furthest most inaccessible place. Plodding there and back through the mud, darkness and rain (which comes down in stair rods), while trying not to nose-dive over a vine or poke my eye out on a hazel branch and endeavouring not to think about coming face to face with a wild boar sheltering in the bamboo and brambles, can take fifteen ghastly minutes. And in the back of the mind is always the thought that if the storm does a U-turn you will have to do it all over again.

That first spring the thunderstorms were usually in the middle of the night and, unless one of our friends warned us one was forecast, we were never prepared with torches and candles. Once, after a session on the internet, I'd foolishly left the computer modem plugged in and a strike on the phone line blew it off its hinges. For half a day I was convinced the whole computer and all my work were fried. The only person I could think of with a computer in the village was Nuria, the secretary at the *ajuntament*, so I rushed to the civic offices and burst through the door clutching a prepared speech about how the ruddy *tempesta* had ruined my life and did she know of a good engineer?

'Don't worry, Marteen,' she said in Catalan. 'You are the sixth person. Josep tells me it may only have killed the modem not the computer. He will come round later today.'

'Josep?'

'My husband.'

I could have kissed her.

We've come to love gentle rain, especially at dawn when it surprises us to break the cycle of sun and heat and washes away all thoughts of rising with the lark. 'You think about it differently here,' Maggie said one day, after we'd woken to the gentle sound of water falling onto the fig and walnut leaves close to our open bedroom window. We'd been warned that even when the region was set to get a welcome soaking our valley was inclined to be bypassed. There have indeed been strange days when dark clouds have clustered around the mountain and promised much but delivered nothing, prompting neighbour Pere to pull a raised-eyebrows 'I told you so' expression. His response was swift when we told him we were going back to England for Easter week and asked if there was anything he wanted brought back. 'Of course. Some of your rain, please.'

At the beginning of May we had one particularly bad nightstorm that plunged us into darkness, significantly changed the temperature and left piles of hailstones beneath the roof channels. I was due to drive through the mountains to Reus airport in the middle of the night to meet my oldest friend Mike and his girlfriend Kirby. (No kidding, that's her Christian name, borne of a parental love of the singer Kathy Kirby and a dislike of the name Kathy. Needless to say I approved.) They were due in on the 2.30 a.m. charter flight from Bristol and, having stomped up the land to flip the switch, I skidded off down the track in the car, looking as if I was kitted out for a December stroll in the Cairngorms.

The scene at the airport was strangely sad. A fair number of British holidaymakers spilled off the flight in shorts, T-shirts, assorted football shirts or shell suits expecting to be hit by a wall of Mediterranean heat only to be greeted by fixed-grin package holiday reps decked out in padded jackets. Poor souls, you couldn't help but feel sorry for them. Their excitement, first weakened by the ungodly hour, must have been crumbling at the thought that, having counted down the weeks and days, their holiday was likely to be far removed from the blue sky brochure pictures that had prompted them to part with a few hundred hard-earned pounds. Some put on brave faces, others looked positively depressed. Most were just bewildered. I found it all rather depressing, because I knew (and they probably didn't) that the rain was forecast to stick around for much of the week.

Mike and Kirby's stay was a bit special as it turned out. The dark, low clouds lining the coast failed most of the time to clamber over the mountains and reach Mother's Garden, so our visitors went home with a little colour in their cheeks and six rolls of film to show their friends and families.

We stayed close to home for most of their seven days with us and they were happy pottering about, wielding a mattock between the vines and snoozing in the deckchair by the *balsa*. But towards the end, to change the scenery for them for at least one day, we decided to venture down to walk on the beach. It seemed daft to come on holiday to the Mediterranean and not get your feet wet.

Our stretch of coast is the Costa Daurada, running from just south of Barcelona to the Ebro Delta wetland. Tarragona, with its mix of port, modern industry, oil refineries and beautiful old quarter loaded with Roman history, is the main administrative centre although Reus, just a few miles inland, is almost as large.

The nearest beaches are about an hour away from the farm,

but in those early months we'd only been a couple of times and didn't have a clue where to go and where to avoid. We knew, of course, that the Ebro Delta was wonderful, but that was a very long drive south. We knew of a nice beach about twenty miles north of Tarragona, but that didn't have happy memories. We'd gone there on the advice of friends for our first beach break from the farm in late February, only for a thief to smash two locks on the car and steal our camera while we were sitting just yards away outside a café. So after that we stayed away from the coast for quite a while.

As we weaved our way over the mountains and down to the sea with Mike and Kirby it became clear that the gloom and cold had not gone. We made for the nearest beach, the one we'd popped down to see during the four-day olive harvest trip back in the November. There was a cluster of predominantly German-owned villas on one side of the road and a campsite on the other, but it was quiet with a few trees and there were no towering hotels.

We took off our shoes and rolled up our trouser legs but the skies and even the water were grey. The cold wind soon chased us back to the car. At that point we should have turned tail and headed for the hills again, but we decided to explore and drove south along the coast. Finally, with tummies rumbling and drops of rain speckling the windscreen, we began looking for somewhere to have a drink and meal. The trouble was we didn't have a clue where to go. We'd been told that there were excellent seafood restaurants to be found, and we wanted to give Mike and Kirby, both accomplished cooks with a penchant for culinary adventure, a true flavour of Catalonia. But trying to find authentic local cuisine and a quaint eating place frequented by locals when you were stuck in a car on a rainy day in the coastal holiday sprawl was, we soon realised, like looking for a double yolk in a crowded henhouse. We learned many months later of scores of places that would have fitted the bill, but that day we were bewildered as we drove along the seafront beside the wind-blown palm trees.

The sweep of sand was deserted but between the flats, hotels, restaurants, pubs and gift shops the pavements were crowded with people in anoraks. Again I felt so sorry for them, especially the families with children. We drove for miles and every time we thought something was worth investigating, there was nowhere to stop. Finally, as the light was fading, I found a little bar whose main attraction was a parking space right outside which meant we could see the car. That was a priority because we still hadn't fixed the lock on the rear door.

The bar overlooked the back of a vast hotel and adjoined a gift shop loaded to the gunnels with unnecessary plastic objects where Ella sorely tested Kirby's reflexes by holding up a penis key ring and asking, 'What's this?' We ordered beers and opted for a bout of giggling to see us through, but this rapidly dried up as the television suddenly showed the last distressing moments of an exhausted and bloodied bull. There was no time to cover Ella's eyes and we rapidly downed our drinks and gathered our things as first the sweating matador gave a brief post-fight interview, and then, before we could reach the door, another battle commenced and a fresh bull promptly felled a man on a horse.

The rain began to fall as Robbie climbed away from the coast and we talked about bullfighting. On the one hand it was a clear case of a cruelty I can't abide, and on the other it was the product of a deep-rooted culture that I still don't feel qualified to criticise. We discussed how the camera shot of the bull sinking to its knees was juxtaposed with sweep shots of the audience, rows of well-dressed men and women seated shoulder to shoulder, all applauding in a dignified and attentive way as if they were at Lords or Wimbledon. I made a mental note to reread Hemingway.

Spreading Our Wings

mother's garden

'*E*nron no! Enron no! Enron no!' came the cry from behind us.

'Respect the Ebro! Don't take the water!' came the clamour from in front.

The red and yellow striped flags of Catalonia and Aragon, rippling in the February breeze, sailed down the broad Barcelona streets as far as the eye could see. Troupes of musicians, marching and playing what sounded like small oboes and snare drums, energised the masses as we all flowed gently towards the city's gothic quarter. There were banners galore too, raging at the Machiavellians in Madrid, carried by people of all ages and (it seemed) of all political persuasions – children, the well-heeled, the proletariat, artisans, students and a veritable army of the common multitude.

There may have been a slight nip in the air but some people

were determined to make their point, for in the middle of this pot pourri of society, between the moustachioed señors in cravats and señoras in Sunday coats, came half a dozen naked men and women painted blue from head to toe holding aloft a stream of aquamarine fabric.

I'd only been in Spain for a month and I was already taking part in the first major protest of my life. (A career in journalism can make you a perpetual observer not a participant.)

'You should come,' some friends had urged us. 'It's so important. We have to make a protest because these plans will affect us all.'

'What's all the fuss about?' We hadn't really thought about it before but, inevitably, when you move communities, let alone countries, your life is still affected by local issues and you can't dodge them. We weren't naive enough to expect seamless pastoral serenity, but before we'd barely got our bearings our integration appeared to be going into overdrive.

There were three bones of contention that dovetailed into one general outcry about the damage that could be done to the environment in the name of progress – and profit. The local people who rallied us to the cause were particularly outraged at proposals by the then seemingly invincible American corporation Enron to build a mixed gas and oil power station in a valley not a million miles away from us. We'd noticed a sudden proliferation of T-shirts featuring a skull and crossbones and cursing Enron. The dread was that pollution from the power station would blight the pure mountain air and cast a veil over communities for miles around. The subsequent scandal in the American courts, when Enron fell apart, nipped it all in the bud thank goodness, but at the time locals like Alex were spitting feathers over the threat to our community as well as the general issue of global warming.

Then there were the wind farm protesters, people who wanted to ring alarm bells about the proliferation of turbines without, they felt, due regard for nature or local opinion. They weren't against wind power, far from it, but their voices called for the authorities to respect agreements about the number and locations of future sites – there were already a significant number in mountainous southern Catalonia – and to leave areas of outstanding beauty well alone.

But by far the largest clamour, and that which included the blue nudists, was against an audacious government project to take vast amounts of water from the Ebro river and channel it to parched stretches of the Mediterranean coast, chiefly beyond Valencia, where it was needed to quench the thirst of ballooning development and tourism – and (the protesters were quick to add) a string of new golf courses.

I don't suppose you worry about it when you're on holiday on the Costas. I certainly didn't when I took my daily showers during a holiday on the Costa del Sol back in 1997. But it helps to get a handle on the acute water crisis when you think some forty million tourists fly to Spain every year and turn the taps on.

Ironically, the Spanish and Portuguese peninsular, which ancient cartographers compared to a bull's hide stretched out to dry, was named Iberia – the Land of Rivers – by desert tribes who crossed over from North Africa. It may well have looked more fertile to them, but there are only a few rivers in Spain that are plentiful enough through the summer to be useful for irrigation, one of which is the mighty Ebro.

The National Water Plan was the conservative government's answer to Spain's undeniable water crisis, and it was colossal. It declared the need for scores of new dams on the river, along with more than nine hundred kilometres of tunnels and pipelines to carry water to the south. The idea was that each year about a thousand million cubic metres of water would be taken from the Ebro – more than enough to unite people from several regions, chiefly Aragon and Catalonia, who all feared the worst for the ecology and the future of the farming communities that relied upon the country's biggest waterway. On top of this was the effect any drop in water levels would have on the wetland nature reserves and rice fields of the vast delta where the Ebro reached the Mediterranean, one of the main staging posts for birds migrating between northern Africa and western Europe. The National Water Plan, specialists warned, could well spell the end for the delta.

We felt there was no way we could bury our heads in the sand. The Enron plan had a direct bearing on our new lives and we also wanted to add our voices to the other two causes. But we agreed it would be too long a day for ten-month-old Joe Joe, so Maggie said she'd stay at home with him.

Ella and I joined some familiar faces as we clambered onto the early morning Saturday train, only to find it was already packed with people holding placards. By the time we got to Barcelona it looked like a *Guinness Book of Records* attempt at how many people you could squeeze into three coaches. Thankfully Marta and her seven-year-old daughter Paula were there, too, which pleased Ella no end.

Mac and Conxita took us under their wings, and as we made our way into the 300,000-strong march we nipped into a fast-food restaurant for a coffee, and cheekily munched our homemade sandwiches. We had a moment to admire Gaudí's shining and undulating Casa Batllo before we pressed on to meet up with Pere and Nuria, and other people we recognised, all waiting patiently at the tail end of the throng which was slowly moving away from the university. Ella and Paula stuck together like glue which made keeping an eye on her in the vast crowd a little less stressful (although I nonetheless insisted she wore a Paddington Bear label with her name and address on it).

For one so new to Iberian politics and the fervour it can engender it was an astonishing experience, with an unforgettable rhythm of drums and sense of energy. And Ella and I must be the only people who, on their first visit to Barcelona, walked for hours and barely saw a thing – save the extraordinary spectacle of Catalans and Aragonese on the march.

Away from farming matters, two other things were on our minds. It was clear very early on that conducting business of any sort was all the more fraught because we were not Spanish residents. We had to get organised and apply. Also, we were set to return to Norfolk for a week at Easter, which was bound to be a bit of an emotional roller coaster, what with my mother's illness and the prospect of seeing again all the people – and some places – it had hurt to leave just three months before.

'Oh . . . my . . . gawd.' Both of us had to override the urge to turn and bolt.

Conxita had made an appointment for us in Tarragona and we were told the whole family needed to be present at the residency interview. We arrived to find every desk in the overheating reception area besieged with people, and sensed, unhappily, that because of the cross-section of nationalities represented, it must be the right place. I remembered reading an article somewhere about Spanish bureaucracy which helped confirm my suspicions. It warned against feeling pleased if you turned up at an office and found it devoid of people waiting – because you were almost certainly in the wrong place.

We stationed ourselves at the back of the crowd and as the time ticked by and we were just beginning to wonder if we'd got into a tangle over the date, Maggie heard what could have been our names being called out above the din. We shouldered our way to the front where a very patient woman, who was continuously interrupted by members of the throng pushing at our backs, spent nearly half an hour trying to guide us through the forms. It soon became clear this wasn't the end of our application but just the beginning.

A few weeks later, after we'd posted off the necessary

copies of various family documents, along with the completed forms and some passport photographs acquired in a booth at the supermarket, we were told to report to a police station in the city.

We assumed that the scrum-down part of the process was over and the chance had come to create a good impression, so we put on our best clothes, combed the children's hair, and headed off down the mountain again. Nearly everything at that early stage of our new lives was a puzzle, but you wouldn't think finding a police station would be that difficult. Well, the tricky question was, which of the three police forces did they mean? Was it the national Guardia Civil, Catalonia's new police force, or what is known as the local police?

When we eventually found the right building we brushed ourselves down and, without a second thought, headed for the main entrance past a queue of predominantly north Africans kicking their heels. A guard standing on the steps put out his arm to stop us entering.

'Can I help you?' He inquired politely, but very firmly, in Catalan.

'Residency?'

The officer didn't say anything else. He just leant out of the door and pointed to the end of the queue. Children aren't keen on queuing at the best of times and Joe Joe, by then an Olympic-standard wriggle bottom, was having none of it and began wrestling. We hung in for an hour before, much relieved, we were ushered in, although by this time our efforts at looking like the perfect, well-ironed immigrant family had gone by the board. The woman behind the counter was pleasant enough, checked the forms, asked all four of us to be fingerprinted and then announced that Joe Joe's photograph wasn't acceptable.

'What? Why not?'

She tapped the photograph. Behind Joe Joe you could clearly see me grappling with him. 'The background needs to be white,' she said slowly.

I wanted to ask her if she'd ever tried to get a tot to sit still in an automatic photo booth and look in the right direction at the critical moment, but my Catalan failed me.

Maggie pointed out the registration office would be open for another thirty-five minutes so there was still time. The woman nodded.

'Head for the supermarket,' said Maggie. 'It's only about a mile.'

'Hang on a minute – if I take the car I could get stuck in traffic and there may not be a space when I get back. Come on Joe Joe, we've got to leg it.'

I ran like a madman with my wide-eyed son clinging to my chest like a baby chimp only to find the booth occupied. I'd passed the stage of fraying at the edges by then and knew, given the time it took the machine to process the shots, we'd only have one bite of the cherry.

For the first of the four flashes I tried kneeling and begging. Joe Joe swivelled round on the chair and we got a picture of the back of his head. The second flash, with me yelling, 'Look! Look!' and pointing at the camera, had no effect whatsoever.

Top of his head. Third try, but neither of us were remotely ready. Picture of back of my head. So it was down to the wire. I knelt again and, relinquishing all remaining dignity with my bum sticking out from under the curtain, held Joe Joe under his arms, stuck my head next to the camera and blew an enormous raspberry. Bingo.

Back we flew like John Cleese in *Clockwise* and made it with seconds to spare.

We'd always said we would budget for regular trips back to Britain so we could maintain as much contact as possible with our families, who would help fill in the long gaps by coming to see us. But that Easter journey just three months after we'd moved countries was exceptional. Both of my parents were very ill. We were only going back for seven days but it was as long as we could expect our friends here to walk and feed our dogs and water the garden.

The day we were due to travel didn't start swimmingly. Reliable Pere rolled up at the farm at 6.40 a.m. to take us to the station to catch the first train to Barcelona, which should have got us to the airport with about an hour to spare – a tight squeeze, but with Robbie the Range Rover in the garage having another problem sorted out, there was no alternative. The 5.30 a.m. alarm split my head open and the pain never left me all day. Shortly afterwards nausea set in.

The railway station was ominously deserted. We chatted as the minutes ticked by and the day – and truth – slowly dawned. At 7.15 a.m. I found a bent timetable in my rucksack and our niggling doubts, which were rapidly blossoming into worst fears, were confirmed. No early train, the small print confirmed, on Easter Saturday, 14 April.

Bugger. Now what?

Pere, bless him, immediately volunteered to drive us down the mountain where we could pick up a coastal train that might, just might, get us there on time. We belted down the twisting road towards the sea while Ella said she felt sick, Joe Joe was in a dawn stupor and Maggie and I chatted idly with Pere as if nothing was going wrong.

But things were going wrong, big league. We knew we were unlikely to find a train that would get us there in time. We were heading in the right direction, but sod's law said that there would be no fog or snow in the UK to delay the plane and whichever train we caught now we were sure to roll up late to watch the Go flight to Stansted soaring off through the haze. And like Ella I wasn't sure I'd make it down the mountain road without gagging.

We faced facts as, finally, the road straightened out and the Renault 4 screamed. It would have to be a taxi. There was no way we could ask Pere to press on to Barcelona and we didn't want to put him, the car or us for that matter, through the ordeal. We unloaded outside the town railway station just as a large, new taxi with a friendly driver rolled up. Pere negotiated and said it would cost 18,000 pesetas. At first I thought he said 80,000 and I stuttered, 'H-h-how much?' Despite my stubborn inability to fathom the old exchange rate I still managed to figure it was well into the hundreds of pounds. I went weak at the knees. Pere seemed to notice the colour draining from my face and tried again, saying the figure very slowly and loudly, like a game show host revealing a star prize.

'This is about seventy pounds, I think, including the road tolls. It is a lot of money, of course, but at least you will catch the aeroplane. Don't worry. There is no need to worry.' Then he added. 'But I have no money I am afraid.'

'No, no – we have enough, don't we, Maggie? Just. Brilliant, yes, great – let's do it,' I blurted and shook his hand frantically. We couldn't afford to blow that much, but neither of us mentioned it.

We tried a bit of chitchat with the driver which he sensibly fended off, so we followed the children's example and dozed as the people carrier whizzed along at up to 140 k.p.h. Things, and my stomach, finally started to settle down. The flight was on time and only half full which also made things a little less stressful. Maggie's sister Liz was at Stansted to meet us. Ella joined me inside my coat to escape the cold wind as we waited by the car while Liz ran to pay for the parking. It was blasting cold air up my trouser legs and threatening rain, which duly arrived as we drove north into Norfolk.

After a quick bowl of soup at Beryl's farm we left the children with her, and Maggie drove me in her mum's car to see my dad and mum. It was drizzling. I felt very strange and unhappy. I suppose I hadn't planned on seeing such familiar landscapes like that, so soon, for such a sad reason.

Kelling Hospital was en route so we called in to see Dad first. We found him sitting in the day room in his dressing gown, full of smiles, much thinner but bright as a button and eager to talk about his new friendships. Other patients told me he had been playing the piano. He said he'd proposed a tug of war between the males and females but relented when it became clear the men would lose. The old humour was alive and kicking and I was much relieved. There was every chance he would be home by the end of the week.

At Sheringham I picked up the key from a neighbour and let myself into Mum's deserted house, Pebblegate. I'd been warned about the ants emerging from beneath the sink and patrolling the work surfaces. Otherwise the place was much the same. But despite the gas Aga rumbling away in the kitchen I still felt chilled. Perhaps it was delayed shock. Perhaps it was the Aga, warming a false sense of normality when in fact the house was no longer a home. I hurriedly sifted through the pile of mail that had been pushed into the hall by the front door and checked Mum's Volvo keys were still hanging by the dresser in the kitchen. Having pointlessly swept a couple of the ants off the table I lugged three boxes of my books to Beryl's car which Maggie would take back with her to her mum's farm that evening. These were books which Mum and H had readily agreed to let us store in their loft. I'd struggled up three flights of stairs with them just five months before, when life was rolling on at Pebblegate as it had done for twenty-five years.

As I made my way back downstairs again I took down a poem about inner peace that was hanging on the first floor landing. With Maggie's help I picked out a picture of my sister and I as children playing on a Cumbria hilltop farm in matching yellow polar-neck jumpers during a distant family holiday. I didn't want to go empty-handed to the nursing home.

Maggie waited until she heard the roar of the Volvo from the garage before heading off back to the children. She knew I wanted to see Mum on my own first of all, and it was agreed she would bring the children to see my parents in their respective nursing home and hospital on Easter Monday.

Ma was in the lounge when I arrived at Sun Court. We both cried a little and held hands while another resident watched 'Blind Date'. I wanted to turn it off. I produced my offerings and tried to talk about Mother's Garden. But Mum was obviously tired, contented after a few attempts to respond to my stupid questions just to look at me and smile and wrinkle her nose. So we fell silent as Cilla rattled on. 'Oooo you've got-a-lorra things going for you luv, an' I don't juss mean your face!' I thought again about pulling the plug, but the other resident seemed transfixed. I couldn't. Mum didn't seem to care or notice. Earlier, when I had sought water for the flowers, I'd tried to tell a member of staff that my mother had been a ballet dancer, a nurse, a guesthouse proprietor in nearby South Street. I wanted them to know. The woman said Mum was a gracious, gentle and beautiful lady. When I picked up her hand again I told her and there were more tears. I kissed her, promised to be back in the morning and wandered out on to the street feeling utterly useless. I started to head for the car, but despite the drizzle doubled back and edged along the footpath until I could see into the lounge. Mum was watching 'Blind Date'. The beautiful lady could neither say nor stand to turn it off. Maybe it wasn't important anymore. Five months before it would have been.

The week rolled on in much the same vein. Maggie brought the children to see Mum on Easter Monday and her eyes glistened. She hugged Maggie like I'd never seen before. Every meeting that week was deeply emotional and we sensed she knew – she knew far more than her body would allow her to express and she knew she might never see the family again.

Maggie had arranged for Ella to meet up with old school friends and so she took the Volvo. I ploughed backwards and forwards on foot between the nursing home and Pebblegate on the far side of town, along familiar streets and through hailstorms and North Sea blasts that whipped my long hair into a mop. I hadn't walked across town like that since I was dating an old girlfriend, Sue, twenty-five years before. She lived on the Hump, the eastern hill on which Pebblegate was perched, while I grew up across town in Honeylands guesthouse, South Street, just a stone's throw from Sun Court.

Day after day I walked backwards and forwards between Pebblegate and the nursing home. I varied my route, covering old tracks. Little seemed to have changed – the view from the Hump across the muddle of red tiled roofs to the golf course in the distance; the rhythm of the train, high on the embankment amid the chimney pots, as it slowed at the end of the branch line; the High Street crowded with Easter weekend tourists, some huddled on benches eating chips and trying to ignore the fickle weather; the familiar faces in the crush. Faces like the old boy, his cap at a jaunty angle, swaying from side to side on his 'sit up and beg' as he pedalled up the hill past the site of my old primary school. Retirement flats now stand where we used to rush through the rain to the outside loos with the shiny brown bricks and play catch and take our cycling proficiency in the playground. Just around the corner was the old hall where Mark, Clive, Alan and the gang had come to my pirate party. I think it was my ninth birthday.

In Barford Road I hesitated. The gate to the old refectory through which the class of '66 had processed in pairs, was open. The building, a concrete blocks and iron windows relic from the forties or fifties, was still standing. It was used for storage now, the white walls a dusty grey, the inside stacked with furniture and boxes. I walked round to the locked double doors where the smell of lunch would pour out as we flooded in. I can still remember clear as day the motherly, smiley ladies who served us, the ranks of long tables and benches, head-master Mr James standing in the middle of the room leading the prayer and then watching over us, and the shrieks when we found a cloth in the steaming bowl of semolina pudding.

Further on I dithered by the shallow, swift beck flowing from Beeston Common into town, where we used to take off our shoes and socks and walk along the shiny shingle bed trying to catch sticklebacks. To and fro I went, trying to fathom out what to do next and forever colliding with my childhood. Mother's Garden was a million miles away.

By the Friday I had marshalled Mum's documents into one large file, squirrelled some of the more precious household items into the attic room and managed most days to see Mum morning, noon and night. As the days passed I understood why Jackie was so set on her going to Sun Court. The place buzzed with life and had such a happy atmosphere, and the care and affection were a real comfort while I struggled with the sense of betrayal – planning to sell Pebblegate and disposing of the contents as if Mum had died. The law said we had to fund her care. She needed full-time nursing care. We faced fees of £1540 a month and there was no other choice – the house had to go. But while we all desperately wanted her to recover some quality of life, I was certain she would be heartbroken to know her home had gone. That week she kept repeating the words 'perhaps soon'.

Before we left to spend our last night at Beryl's farm we dug up two yellow primroses from the garden and drove to the town cemetery overlooking the raging North Sea. H's grave was on the far side and by the time we'd reached it and dug in the plants, freezing near-horizontal rain had soaked our legs and all but crushed the brolley. I'd wanted to visit my grandparents' grave too, but the storm chased us away.

Twenty-four hours later we were eating a bland café meal in Barcelona's bustling Sants railway station, watching beggars as they worked the crowd. We'd sprinted off the plane but missed by just a minute the only train that would get us all the way home. We were beleaguered, bemused and weighed down with bags and winter coats. Ella was hyper and all we could do was bellow. Joe's nose was running like a tap and he didn't know whether to laugh or cry. We finally got home at 9.30 p.m. after taking a train two-thirds of the way and resorting again to an expensive taxi ride. The driver, thankfully, insisted on risking the lumpy track up to the house and we carried the sleeping children to bed before resorting to the vermouth.

Four weeks later, the day after I'd booked a flight for me to go back for a few days in June to continue to empty Pebblegate and to organise the sale, the BBC World Service told us that Perry Como had died. Mum, like so many women of her generation, adored his style and loved his music which had often drifted through both our childhood homes. An age was passing, we reflected. Ella put her fingers in her ears as we sang 'And I Love You So' and 'Catch a Falling Star'.

Desperanto

mother's garden

'Ella, would you get that please!'

'YEP!'

Thank heavens for bilingual little six-year-olds who like answering the phone. It's been an extraordinary experience watching our daughter soak up another language like a sponge and then for us to have to rely, on occasions, upon her greater understanding. It's been edifying for us all, adding a new dimension to our relationship and friendship that she clearly understands and appreciates too. And, thankfully, such is her age and happy disposition that Ella has never been remotely bothered or embarrassed by her father's painful progress, which on bad days could best be described as a learner driver crashing the gears and leapfrogging the wrong way down a one-way street.

Joe Joe has had reason to be grateful to her too.

A few months into our new lives, when the temperature was nudging into the nineties during the day, he suddenly developed a terrible fever which raged for a couple of days and nights and was impervious to the usual bathroom cabinet remedies.

We rushed off to the medical centre with Ella in tow where a very pleasant woman doctor checked him over. Maggie and I were doing reasonably well on the dialogue front until she kept repeating the same phrase which neither of us could grasp in Spanish or Catalan.

'Ella, do you understand?'

'Yes, Daddy.' She was sitting on the couch swinging her legs. 'They want to put a bag on his willy and take some pee pee.'

'Oh – right,' we said, doing a double take and wondering how on earth our girl had broadened her vocabulary that far.

I've lumbered on with the language, occasionally kidding myself that I've turned the corner at long last, but I rapidly lost count of the horrible misunderstandings due to my dreadful habit of saying '*Sí*' and trying to give the impression I've understood when I haven't. It was a ludicrous way for a person with a fingernail grasp of a language to carry on. Our good friend Marta has been on the receiving end more than most and, after a few disastrous calls when I'd got completely the wrong end of the stick, I'd hear her sigh heavily down the phone as soon as she realised it was me on the other end and then ask if Ella or Maggie were around. Maggie lived near Seville for nine months in the early nineties and at least had a working grasp of Spanish from the outset.

We've tried hard to find the time to put into practice what sinks in from weekly Catalan lessons we've arranged with Cristina from the tourist office, and also what we glean from Ella's homework. But it's been slow and that's been particularly hard for Maggie who has sorely missed her family and friends and the chance to talk freely and have the occasional heart to heart. Subsequently our telephone bill has, along with the car, taken the biggest bites out of our cash reserve.

A little knowledge is, of course, a dangerous thing.

We avoided showing our faces at the school parents' group for a long time knowing it would be pointless, but after nearly a year and after one particular good day on the language front when my confidence was high, I told Maggie I'd give it a whirl.

The assembled parents were surprised but obviously pleased to see me. I sat at the back trying desperately to grasp what the hell everyone was saying, which as far as I could make out seemed to be oscillating between the agenda and ribaldry. Suddenly there was a brief but earnest exchange between the chairwoman and a mother. It was impossible to decipher but it seemed important and I found myself requesting an explanation, only to be told the woman had a weak bladder and was desperate for the meeting to end.

That wasn't the end of it. I'd gone to the meeting with a rehearsed address, namely that we were sorry for being absent for so long and that we would be willing to do anything to help. Big mistake.

'*Patge*! *Patge*!' Someone shouted and there was a roar of

laughter. One man was beside himself and almost pitched sideways out of his chair.

'*Sí*, Marteen?' I was asked.

What exactly does it entail, I inquired. There was another burst of giggling.

It soon all became horribly clear.

While parents across the rest of Europe worry about what hugely expensive plastic toys Father Christmas has to deliver to wide-eyed Annie and little pickle Johnny on Christmas Eve, many children in Spain have to wait until the Feast of Epiphany on the 6 January – the twelfth day of Christmas – to receive their main presents. This, any self-respecting Sunday school ex-pupil should know, was when the Magi (the Three Kings, Caspar, Melchior and Balthasar) followed a bright star to Bethlehem and presented the newborn Christ with gold, frankincense and myrrh. Which all makes sense when you think about it.

Please don't worry, though, if you feel the children here are being denied any early Christmas excitement. The festive street decorations are up in good time (but, mercifully, not before the first or second week of December) and the big man from Lapland is getting bigger by the year with, one might cynically observe, the onset of rampant commercialism in a country which is modernising at an incredible rate. Once, while we were doing a December shop for toilet rolls and cheap beer at the big supermarket twenty miles away, we bumped into Ella's English teacher beside the Christmas trees display. As Bing Crosby crooned from the loudspeakers and people wandered by pushing trolleys heaving with Barbies and Action Men, she made it very clear she wasn't buying her daughter's Christmas present. 'No, no, no,' she insisted as if she'd been challenged (which she hadn't), 'We are buying for the Three Kings. Very important.' Sadly, you can't help but feel the tradition is slowly being squeezed out.

If this all sounds a little confusing for the children, they don't show it because, I suppose, if you stand a good chance of two hits of presents instead of one you shouldn't rock the boat by asking awkward questions. You just cover all the aces by firing off your letter to Santa while also making sure the Three Kings are in the know about what a very good boy or girl you been all year. And how do they do that?

That's where I come in.

'Er . . . sorry,' I repeated at the parents' meeting. 'But I don't know what *patge* means.' It was an ambush. No way out. Yours truly had solved that year's panic to find a volunteer daft enough to be decked out like an extra from Lawrence of Arabia before attempting to fool twenty children that the Kings had indeed sent a special envoy to their school. The other dads couldn't believe their luck.

'Don't worry,' said Pere on being told. 'You don't have to say anything. Just bring sweets, collect the letters and go. That's all.'

'Then why are you laughing?'

'It's nothing, don't worr— HA! HA! – No, sorry, don't worry, my friend. Just come and go.'

'But what if Ella recognises me?'

'I doubt it.'

So, it came to pass that an hour before the page's expected arrival I was sitting on a desk in the village civic building having my face, neck and ears smeared in black grease paint that stung my eyes and itched my nostrils. Gemma and Roser, two other parents invested with the responsibility of transforming me, then fussed about gathering together the elaborate disguise from an assortment of huge boxes and debating what went best with what.

They finally settled upon a rather fetching combination of a false black beard, a gold and black ankle-length robe, a huge piece of red and black material which was draped over my head and flowed behind me like a cape, a pair of black gloves and black wellies – and a white turban adorned with red star and long pink feather to top it all off. All this was layered over jeans, sweatshirt and a cushion tied round my tummy to give me a fighting chance at fooling my astute six-year-old daughter. She'd looked incredulous that morning when told that for the first time ever I'd been called to an urgent meeting in the big town near the coast.

The aim was to make me look like a distinguished courtier from the East and all the ingredients were right, save the deportment and general demeanour of the man underneath. Finally Gemma and Roser thrust bags of sweets into my hands and guided me out of the building into the plaza where, to my horror, a small crowd of locals couldn't resist having a gawp at the *patge*. There was a lot of elbowing, whispering and smiles as those who didn't know it was the English twit in disguise were told who was behind the beard.

I thought Gemma and Roser were going to stick with me, but they peeled off and I was left to make my own way along the path to the school where the staff and a few children were peering through the gate. It was then, in a desperate attempt to avoid being recognised by Ella or any of the children for that matter, I made the horrendous decision to develop an exaggerated waddle and severe limp which, of course, I had to persist with for the next forty-five minutes.

The first two toddlers I waved at dissolved into tears and clung to their mothers' skirts in abject fear. Pere had warned me this might happen with the younger ones, but burdened with so many clothes and an increasing doubt that I could pull it off I felt a bead of sweat cut a line down my blackened fore-head.

Pere led the way through to the first classroom where everyone was waiting and I was invited to lower myself onto a dinky nursery chair facing the throng. There was a painful pause and then the first child, urged on by his mum, edged nervously towards me. We exchanged his letter for sweets and then the ice was broken and one by one they stepped forward to shake my gloved hand and be photographed, while some of the older and wiser pupils busily scanned the crowd of adults to see which one was missing.

Of course I kept my mouth firmly shut, and just smiled and nodded approvingly as every letter was given to me.

Then, to my utter amazement, there was one point during the concluding melee when the now confident, curious chil-dren were beginning to prod and tweak, and shortly before I nearly lost my hat while attempting to bow out gracefully to limp as fast as possible back to the civic hall, I had one-year-old Joe Joe on my knee and Ella at my side. The consequences of being unmasked by the kids didn't bear thinking about and as I hobbled away from the school (suddenly conscious that my limp had switched legs) I thanked my lucky star that neither of them had twigged it was Dad.

Some people have argued that we should have opted to learn mainstream Spanish first, as everyone understands it and it is a global language. But Catalan is the living word here, an ancient Latin language spoken by nigh on eight million people and a major plank of this autonomous region's defiant claim to be a nation within Europe. Feelings run deep. The woman in the bread shop declared she was unable, or unwilling, to say anything in Spanish.

Early on, queuing patiently in shops and listening to the locals chattering away in Catalan, or tuning in to Ella playing with her school friends, I noticed a significant weave with French which I thought would help me as I'd kept plugging away with it since doing it at A level and could get by quite well – or so I thought. But my brain couldn't compute all the mixed messages. My frail French topped with a smattering of Spanish gleaned from Maggie and decorated with a handful of Portuguese words picked up in Africa fused into a lumpy linguistic loaf I've dubbed Desperanto that was not the answer I or anyone stupid enough to speak to me was looking for.

I'd offer up vignettes of complete tosh, monologues without meaning that at best might prompt flashes of understanding on the face of the person I was talking to when a familiar word spilled out. Most of the time, though, they looked puzzled, pinching their faces in sympathetic constipation and willing me to string a coherent sentence together.

Joaquim has equally frail French too, so at least he and I could muster what you could almost call conversation. It was not the solution but at least I limited that weird, sweating palm sensation of not knowing what my freewheeling gob was going to lob out next. I've even resorted to German.

There can be few tougher tests for the language dunce than to discuss the vagaries of a car's dodgy power-steering with an engineer who has had earlier dealings with you and knows he's in for a rough ride.

Robbie the Range Rover – hero of the big journey south through France when he was weighed down to the gunnels and thrashed mercilessly – started showing signs of distress a few weeks after we arrived. He began dribbling fluid from the powered steering and, despite regular top-ups and gentle chats and pats, the occasional squeal from under the bonnet rapidly turned into a perpetual, mournful wail. He was fine when driven in a straight line, but there are not many of those in the mountains and we were suddenly struck by the concept of life without him. Fighting the leaden steering I set off at daybreak on a Friday morning on the long, twisty trek through the valleys to keep an 8.30 a.m. appointment at the (luck would have it) Rover dealership in the nearest large town.

Having ferreted around under the bonnet for several minutes the service manager finally made me understand that I had to come back at lunchtime.

'*Bien sûr. Adieu,*' I said in masterful Desperanto which provoked such a look of bewilderment that I spluttered: '*Muy bien, monsieur* – er, I mean *señor*. Er, bye, see you in-in . . . er . . . no . . . at *uno hora*?'

The sun was just breaking through as I stumbled out of the garage onto the pavement and took a few deep breaths. Traffic was thundering by and the air was mildly yellow and noxious. But there was another more disturbing rotting smell which I couldn't figure out. I struck out for the town centre with the vague plan of tracking down the tourist information office to get some sort of map.

I planned to spend the morning sussing out the place, checking out the price of grass strimmers at a shop which Mac and Conxita had recommended, and also finding a computer shop we'd seen during our few forays to the supermarket to stock up on loo roll. I also wanted to try and find a Spanish internet provider.

My first port of call was the Sol Bank to pay in a very welcome 45,000 pesetas rebate from the notary (for quite what we're not sure) and then headed for a town map we'd seen in the main square beside the statue of a man in armour on horseback. It was there, back in September 2000, that we had sunned ourselves outside a café and, full of cheer, toasted with our mothers the safe arrival at the bank of our £95,000 cash transfer to buy the farm.

I discovered from the map that it was just a short hop down narrow streets to the tourist office where, like at the bank, they spoke English. No need for Desperanto. Things are looking up, I thought. Twenty minutes later I was in the hardware store Mac had told us about, where my head was turned by a dinky Ferrari-red tractor which would fit perfectly between our rows of vines and only cost a million pesetas (about £4000). All worries about finding the £300 needed for a strimmer were lost in a moment of daydreaming that had me patting the driver's seat while the shopkeeper grinned and rubbed his hands. Suddenly sensing things could get sticky I ignored him until he was distracted by another customer, then grabbed brochures for strimmers and the tractor and made a quick exit. I dipped in and out of two similar shops, made a mental note to tell Maggie about the man selling cheap dog food from a garage nearby, and then went in search of the computer store. By noon, clutching a Telefonica disc and my town map (which I'd marked with the locations of all my discoveries as well as a second-hand clothes shop and health food store), I was feeling particularly pleased with myself. The sun was out and the place was more than manageable I thought as I veered into an indoor market on my way back to the garage.

It being Friday I splashed out on four frozen fish fillets and carefully wrapped them in a copy of the *El Mundo* newspaper (which I'd tried to comprehend while treating myself to a coffee and doughnut) and put them in the bottom of the rucksack. They would have just about defrosted by the time I got home at around 2 p.m.

I knew as soon as I entered the garage things were not going smoothly. Robbie was still up on the ramp, bonnet open. The service manager, head on one side and hands clasped together, had a sympathetic expression like a doctor with bad news.

'*Problema, problema*,' he said softly. I sat down. It was one of those gut-wrenching moments when you weren't sure you wanted to know the truth, and in this case I couldn't be sure I'd understand it anyway.

'*Momento*,' and he was gone again, leaving me to gaze numbly at our mud-splattered car which looked a wreck alongside the polished Rover saloons. Men in neat overalls were fussing over all the vehicles except Robbie. I imagined them laughing and walking away from him after some dreadful, fatal flaw became apparent, leaving him suspended in mid-air as a lesson to all who mistreat their cars. I wished I'd washed him.

The manager returned and, after several attempts, was able to explain that the pipe would not fit. '*Gracies*,' I said in relief. He looked puzzled again, then pressed on, tapping his watch and saying something about six o'clock.

'Me, back here at six o'clock?'

'*Sí.*'

A mechanic came by and seemed to be unhappy with the idea that it could be done that day. The manager took him to one side, lowered his voice and pointed towards me as much to say, 'Look at the poor bugger, we can't expect him to try and buy a train ticket, he won't stand a chance.'

'*Sí*, sex o'cock.'

My brain pulled up just short of spluttering, 'I can't thank you enough.' Instead I smiled weakly and wandered out into the sun again. The pong was still there and I headed back towards the city centre with another five hours to burn. Suddenly the fish fillets didn't seem such a good idea. I rang Maggie, then bought pizza, pastries and postcards and looked for somewhere to sit and picnic. The map showed a park and I ended up there munching and watching the world stroll by.

It was a beautiful spring day, like an English June with a gentle breeze to take the sting out of the sun, and I'd long since shed my coat and jumper. Not that the locals seemed to notice the heat. Almost everyone had their winter coats buttoned to the neck. One woman, who zigzagged slowly across the park so her golden cocker spaniel could cock its leg against every tree, was decked out in a designer, ankle-length fur coat. While I turned a true Brit lobster pink the other park dwellers kept their collars up and heads down. The only other people who seemed to appreciate how warm it was were two teenagers clearly in the flurry of a new affair.

By the time I'd woken up to the possibility of killing an hour or two by wandering through the town museum it had closed for the afternoon so I returned to the Placa café and sat and drank a beer at the table I'd shared with my mum, Maggie and her mum five months before. It was 3.30 p.m. and, in the shade of the buildings a cool breeze began to bite.

I thought of Mum and sent her my love. Maybe she will be well enough to come here again, I thought. Maybe.

I drifted through the narrow streets again and then, legs aching, swerved into a smoky bar and ordered a coffee. A television at the end of the bar was on and I watched as what looked like Catalonia's answer to 'Eastenders' unfolded. Violin music ratcheted up the sentiment as a greasy haired old man, apparently beside himself with worry and on the point of tears, meandered round his apartment for an extraordinarily long time, squeezing every last ounce of drama out of the moment, before finally picking up the phone. I grappled with his mournful monologue but didn't understand a word and was left to muse on his off-screen stardom and real life, clean hair, cravat and sports car persona, opening supermarkets and appearing in stair lift adverts. Then the violin accompaniment reached a crescendo, a teenage girl entered – and our star was reunited with his lost dog.

I ordered another coffee.

With still an hour to go before I was due back at the garage I was back on the streets. I continued my ramble, now seeking out estate agents to compare property values and try and gauge if we had bought wisely or been taken to the cleaners. We've always suspected and been advised that Mother's Garden was a bargain and my tour of the agents' windows seemed to confirm this. There were comfortable but not exceptional coastal villas with pools and small gardens for circa £220,000, but the most telling evidence was provided by a variety of seemingly decrepit farms with neglected, uninspiring land of about the same area and yet the agents were asking the same price as we had paid for our 'little piece of paradise' as Maggie calls it.

Rejuvenated, I set out for the garage at 5.30 p.m. in the hope that they'd finished early and had even found time to wash Robbie. I stopped at a hardware store and bought a rat trap, then pressed on past the wasteland that lay between the ring road and garage. The stench hit me again. I glanced to my left and recoiled. The dead dog's eyes were open. So was its mouth. It was a large, beige dog, quite old by the look of it (though I didn't linger), lying on its side facing the pavement.

Robbie was still up on the jack and I, by now drained and befuddled, sank onto a chair and looked on my town map for the train station. The service manager was buzzing about more frenetically then ever and I sensed he was avoiding eye contact. The minutes ticked by and it slowly dawned on me that if there was no point in me waiting around he would have tried to tell me. People came and went as the service area slowly emptied, leaving just a handful of cars and Robbie. Finally, at 6.45 p.m., the manager took a deep breath and approached me. It was sorted and the damage came to just 22,000 pesetas, only about £80. I wouldn't have battered an eyelid if he'd said treble that. With the mental picture of the dead dog filling my mind and the aroma of fish filling the car, I made it back to the farm at 7.30 p.m.

The garage bill proved too good to be true. Three weeks

later I was back. Robbie was still dribbling and this time the news was far, far worse. The whole steering unit was shot to pieces and it was going to cost up to five hundred quid to replace it. I couldn't fathom this out at first but I finally solved what the service manager was trying to tell me when I suddenly broadened my Desperanto.

'*Kaput?*' I said, pointing to a picture of the steering unit in my car manual.

'*Ja, kaput,*' came the reply.

We booked him in to be overhauled during Easter week when we were back in the UK seeing our families and still trying to sort out Mum's care and her finances. We got back to find he'd been fixed, serviced, and polished. He looked half respectable. They'd repaired rather than replaced the steering unit which kept the cost down, and the unknown engineer grew further in my estimation when I discovered he'd been playing my Johnny Lee Hooker blues tape on the car's stereo.

As for Robbie, he continued to grumble and next set his heart on a new clutch slave cylinder. Back down the windy roads we went.

We had a good day, as it turned out. The car wasn't fixed when we went back at 4 p.m., which didn't help the blood pressure, but we'd spent our time in town gleaning information about registering the farm for organic production, a task we'd feared would be arduous, and had also stumbled upon a very chic bar in a back-street square.

I have to say the cars around here are fascinating. I've never been a trainspotter, but as a little kid in the late sixties I used to pride myself on being able to identify cars at night by the size and location of the sidelights and headlamps. Sad, I know, but true. My dad will bear witness. We travelled a lot together and it helped pass the time. I lost interest in the early seventies, about the time a schoolfriend's father took us for a spin in his new, state-of-the-art Morris Marina, and when the little round sidelights and indicators that looked like pimples and popped up anywhere on the bodywork of cars were a thing of the past. Imagine my delight, then, at the discovery of scores of ancient Seats, Renaults and the like, long-gone from UK roads, still trundling about here. I'm not likely to settle down on an apple crate beside the road at nightfall to test the grey matter, but the old motors have brought back some happy childhood memories of long camping holiday car journeys with my dad.

If you've ever wondered, incidentally, who buys those two-seater Toy Town micro cars that are about as long as a motorbike and seem to run on sewing machine motors, it's the rural Spanish. If you feel inclined to giggle, don't.

Who in their right minds would want or need one of those, I tittered out loud the first time I jammed Robbie into third gear and roared past one on the open road just a couple of days after we arrived. They seemed to be everywhere, along with the ageing Renault 4s and 6s and assorted small Seats from the late sixties and seventies.

Well, just try following one of the wee wonders through a hilltop Spanish village. The maze of wafer thin streets and right-angle corners (not to mention the 'tight squeeze' underground car parks in the big towns) are just perfect for parp! parp! Noddy cars and the last place you want to get wedged in in a Range Rover with spongy steering.

Believe me. I've been there – and had to come out backwards. Dipstick.

Echoes

mother's garden

Naturan expelles furca, tamen usque recurret.
('You may drive out nature with a pitchfork, yet she'll
be constantly running back.' Horace, 65–8 BC)

It wasn't long after our move that the land began to reveal its
secrets.

Our life here has always tended to revolve around buckets –
one for the compost, one for scraps for the chickens, another
for weeding the veg patch or for despatched rats, one where
washing up water is left to cool before being poured on to the
garden, and so on. They are precious vessels and we inherited
quite a few with the farm, but you can never have enough and
I was none too pleased during an early 'I need a bucket!' panic
to discover that what seemed like a perfectly serviceable one
(that I'd spied on a high shelf in the barn) was brim full of

stones, shells and broken pottery. I would have jettisoned the contents had a suitable spot sprung to mind. Thankfully it didn't.

A couple of weeks after we arrived we suddenly woke up to the historical significance of our new home when Rob, who'd stayed on for a while after the move to help us get settled and to help Maggie while I went back for Horace's funeral, came back from a cross-country yomp with a tiny coin in the palm of his hand. We knew how important the coastal lowlands had been in Roman times, but we hadn't considered the relevance to our valley. I started ignoring the views as I walked about the land, instead stumbling into branches and snaring myself on brambles as I scoured the ground for artefacts. Ludicrous, I know, but the next day I charged back to the house waving my arms in the air having found what looked like a handmade square-sided nail, about three inches long.

Later that week Mac and I were returning from a trip down the mountain where we'd hunted in vain around a junkyard for a spare part for his Land Rover. We trundled back up the mountain and had just turned into the mile-long sandy track to his house when I told him about the coin. We stopped on the brow of a hill beside a sun-bleached dry-stone wall in the shade of an ancient olive tree. 'It's incredible to imagine really,' he said softly, leaning forward on to the steering wheel and gesturing to the mix of olives, vines and hazelnuts that rolled away across the south-facing slopes of the valley. 'The Americans marvel at Britain's history, but boy, the Mediterranean, this place, is steeped in it. I know wine production may not quite be the world's oldest profession, but there were vines here thousands of years ago and the Romans left their mark for sure. Goodness only knows what these lands have seen.'

The next day Pere further fired our imaginations. We were driving to pick up Katie, our new, jointly owned Ferrari red rotovator. During the car journey home in the fading light we told him about the coin and nail. We asked what he knew about local Roman history and then said it would be fascinating to check out the land with a metal detector. He roared with laughter and shook his head.

'You cannot do this thing – the law will not allow it. Believe me, it is not allowed here, I think. If nobody knows then that is your risk, but I would not do it.'

The ban seemed illogical, given our thirst to know more, but as time has passed we have grown to understand. Such is the enormous legacy it is better left alone. Things will show themselves occasionally and the last thing anyone wants is a plague of people tramping across farms prospecting for treasure.

Pere said he and Nuria had found nothing on his five hectares of land in the six years since they'd moved there, but added that everyone knew the valley was probably farmed during Roman times and was loaded with history. 'The village was some sort of Roman settlement for sure. People find pots and things and a great many of these pots were found in one place. It is thought the prefects and rich people from Tarragona had villas here in the valleys. Of course, there are a great many things we do not know. Maybe there was a Roman farm where you are!'

By now I was buzzing with excitement. What if it was true?

I had seen something between the two almond groves right at the top of the farm near the brow of the hill where there was a panoramic view of the whole valley. Sticking out of the side of the sandy bank, about three feet down, there appeared to be some sort of floor, and the area was strewn with what looked like sandstone blocks with clear, straight edges and right-angled corners. Perhaps it was just the remains of an old terrace wall, but why was it only in one place? It could just be a strata of rock, but it seemed so flat.

The sky was leaden and it was tipping it down the next morning but that didn't stop me. Decked out in my Spanish wellies, jeans, stetson and Maggie's ankle-length Aussie range coat, I went foraging. With Maggie calling after me that I looked a right tulip I pressed on through the undergrowth until I reached the almonds. The low cloud meant you couldn't even see the mountain ridge less than a mile away and the rain which Pere said never came was pouring off the front of my hat as I burrowed with a stick. What I thought could be a section of floor was about five feet long and appeared to be in three sections. I scraped away enough soil to expose at least two feet, possibly much more, but by now the terrace was sodden and there was a risk of landslide. Megan the mad hound got the idea and started digging furiously further along the bank while her brother Charlie looked on puzzled. Then a hefty lump of rock whizzed past my head so I gave up and trudged home frustrated. If I continued to dig there was a real risk the upper terrace might collapse.

That afternoon we were due to make the long trek to Tarragona to resolve a few problems, namely to try and sort out our car insurance, possibly buy a new washing machine and hunt for a baby bath. We were also due to meet Maggie's mum at Barcelona airport late that evening, so we decided to allow some time to wander around Tarragona's ancient quarter.

Ringed by vast oil refineries and with a queue of tankers and cargo ships at anchor offshore, Tarragona doesn't look inviting from a distance. It pays a price for its modern-day importance, and driving down from the mountains you can both see and smell how the industrial sprawl taints the air. We were nervous, too, about plunging in to what people had warned us was a bustling city with a maze of narrow streets teeming with traffic. But we are immensely glad we did.

At sunset we were standing about five floors up on the roof of part of the Roman provincial forum, the Praetorium Tower, looking in wonder over the amphitheatre and assorted ruins of what was one of the most important Roman imperial cities in Western Europe. Step by step we learned so much: how Tarraco, as the Romans called it, was an outpost of the empire as far back as 218 BC, growing to become the capital of Hispania Citerior – later known as Tarraconense – before being made a colony in 45 BC by Julius Caesar. Better was to come – twenty or so years later it was regarded as the cultural centre of Roman Spain and Augustus Caesar ruled the empire from Tarraco for two years.

We were in a bit of a daze looking out over it all, having

just explored the tunnels beneath the Roman circus where chariot races and tragedies were staged to keep the population's mind off revolution. Below us was the remarkably well-preserved amphitheatre, where thousands of people would watch the blood of gladiators and other hapless souls being spilled. It was the perfect fuel to ignite the mind of someone who'd just discovered what could be Roman ruins in his garden. Even Ella got a real buzz out of the visit to what we all agreed was a beautiful and, in places, peaceful city that's justifiably a World Heritage Site.

Back at the farm I emptied out the bucket of bits and looked closely at the contents. They seemed to be an assortment of Mother's Garden discoveries. The fossils and shells were a complete mystery, but the fragments of pottery, some of which were painted with fish, were enthralling and one jug handle in particular has lived in the house ever since. I also found what could have been a Stone Age hand chisel and flints for cutting.

We talked excitedly about what might lie beneath the surface of the land, but as the days and weeks passed and little other than tiny bits of pottery of indeterminate age were discovered I calmed down. We still have the Roman coin, but now it's at the bottom of the *balsa* after a depressing butterfingers incident while we were chatting with friends and watching the sun go down, all sitting on the low wall round the reservoir. The pot handle makes occasional dinner party appearances, but these are waning, and I have decided not to excavate any more of the terrace where I thought I'd found a section of floor. The compulsion to dig further has given way to the realisation that we have so many other things to occupy our minds and that, all in good Mediterranean time, we are bound to discover more as we work the land. Meanwhile, another incredible chapter of local history has come to the surface.

The back wall of the farmhouse is more pitted and scarred than the rest, but we thought nothing of it until I saw something sticking out of the soil close by. It was an eerie discovery – the very heavy, rusting cylinder of a revolver with its six empty bullet chambers. I felt numb, like I have always done when I've seen a handgun or on the only occasion I've held one (while reporting on Ghurkha Regiment manoeuvres on Stanford Battle Area in Norfolk in 1980). I couldn't believe the weight of it.

I hate guns. Despite my teenage TV diet of 'Kojak' and 'Starsky and Hutch', I remember my shock when I first visited America in 1978 and a policewoman with a holster round her hips watched us troop off the plane at Boston. I'm still haunted by the memory of how, during a later visit to the US, a young boy in a pick-up parked alongside my hire car at an all-night diner in the Texas desert pulled a huge revolver from the glove compartment and, illuminated by the flickering blue neon sign above the diner's door, struggled to point it at me.

A few days after I found the gun carriage at the farm my stepsister's partner Steve took a knife to one of the holes riddling the wall and dug out the head of a bullet.

'You should be careful working on the land,' someone said later. 'They're still finding grenades and ammunition. Only recently there was a fire in the forest about ten kilometres away and you could hear the explosions.'

What rapidly came in to sharp focus was something we had only been vaguely aware of – that the farm was not a million miles away from the scene of the last major battle of the Spanish Civil War. The battle of the River Ebro in 1938 was one of the conflict's longest and bloodiest engagements as the Nationalist army of General Franco, backed by Hitler and Mussolini, homed in on the Republican bastion of Barcelona.

One day at the school gate I told fellow parent Josep about the gun carriage and asked how the community was affected by the war. As the children raced out through the gate he told me to track down and read the book about the village's history and that we would talk some more another day. I made a few inquiries but it slipped down the agenda as we battled away on the farm and hosted a procession of visitors. The school term ended and the long summer holidays began. My sister Jackie was among those visiting Mother's Garden and we showed her the gun carriage and recounted the stories of the war. I told her about the village history book and that it was on our wish list. She later saw it for sale in the hardware store and bought it for us.

I was stunned by what I read. During the blood-letting in what was an appalling conflict, seven people from the village were shot, thirty four were killed in battle, five died when the village was bombed, six were claimed by disease and two disappeared – fifty four out of a population of a few hundred, and there was no figure for the number injured. It was one of the worst-hit communities in all of Spain.

Those who survived hid in the caves scattered through the valleys around us as the area was bludgeoned by air and artillery bombardment for more than three months. We later learned how a local woman, then a little girl, took refuge in a small rural house. It suffered a direct hit. The girl was maimed and the grandmother was killed. The book told, too, how thousands of soldiers were billeted across the area in the weeks before the beleaguered Republican army's last ditch offensive across the Ebro in a valiant effort to regain lost ground. That, said Josep when we bumped into each other in the village square, was the probable explanation for the gun carriage and bullet holes.

'My mother was one of those taken to hide in the mountains,' he added. 'She was four years old. The family was from the next village which suffered greatly too. Her father, my grandfather, died in that final battle and I am trying to find his grave.'

'Is that possible?' I asked. 'I mean in the chaos of war it is so difficult . . .'

'I have been trying for some years now and I won't give up.'

He also told me how some villagers fled abroad, including his uncle. Many never returned. I told him there was something else in the book that had leapt out at me. It was a grainy photograph of a parade on the old football pitch below the civic building where the school now stood. The caption said these were the men of the 15th Division of the International Brigade – some of the thousands of foreigners who defied their governments to fight for the Republic against Franco and Fascism. And they were here, in our village.

'Yes, they were here, scores of them,' Josep confirmed. 'Apparently there is a grave somewhere in the valley, the grave of an American who was wounded and died while being taken to the hospital set up in the railway tunnel at the top of the valley. But I have looked for it and cannot find it.'

'I know where it is!' I blurted. Pere had pointed it out shortly after we arrived.

Josep couldn't believe it. 'But I have been looking for so long.'

The next day we drove up the valley, parked close to the snail farm compound on the edge of the forest wilderness, walked a small way and then clambered down towards the dry riverbed. The gravestone, etched with the star of the International Brigade, was barely visible in the dappled light beneath a fir tree. As we approached we could see that a neatly folded flag of the Republic, weathered by rain and sun, lay at the head. We stood in silence for a moment then Josep said how grateful he was – he'd scoured the lower section of the valley and had given up his hunt just fifty yards away.

All this coincided with other events and discoveries. Back in the village a building I'd walked past countless times without a second glance suddenly became hugely significant. It's a fairly uninteresting terraced house of the standard proportions with accommodation upstairs and large, ground floor double doors that had clearly seen better days. In fact the whole of the building looked battered and in need of repair. Above the large doors I could make out a few faded letters and I assumed it had once been a business of some sort, like the carpenter's next door. Then, during a lazy afternoon during the August fiesta when people were milling about the village, I was introduced to a nice guy called Charlie from London. His wife was Catalan and from the area and they'd come back for the festivities. He was keen to know how we were getting on and what we liked and disliked about our new life, and I told him about our various discoveries.

'It's amazing to think,' I said, 'that so many foreigners who came to fight in the International Brigades were here. It's hard to imagine.'

'Yes,' he replied and then turned and faced the old house. 'You can still read it, though, can't you?'

'What?'

'The lettering above the door of that house. It's worn, but you can just about make out "*Intendencia Brigada*".'

As I looked up at the sign open mouthed he went on: 'It was the division's stores, apparently. It all looks tatty at the moment because I think it was painted over during Franco's time, but now it has been revealed again.'

If that wasn't enough, within weeks I was sitting in the restaurant next door chatting to a bright-eyed ninety-year-old Brigade veteran called Steve, from Scotland, complete with beret, blazer and badge. We'd heard English voices at another table and having started a general conversation I was soon engrossed as he reminisced about his time in Catalonia. But his memory of the village was hazy and he asked if there was a dry riverbed nearby. I told him about our valley and the grave.

He said he'd trained for weeks on end along a riverbed before the final Republican push across the Ebro, and he'd all but given up hope of finding it again. With that he was gone, jogging down the hill the way I'd pointed, pursued by his younger companions who were accompanying him on what we later discovered was a reunion of Brigade survivors.

One of his companions, Rachel, an English woman living and working in Barcelona and helping on the tour as an interpreter, invited us to meet up again the next day, close to a remote village about an hour's drive north into the mountains where a ceremony of remembrance was being held. The exact location was a vast, cool cavern, site of a Republican army field hospital staffed in part by English doctors and nurses in the last desperate months of the war. We joined the throng to listen to speeches by several veterans above whose heads you could still see remnants of old wiring dangling from the rock. It may have been more than sixty years since the war but there was a real sense of the appreciation and admiration among the assembled Catalans for these foreigners who had risked and often given their lives to help them.

One of their number had died just a few weeks before aged ninety-two. His name was Dr Len Crome. Billy of Ricochet Films had sent me his obituary from the *Guardian* which described in great detail how the doctor had run a cave hospital near our new home, but at the time we were not sure exactly where. It was the same place. Len Crome was a Latvian who studied medicine in Edinburgh and worked as a junior doctor in England before signing up in 1937 for the International Brigade. He probably knew our village well. Later, serving with the Royal Army Medical Corps during the Second World War, he was awarded the Military Cross for clearing casualties under fire during the battle for Monte Casino in Italy.

What echoes. What food for the mind on a peaceful Spanish day as the distant church bell tolls.

As for the predominantly friendly older people in our village I've long wondered what horrors they've known, but I've never judged there to have been a good moment to ask and doubt there ever will be. Yet about the time I first read of the delicately named Association for the Recovery of Historical Memory – the force behind one of the most heart-rending and politically sensitive episodes in this country's history and a touchstone for many tears – one old boy's past was whispered to me.

I vaguely remember seeing him (his name was also Josep) that first summer, seated in typical Latin fashion outside his front door in the evening sunshine watching the world go by. I paid little attention save to exchange a simple greeting. Then he was gone. His name came up in conversation when I mentioned the association to my English class and asked if it was relevant to our part of the world.

In truth I knew it must be, but I wanted to gauge how sensitive things remained about the consequences of the civil war and the subsequent Fascist regime which suppressed all Catalan culture and made exiles of many of its leaders and academics. The paradox was, of course, that such suppression merely served to strengthen local resistance and identity.

Josep, I was told in hushed tones, was an invalid who'd lost both his legs during the civil war. He was among several locals who'd been taken away by Franco's victorious forces before being lined up in a ditch and shot as the bloody conflict was coming to an end in 1938. As the men were executed they fell on top of Josep who, despite wounds to the legs and body, survived for two days until he was discovered and saved by relatives.

Only now, after nearly three decades since Franco died, do some of the families of the estimated thirty thousand people executed during the conflict all those years ago feel able to call for the return of their loved ones. And that, we've learned, is what the Association for the Recovery of Historical Memory is all about.

It's easy to imagine some governments dodging such a thorny issue, particularly when the country is blossoming on the international stage and trying to forget its past. But the key to the movement, as I gleaned from the BBC World Service, has been the ten-year-old UN resolution stating that, in cases of forced disappearances, governments are obliged to investigate, find and identify these people to give them a fitting burial.

There have been no local meetings yet, but excavations

have begun in other parts of Spain and a few bodies have been retrieved. Why, though, I asked, had it taken so long since the death of Franco in 1975? The skeletons of Bosnia's victims were already being recovered. I was reminded of the attempted Spanish coup d'état in 1981 when disgruntled army officers took over the parliament building and fired bullets into the ceiling. It seemed for a moment that the fresh democracy would die young. The drama proved short, but it unnerved the nation to such an extent that, some believe, it set the cause of justice back decades. Spain, for many people in the rest of Europe, may just be an affordable Mediterranean beach holiday far away from recent war zones. But this country is still coming to terms with its ghosts.

We have gained something else through the civil war revelations – acquaintances which have blossomed into important friendships. Rachel, who illustrated a local book about the conflict, and her Catalan fiancé Gerard are regular visitors and helpers at Mother's Garden, and through them we have grown close to another like-minded English couple keen on history and with a 'smallholding' past who have bought an equally challenging house just a mile from us. Angela Jackson was the driving force behind the cave hospital commemoration, having reawakened interest in the cave's significant recent history while researching her Ph.D and subsequently through her absorbing book *British Women and the Spanish Civil War*. She and her husband Roger, a photographer-turned-house restorer, have dovetailed into the Mother's Garden support network, sharing ideas, knowledge, and jokes, putting their shoulders to the wheel when things have got sticky and imbibing the odd glass of wine or two at sundown. They, along with Conxita, Mac and other close friends, have become our essential Catalan family.

Blisters and Blushes

mother's garden

*C*onxita has a cast-iron grasp of English, but she was flummoxed by my indomitable eighty-year-old father's Norfolk dialect and the broad Norfolk joke about the honey cart.

Dad, who's both partially sighted and hard of hearing, had bounced back after his health scare early in 2001 and even in his hospital bed had been declaring his determination to get to Spain 'some blummin' how' to see Mother's Garden. I knew he'd come. When I visited him in hospital that Easter he looked thinner and pale but the twinkle in the eye was still burning bright.

Escorted on the flight to Barcelona by John, a friend from schooldays, Dad brought with him his what we call his 'Jack Lemmon' pale blue sun hat and his gentle Norfolk humour. The honey cart yarn from days gone by is one of his favourites.

You may have heard it – the one about the old boy who trawled through the village on the horse and cart (before the dawn of modern plumbing) collecting . . . er . . . buckets full of thoughts from the smallest room, and who accidentally knocked his jacket into the mire and started fishing for it with a stick. 'You can't want that now,' said his partner. ''Corse not,' came the reply. 'But m' blummin' sandwiches are in the pocket.'

Bizarrely, the joke, for all its fragrance, was to prove potently prophetic. Three days later I was knee-deep in it, so to speak.

It's a well-known fact that cows produce vast quantities, and I'm not talking about milk. A few weeks before Dad's visit we'd buttonholed Joaquim and asked for a couple of trailer-loads of cattle poo to be deposited in distant corners of our higgledy-piggledy ten acres, to mature and await the day we would use it to encourage the crops. He assured us the delivery would all be over and done with in a jiffy, without so much as a whiff of fuss or bother. Marvellous, we said, and set about discussing prevalent wind direction and a wise place to deposit it.

Tractor driver Josep (yes, another one), a familiar smiling face around the village, was asked by Joaquim to make the delivery and seemed jovial enough when he and a swarm of flies turned up early one Tuesday. 'Top of the olive grove, please!' we gestured from a safe distance, only to watch him roar off, veer right and plough through the vegetable patch. Maggie went a funny colour, walked slowly along the tyre track through her onions and then tensed. Her body language as she advanced towards Josep didn't need translating and, perhaps sensing time was of the essence, he tipped the trailer and was gone in a flash.

Maggie was ready to chase him down the farm track, but listened to reason. The damage was done.

'Better if you go to market and I'll see him when he comes back with the second load,' I suggested. 'If he comes back.'

'All right,' she said finally. 'But make b— sure he doesn't do any more damage. Get him to put the next lot at the top of the land. That way you should be able to keep him away from the vegetables.'

'Right,' I said. 'Leave it to me.'

Back he came an hour later looking flushed but clearly relieved to find the car and Maggie absent.

'This way!' I yelled and walked ahead up the track to discourage any further vandalism. I was nearing the top of the farm when the pitch of the tractor engine suddenly changed. I turned to see Josep halfway up the track bouncing wildly on his seat like a rodeo rider, but he was going nowhere except slowly earthwards. The tractor had lost its grip and, wheels spinning, was doing a remarkably efficient job of burying itself. What I'd forgotten was that the main pipe from the well to the house had been leaking for weeks and had created a hugely effective mud trap. What followed (witnessed by my father leaning on his stick and grinning from ear to ear) was farcical.

Assorted efforts to free the tractor and trailer only made

matters worse and so Josep, by now looking manic and (like me) smeared with *caca* and sweat, declared he'd have to unload right there – plum in the middle of our only route to half the land.

'But-but-but . . .,' I cried to no avail.

With a shrug of the shoulders as if to say, 'There's nothing else we can do,' Josep clambered aboard his tractor again and pulled a lever. I watched helplessly as a head-high ton of foul-smelling fly food slid off the trailer and blocked the track. As the tractor clawed its way out of the hole and Josep disappeared over the horizon, I stood staring at a steaming pile. It was hard to think of a worse place to put it, save on the doorstep.

It had to go.

I'm not entirely sure what the rights of passage are regarding farming, but shovelling and carting a mountain of glutinous you-know-what has to be in the small print somewhere. By the time I'd finished the moon was high. Just like me.

It was, or course, by no means the first or last time the bones have creaked and blisters bulged. From the outset both of us suffered for the cause, whether it was digging up spuds, scavenging for wood, reaching for blackberries and rosehips or toiling with the saw, secateurs, shovel or scythe. Wounds and stings have seemed to take longer to heal here for some reason, while aches and pains have had to be endured without the solace of a hot bath.

One of the hardest physical challenges was presented

shortly after we arrived by those tenacious white-flowering weeds choking the vineyard and which proved too much for the new rotovator. For weeks after our battle to pull them all up by hand, Maggie had problems with her right arm. She would wake with pins and needles in her hand and tears in her eyes and this, combined with Joe bellowing to be fed every four hours, was taking its toll. In the dead of night a few serious illnesses sprang to mind as we contemplated Maggie's pain, but we quickly figured out what was to blame. As we bent double for a few hours every day, tugging away trying to get the plants out roots and all before the blighters went to seed, we urged ourselves on with the logic that there was no alternative if we were going to be true to our organic principles and avoid spraying.

Even the rotovator work was giving me grief. After a few hours with Katie I was wide-eyed and giddy, and looked like I'd been wrestling an alligator. The vineyard looked wonderful afterwards, but it had been hard graft and we were not sure, given the small fortune we spent subsequently on the osteopath, if it wouldn't have been faster and cheaper to pay someone to plough it. We were to resort to that at a later date.

With no let-up in the pain in her arm and her back, when Maggie got wind of an osteopath in a town about twelve miles away we booked her in. Twice her appointment meant she'd have the car and I'd have to walk with Joe Joe in the pushchair to meet Ella from school, which seemed like a nice idea at the time. It's about a mile to the village and Maggie had done it once before, when I'd been in the large town at the foot of the mountains trying to get the car fixed. Strolling there and back would be a pleasant distraction from the piles of work at the farm – and we worked out that Maggie would be back in time to take Ella to school for the afternoon session.

As she headed for the osteopath she shouted out of the car window that I needed to allow fifteen minutes if I was to get to the school on time. 'Give yourself plenty of time. Bye!'

Once you're out of the farm track and on the road it's slightly downhill for about five hundred yards so I strolled along enjoying the almond blossom and pointing out wild flowers and butterflies to Joe Joe who seemed to find the whole experience somewhat soporific. It was only when we began the long, very steep climb up to the hill village that I realised we were seriously off schedule. Joe was shaken awake as I tried to up the pace and I arrived at the school utterly shattered, labouring up the last excruciating yards with my head down, body bent over and arms stretched forward like someone pushing a hefty car stuck in snow. The assembled parents stopped talking to watch and whisper, while Joe Joe rocked back and forwards and waved his arms in an animated appeal for more speed. Never again, I told myself, perspiring profusely. Get a lift or allow yourself at least half an hour.

The next time Maggie had a late-afternoon appointment that coincided with Ella leaving school I suggested she drop me and Joe Joe somewhere in the village and we could kill time wandering around.

'I'm not going to attempt that hill again. Not pushing Joe, anyway.'

'It'll do you good.'

'It nearly finished me off – and I've not intention of making an arse of myself again, thank you very much.'

Maggie left us beside an abandoned tractor on the top road so it would be downhill all the way home apart from the last gentle rise to the farm. I waved her off, loaded Joe Joe into his pushchair and looked around unsure which way to go. We had half an hour to spare before school finished. It was hot as usual and I cursed myself for putting on trousers rather than shorts. I was just starting to dabble with the idea of popping into the bar when a group of women meandered by, deep in conversation, cardigans round their shoulders and seemingly oblivious to the afternoon sun. They left the road, walked along a sandy track and disappeared behind a wall. I took a swig from a bottle of water and followed at a respectable distance. Most afternoons the village's more senior residents, mostly women, can be found in groups of three or more, chatting and strolling along the lanes around the village, so I figured they must know a pretty route.

The pushchair got bogged down in the sand and by the time we got to the end of the wall the women were heading back towards us on the last leg of their lap around the edge of the village football pitch. Figuring they were leaving I avoided them by veering right and setting off round the pitch the way they must have gone. But they didn't leave. They followed and the race was on. I tried to keep ahead with the pushchair from hell, but gave up after two laps and sat down on a bench. They came by and cooed at Joe Joe before heading off round the touchline again.

It was one of the most remarkable football pitches I'd ever seen. Through the high wire fence that stops the ball bouncing down the valley you could see for mile upon mile across the valley and rolling hills to distant mountains. A centre forward could be forgiven for stopping in his tracks to admire the view. I could also see another good reason for players to take things gently. The pitch's sandpaper surface looked like the stuff of the gladiatorial arena, where any self-respecting grass surface player would think twice before making a sliding tackle. Reflecting that the trainer would need more than a magic sponge in a bucket, I heard the clock strike a quarter to five and we headed off to meet Ella.

Struggling back through the sand trap I remembered Pere had suggested while we were watching Barcelona on his television that I could be the village team's next coach.

'Why on earth would they want me?' I'd replied. 'I played rugby – at senior school and for Dereham Vipers for a few seasons fifteen odd years ago – but not football. Not since I was a kid, anyway.'

'Oh,' he said. 'That will not matter, I think. It is just that they are wanting a foreign coach, like Barca likes to!'

Barcelona FC is big news in this neck of the woods, of course, and some of the boys and fathers sport club caps and the blue and burgundy shirts. It's a huge part of the whole Catalan pride and independence thing, an institution that brought solace and enjoyment during the bleak Franco years and which now continues to challenge Madrid in more ways than one. But did you know there is another top-flight Barcelona club called Espanyol? I didn't. It appears to be despised with a passion around here and, unless it wins the league or a European trophy, seems destined to live forever in the shadow of its giant neighbour. A few weeks earlier I'd wandered into the smoky bar to find the local derby on the TV, and from the roaring and gesticulating among the assembled I couldn't see anyone supporting the team in the blue and white stripes. That explains a lot, I thought – why I'd been getting filthy looks the few times I'd worn my replica 1950s Huddersfield Town FC shirt given to me by my mate Nigel who hails from the Yorkshire town. Yep, blue and white stripes. I've tried to explain to anyone who'll listen, pushing out my chest and tapping the club badge, but only the Mayor, Quico, whom I cornered at a school paella picnic, seemed to twig.

Walking down through the village that humid afternoon I promised myself I'd drive up to the pitch one Sunday to cheer on the local team in which, I'm led to understand, the Catholic priest is a canny midfielder. Odds on the team colours won't be blue and white.

Joe Joe and I arrived at the school gate just as the children were emerging. The school had been built two years earlier on the site of the old football ground opposite the bar and beside the village spring and ancient *lavadero* where, for the first and only time, I saw a woman washing clothes.

When I recounted my soccer pitch visit to Pere he told me

that when the site beside the top road was cleared they found Roman pots and other evidence of a major villa, which made sense given the stunning position and sweeping views.

The sun seemed to have lost none of its heat as we made our way home. Ella hitched a ride by standing on the front of the pushchair and I battled to stop it running away down the steep hill, only loosening my grip with one hand for a split second to wave back at passing villagers. Hard as I tried to blend in there was nothing I did, it seemed, that didn't bring looks of bemusement.

I daydreamed about the day we would take that ruddy pushchair to the dump where the ants could eat it. We got it second-hand after Ella was born and from day one it has refused to open when we've wanted it to and more often than not has sprung to attention when we didn't need it to. The wheels had a mind of their own and I was forever belting my toes as I pushed it, so I was forced to walk at forty-five degrees. We had names for various contraptions in our lives – Robbie the car, Clyde the new orange mower and Katie the rotivator – but the pushchair never qualified. We hated it with a passion and looked enviously upon people with those new-fangled, go-anywhere three-wheel buggies. We just wanted to go in a straight line.

I felt quite pleased, though, that on the return journey to the farm Ella contrived a way to get both her and Joe on to the pushchair. At least the stupid thing was doing something surprisingly useful for a change and with luck the stress might shorten its life. Two days later it got its revenge.

I had been at Mac and Conxita's house all day, helping them chisel off old cement in readiness for the arrival of a British builder friend who was going to re-render the outside of the house. Maggie had dropped off me and Joe Joe before going shopping. Ella was at school and the plan was for me to walk home with Joe Joe later in the afternoon down the mile-long track from Mac and Conxita's house.

Joe Joe sat in his pushchair watched Conxita working in the garden while Mac and I chipped away. It was windy and the old rendering, complete with bullet holes dating from the Spanish Civil War, threw up a cloud of white dust that found its way into our noses, eyes, ears and mouths. In desperation I wrapped my head in my old Middle Eastern scarf and donned some old ski goggles that made me look like a desert rat in a sandstorm. But it worked. It meant the only parts of me that got a dusting were my nose, cheeks, forehead and what's left of what I kid myself is a fringe.

At the end of a knackering afternoon with the chisel and hammer I took off the scarf and goggles, left Mac still battling on in a cloud of white mortar, waved a farewell to Conxita and trundled Joe Joe off down the track. His strange looks should have warned me that something was amiss but I failed to catch on and the poor little fellow couldn't tell me. Besides, he was soon too distracted by the ride of his life to worry about pointing out that I looked a sight and potentially terrifying.

The pushchair pitched, dived and occasionally stopped dead in its tracks, turning a ten-minute stroll into a half hour of horror for us both and the air blue with cursing. Twice the little lad was saved by his seatbelt as the damned chair made a beeline for the largest rocks. By the time we'd reached the railway station my shins were sore and Joe Joe had eyes like saucers. I sat down beside the old engine sheds to give us both a rest and to promise him I would never attempt it again, not with that hopeless contraption anyway.

Every time we've driven by I'd wanted to stop by the old station yard. I could see that part of the yard was used by a builder for storage, but the station was deserted, an unmanned stop on the line. I'd been told it was once a major depot with fifty people working there – and a vital lifeline for the Republicans during the civil war. Joe was still dumbstruck so I left him for a minute and looked over the wall at the roofless sandstone shed with its two glorious arches and round window and imagined the steam and scent of engines. The old water tank, taking an age to rust away in a place it rarely rains, towered over the yard and there were bits of old iron scattered round its base. The place was alive with echoes and, despite the decay, all strangely beautiful.

We pressed on again, up to the top road and then left down the hill past the guesthouse at the top of our road which, we've been reliably informed, was once a bordello with a well-trodden path from the rail yard. I'd always wondered why the place had so many small windows and lots of rooms.

It was about six o'clock and one of the village women taking her evening stroll appeared round the bend in the road and headed towards me. She was looking down, deep in thought, and only glanced up when we were about twenty yards apart. I smiled. She froze for a second, pulled her cardigan across her neck and turned on her heels. Joe glanced up as much to say I warned you, but only later, when I faced myself in the shower-room mirror, ready to clean myself up. did I realise why. I looked like a crazed panda.

On the whole our aches and pains have been what you might have expected for overnight farmers exchanging Marigolds for work gloves. But the creaking joints have been holding out and so too, remarkably, has my dodgy back which took a regular beating when I used to play rugby and which forced me to give up after I finally landed in hospital with a trapped nerve. In fact, I'd risk saying the workload seemed to be doing it some good.

Of more concern has been the risk from the various creepy crawlies.

The mosquitoes were to be expected and despite the net over the bed and us slapping on various lotions, not to mention the sterling efforts of the spiders and geckos waiting on the bedroom walls and ceilings to catch them, the blighters have drawn more than an ounce of blood. But it's the flies that have been the real nuisance, especially one little variety that hangs out in the vineyard and whose bite can cause a huge, painful swelling. We've got 'his' and 'her' fly swots for the house and my backhand is pretty good now, but despite the mesh at the windows and a bead curtain across the open door it was relentless during that first spring and summer. As for eating lunch outside, I've been meaning to rig up some sort of net to spare us the stress of constantly waving our arms over the food and slapping our legs like Austrian dancers. It would also serve to fend off the mosquitoes in the evening.

In the middle of the cow poo debacle, when you could barely see for flies about your head, I hit upon the idea of gathering rocks to put under the wheels to help the tractor get out of its hole – and us out of the mess – as quickly as possible. Josep raced after me and physically held me back before sternly offering up a dollop of advice that has dramatically changed the way I approach certain tasks on the farm.

'Be very careful,' he said in Catalan, shaking his head. 'Check under the rock first.'

'Why?'

'Scorpions.'

'You're kidding,' I said. 'Here in the mountains?' I remember finding one as a boy when we'd camped in a wood bedside the sea in the south of France. I'd managed to get it into a matchbox before terrorising my mother who eventually got it into my thick skull how unpleasant they were. Somehow I'd never related that parched grass, midsummer encounter from my childhood with our mountain farm.

'Oh yes,' said Josep, now more serious than ever. Pointing beyond the village he added, 'My friend had a nasty experience last week.' I decided not to dig any further or to lift up any more rocks but in the following weeks and months couldn't fathom out why I hadn't at least glimpsed one of the critters.

Then a friend, Delfi, explained.

Mother's Garden is, I should point out, an island in a lumpy sea of soft red rock which either lies just beneath the surface of the otherwise fertile land or stands proud, weather worn and smooth. The house, barn and most of the dry stone walls of our terraces are made from pieces of it, understandable given the relative ease with which it surrenders to the chisel or pickaxe.

At first I thought the walls lacked the charm of those to be found just the other side of the village (and around much of the Mediterranean) cradling ancient olive trees or forming endless flowing steps across the countryside. Everywhere else, it seems, the rocks – sharper, harder and as mellow as beach sand, decorated with lichen and sometimes seamed with quartz that catches the sun – create mesmerising patterns and so beautifully reflect the timeless quality of the patchwork of vineyards, groves and pine forest. Our walls, on the other hand, are dark, dusty and devoid of sparkle.

Rain merely darkens them even more.

But I suppose they set our little farm apart and I've grown to appreciate them in more ways than one – not least the willingness of the strata to yield when we've been forced to communicate with them through the medium of a mechanical digger when laying new drains.

Delfi sat with me in the shade of the trees in the village square and as we chatted about the fruits of our labours a scorpion puzzle was solved.

'Have you seen any on your land?' he asked.

'Funny you should ask,' I replied, 'but no, not yet. We were warned and I'm always careful when lifting rocks, but nothing.'

'My brother was stung twice on the foot once,' Delfi went on. 'He was working barefoot with a rotovator when it happened – many people used to work barefoot on the land.'

I told him I'd tried it too on hot days, when it was glorious to feel my feet sinking into the cool, freshly tilled soil. But I made a mental note never to try it again.

'What happened to him? Was he all right?'

'Oh, it was not very serious. Painful, but if treated it should be all right. It was just over there.' He pointed to the far side of the village, in the same direction Josep had done. 'There are many of them there. It is famous for it. And the last house on the road – you know it? – scorpions have been known to come in under the door.'

I felt queasy. 'So why haven't I seen one yet?'

'Because they're not on your side of the village.'

'For heaven's sake, why not? It's barely a kilometre or two away.'

'Because the rock is different. There may be a few, yes, but they don't like the rock. It's more crumbly. There's more dust. This they don't like.'

I told Maggie the good news and said a few quiet thanks that I might be spared a few less shocks. The next day in the barn I found a nest of baby rats in the draw of my tool cupboard.

Scorpions may be scarce but stinger ants have been an entirely different story. They're every bloody where, and invariably bide their time until I'm carrying the log which was their home before making an appearance and bolting up my arm with their bodies arched for action. They're truly unpleasant, aggressive little blighters and infest the old hazel boughs we collect as firewood. I grew wise to the danger and started giving each log a damned good clobbering before attempting to carry it to the wood store, but in those early weeks when we were trying desperately to keep the house warm I discovered what it felt like to be stung repeatedly. The first time it happened they'd made it to my neck before I realised I was under attack, and in that terrifying moment when I saw my arm was teeming with them I started tearing my clothes off and even contemplated leaping into the *balsa*. Once, when I'd gathered a huge pile and left it beside the barn overnight before sawing it up, I found a veritable army of stinger ants all over the wood and ground and trailing up the wooden posts and into the roof.

We've had our house invasions too. A few small black ants have emerged from the brick floor in the kitchen to lead us a merry dance, but our worst moments to date were probably when a sea of them, many with wings, poured out from a tiny hole behind a chair in the lounge and turned the wall black. There was also a minor panic when we found two or three in Ella's bed. We traced the problem to the corner of her room and zapped them with an ecological spray which seemed to end the problem.

Outside, ants of all shapes and sizes abound wherever you go – including a variety which we've dubbed soldier ants that patrol the wall round the *balsa* and can measure up to a centimetre and a half. They look formidable but are quite solitary and just seem to bumble about and never seem bothered by each other or us.

Away from the house, with the exception of the stingers, we've had no problem with the ants and they've been fascinating to watch. As the days warmed up little volcanoes erupted across the ground from where colonies teemed out to clear paths through the undergrowth. Some of these highways covered huge distances along which we've seen the likes of rotting figs and the crumbs from our dining table making steady progress. But perhaps the most incredible sight was the aphid farm on the elderflower bush, where a few ants marshalled and milked clusters of the plump insects. At least that's what appeared to be happening.

One particularly hot day in spring Maggie called me out of the house and gesticulated towards the round table beneath the small walnut tree. 'Look!'

'Look at what?' Everything seemed normal. Ants were on the table as usual.

'There, on the wall beside where we often put Joe Joe's high chair.'

I still couldn't see what all the fuss was about and walked towards the wall.

'Don't be daft – the viper! – can't you see it?'

I rapidly went into reverse. 'Wooooo!' The snake was coiled on dry grass only a few inches away from where Joe Joe's head would normally be. We hadn't eaten yet and if

Maggie hadn't spotted it and raised the alarm I'd have happily carried Joe Joe out in his high chair and stuck him beside it.

It looked at me and I looked at it. 'What do we do now?' I whispered. 'Kill it? We've got to kill it because it may come back. But how do you do it?'

'Be careful.'

'I think I'll put some more clothes on and get that long metal bar out of the barn.'

'Be careful.'

Trying to kill it was, of course, a stupid idea. Things could turn nasty and if left alone the equally terrified snake would almost certainly flee and avoid the spot in future. But I was a parent in a panic. Ten minutes later I emerged from the barn clutching the iron bar and resplendent in wellies, thick sailing jacket and trousers, elbow-length chainsaw gloves and full-face visor. Maggie stifled a titter then followed me round to the walnut tree to watch. Needless to say the viper had buggered off.

Then there was the washing machine monster.

'Now the plan,' I explained as we wandered into the barn, 'is to bring the waste water from the new kitchen sink by knocking a hole through the wall here behind the washing mach—'

I never finished the sentence. As I bent down next to the washer a four-foot long black and grey snake emerged from behind it just inches from my face before proceeding to climb up the wall. I reversed and held out my arms like a PC on crowd control.

'Don't worry, don't worry,' said Mac. 'It's not poisonous.'

'Right,' I said. Maggie, for whom the washing machine is a regular port of call, uttered something unrepeatable.

Mac continued to talk reason. 'Firstly, it's far too big to be a viper and secondly it doesn't have a viper's head. It should help to keep the mice and even the rats down. It certainly doesn't seem bothered about us.'

'You can say that again. Best you check before you put a wash on,' I proffered, only to receive a 'Thank you for stating the bleedin' obvious' glare from Maggie.

The snake continued to slowly ascend the wall and then disappeared into a hole – leaving its rear end dangling for an inordinately long time as if to say this is my manor, not yours.

A much happier acquaintance has been Lilly. That first summer, a lime green lizard with yellow and black spots suddenly started sunning herself on the rocks by the back door and grew increasingly bold as the months went by. She measured about twenty centimetres including her long tail and we grew quite attached to her. Through July and August Maggie left pieces of fruit on the rock for her to munch and it seemed as if we had forged an unlikely friendship. We could get within a couple of feet of her.

Then one day Maggie issued another summons reminiscent of the adder incident. Lilly was nowhere to be seen, but lounging on her favourite rock was another green and yellow lizard, only three times as big and considerably more ugly. Before we could get a photograph, it lumbered away, its saggy neck swaying with every step, before it disappeared

239

down a gap in the rocks beside the barbecue, its long tail slipping slowly into the hole. Somehow it didn't engender the same feelings as Lilly, whom we assumed had either been eaten or chased away after word got round about the fruit. Back went on the gloves while I blocked the hole, and then we looked for information on the species in a book about local wildlife. We discovered that the lizard was rare, harmless and protected. But there were no more visits which was sad in a way, now that we knew there was nothing to worry about.

Since those alarming encounters we've sort of come to terms with sharing our home with assorted reptiles, and, whereas I only saw three or four snakes in Britain in forty years, we've seen three or four a month here during the spring and summer months. We've found them sunning themselves outside the front door or in the flowerbed and they occasionally turn up in the *balsa*.

More numerous than any have been the thin, darting, grey and dark green rock lizards I remember from my Mediterranean holidays, and, of course, the loveable house geckos. Gordon the gargantuan gecko, the one who made his first alarming appearance just after we moved in, flatly refused to vacate the premises, and that first summer did his level best to catch me out by lurking in the shower curtain or popping out from behind the shaving foam dispenser and other bits and pieces on the shelf beside the sink. But, despite his ambushes, I grew rather fond of him and (sad but true) talked to him when our paths crossed.

It's usually been the smaller geckos, though, that we've seen scaling the bedroom walls or biding their time upside down on the ceilings above the beds, and it's been interesting trying to explain to Ella (and several nervous adults we've invited to share the spare room with one of Gordon's relatives) that what look like miniature boggy-eyed alligators are, in fact, our friends who gobble up ghastly mosquitoes. Our five-year-old needed some convincing, too, that the geckos wouldn't loose their grip and drop onto her while she was sleeping. And it didn't take a lot to work out what was going through the minds of visitors who had a tendency to snore.

Niggling worries about the water snakes faded when, during a school outing and parents' paella picnic at the swimming hole across the valley, several children including Ella reappeared after playing in the pools clutching handfuls of them. The other parents didn't bat an eye.

We had one last scare.

We were roused in the wee small hours one night during that first spring by what distinctly sounded like a wild boar snuffling about among the hazel trees at the back of the house.

'Go and look,' said Maggie, nudging.

'Who? Me? It can't be doing any harm.'

'I can't sleep with that noise going on.' By now the dogs had heard it and were going berserk in the living room directly beneath us. It was only a matter of time before baby Joe Joe joined in. 'Anyway, aren't you curious?'

The wild boar theory was reasonable. We'd found black droppings on our land which looked exactly like the ones

Pere had pointed out as being from boar when he showed me a path through the forest.

Being a coward, I opted to lean out of the shower room window with the torch. Nothing. I went downstairs to placate the dogs, crawled back into bed and within seconds the racket started again. Back I went. Still nothing. But when I started reasoning with the dogs the racket reverberated around the room again. Whatever it was, it was in the lounge. With me. Wild boar? Not exactly. A mouse had fallen into a huge, empty, cardboard box and was battling to clamber out. The noise was extraordinary.

Have we seen any boar? At the time of writing no, but the locals say it's only a matter of time.

Swimming with Swallows

mother's garden

*M*any, many moons ago, when I was a young boy venturing off on holiday with my father, I first discovered the other kingdom.

It was just after 4.30 a.m. and we were leaving a friend's Norfolk farm where Dad was based for a short while after my parents' marriage had crumbled. In the first minutes of gentle light and dream-like stillness, when everything was softened by a veil of dew, Dad's faithful old Ford Anglia chugged into life and ventured out onto the lane on the first leg of our journey to Aunty Grace and Uncle Frank's house in Hampshire. An early start meant we'd have time to stop at a greasy spoon café for breakfast and still stand a good chance of weaving through Rickmansworth and Slough before the rush hour. This, of course, was in the days when 70 m.p.h. was going some (or in the case of the Anglia estate, nigh on impossible) and the M25 was still a twinkle in the Minister of Transport's eye.

We drove slowly between the high hedgerows, then the car whined up a hill as we took a short cut across a wartime airfield.

And there they were.

Rabbits, hares and birds covered the old concrete runway and the open ground on either side. We slowed to a snail's pace. I rolled down the window to gaze in wonder at the teeming mass of life. 'We're intruding,' said Dad. The wildlife parted to let us through then closed behind the car like the wake of a boat. It was a time that belonged to the animal kingdom not the human race.

I've enjoyed my fair share of wildlife delights since, but very few unforgettable moments to match that dawn, which is logged indelibly in my curiosity shop of childhood memories alongside the likes of Supercalifragilisticexpialidocious (Um diddle diddle diddle um diddle ay), my aching guilt after stealing a superball from a Sheringham toy store, and sitting on the stairs, aged seven, hugging my knees and listening to my parents' unhappiness. Naturally, in adulthood, it's been love and assorted other emotional agonies and shocks (all of which strangely crush the notion that you're a grown up) that have clogged up the memory banks, but the natural world won't give in. In my early thirties I came face to face with a pair of young stags on the fringe of a wood. Wow. Then, more recently, there was the day the birds came to drink from the Mother's Garden *balsa*.

'Please, Daddy, Mummy, pleeaase!' Ella was desperate for us to stop working in the vineyard and join her for a swim. It was late May and after two months of regular practice she was starting to swim confidently with, and occasionally without, armbands. But the rule remained that she didn't go anywhere near it without an adult.

The sun was high and the air was still – there was some time to go before the reliable late afternoon breeze tickled the leaves and breathed new life into us. I was sweating and there was an abundance of flies, so I didn't need a lot of persuading. 'All right, all right. But not for long, OK? Coming Maggie?'

'In a minute maybe,' she said through gritted teeth while tugging doggedly at a weed near the base of a vine. 'Just want to finish this row.' The heat seemed to be increasing steadily by the day and the vine shoots, already about two feet long, were reaching for the sun. 'You go. And take Joe Joe with you. I'll be there in a little while.'

Joe Joe, nearly one and seriously considering taking his first unsupported steps, was sitting happily under the shade in his pushchair. I took our water bottle out from beneath it and made Maggie drink from it, then dragged the chair backwards across the uneven ground. Ella was waiting by the *balsa* wall, already decked out in her costume and one armband, and clutching a rubber ring.

'More sun block the minute you come out, right?' I said, after stationing Joe Joe where he could watch.

'OK, Dad. You go first. Are you swimming in those?'

'Yep.' I'd shed my T-shirt and sandals and was already

standing on the *balsa* wall in just my cut-off jeans. 'Tally-ho!' I resurfaced to the sounds of Joe Joe grizzling and Ella squealing with delight. The waves created by my belly flop were slapping against the *balsa* wall.

'You splashed us, Dad!'

'Sorry, Ella. Sorry, Joe Joe. Now, get a move on, Ella. Your turn, or I'll splash you again.'

She threw the ring and then launched herself with gay abandon, which thankfully made her brother switch in one breath from cry to chuckle. We spent the next few minutes, laughing and wondering what the goldfish beneath us were doing. The sky was cloudless and I pointed out to the children that the swallows, swifts and house martins were circling overhead again. Over recent days we'd watched them from a distance swooping and skimming the surface, folding their wings back for a split second to scoop water into their beaks. But they'd never been this close before when we were swimming.

'I expect they're waiting for us to get out,' I suggested.

'No, Daddy – look! Behind you!' Ella, who'd made her way back to the steps in readiness for another leap, was pointing to the far side of the *balsa* where the profit of our spring poured in providing the ceaseless music of running water. I was floating on my back in the middle of the *balsa* and swivelled to glimpse a house martin just clearing the wall and climbing away. A swallow dived and drank. Then another.

'MUMMY – COME QUICKLY!'

Suddenly all the birds were doing circuits, seemingly

oblivious to the head floating in the middle of their watering hole. Even my splashing as I trod water didn't deter them and they came closer and closer.

'Oh! That one was just a foot from my nose!' Maggie and Ella joined me in the water and still they came. It was a spellbinding, wondrous treat we have enjoyed repeatedly since, an uplifting reminder amid the various toils of just how wild our lives had become.

That first summer we noticed a couple of other bird species visiting the *balsa* too, but the whistling, aqua-breasted and golden backed bee-eaters were far more timid than the swallows, swifts and house martins and were quick to retreat to the trees if we ever came too close. Yet what a feast for the eyes all the same. As for the grey heron, it was too set on spiking a goldfish to heed our howling dogs and I had to rage out of the shower room window before it budged.

We soon learned to keep one eye on the heavens, and also managed to dig out our *Birds of Europe* idiots' guide in a bid to identify some of the cohabitants of Mother's Garden, not least the huge raptors that drifted effortlessly high above the valley. But they, like other glimpses of movement or colour, were always too far away and too fast for us to identify. By the time I'd sprinted to the house for the binoculars whatever it was had long gone, so I stopped trying. There were also sightings of butterflies and moths large and small – and on several occasions we came across juggernaut caterpillars, some green, others black and red and almost as fat as a thumb, which appeared to have fallen from the fig and walnut trees in front of the house. We thought they must be hawk moth varieties. And there was a bit of a commotion when we uncovered a couple of disgruntled praying mantises, a green one on the grass bank beside the almond grove and a brown one at the base of a vine. They were both several inches long and each took a swipe with a pincer-like foreleg every time it was touched with a finger. We confess to removing them for a while to study them because it was the first time we'd encountered these vociferous hunters known for their hearty appetites for assorted insects and each other. Later a yellow one was spotted on the ripening plums, seemingly biding its time until a wasp came along.

'Apparently,' said Maggie, 'the female eats the male after or even during—'

'Lovely. Thank you so much for that. What's for lunch?'

'It's good that they're around, though, isn't it? Far better than insecticides.'

At night, owls, crickets and tatty-eared, ring-tailed wild cats ruled the kingdom, but despite a brief encounter with a hoopoe sheltering from a shower in the barn and the occasional visitors to the *balsa*, we were gaining far more expertise in vermin, insects and reptiles than other wildlife.

It wasn't long, though, before several birds of a different kind came home to roost. No farm is complete, we kept being told, without some chickens scratching about the yard, and as time trickled by we became increasingly frustrated that we hadn't achieved this particular ambition. Joaquim kept leaving eggs in a basket tied to our front door knocker which didn't help motivate us, but we also knew we had some fairly serious tasks to face before we could get some hens.

Leaving chickens to roam during the day wasn't an option given how partial Charlie and Megan were to game, so we decided to clear out the old lean-to at the back of the derelict house and then fortify an area around it. However, the lean-to was full of thousands of charmless green and white bathroom tiles that weighed a ton and took two days to clear. Classically, we thought they might come in useful one day, so I wheel-barrowed them up to the barn where we had to rearrange our other clobber to make space.

The lean-to door hanging off its hinges was the next task, but I dithered and found other things to do until it was too late. We weren't counting on chickens turning up until we were ready, but out of the blue Antonio presented Ella with a cardboard box tied up with string during a 'come and meet all the family' drink under the tall pines at his farm on the other side of the village. Inside were two bemused white birds that had been liberated from his vast two-storey rearing shed where they, and 39,998 relatives, were just days away from losing more than their feathers.

Very sadly the two escapees didn't last much longer.

We put sawdust down in the lean-to and I wedged what was left of the door closed with a rock, but we were woefully ill-prepared. A few days later I returned from a trip to Barcelona to find Charlie and Megan in the doghouse and chicken on the menu. The dogs had got a whiff of their new neighbours and had sneakily doubled back while Maggie was taking them for a walk in the almond grove. We'd laughingly named Antonio's gifts Sage and Onion but it wasn't funny anymore. We weren't set on eating them, rather we'd been in a turmoil about what to do with two 'factory'-reared birds that may never lay an egg and which couldn't be more differ-ent from our mental picture of our first free-range chickens. The faint hope was that with some tender, loving care they might prosper. But they didn't get the chance. That night I kept looking at Maggie who'd witnessed the carnage, had bravely put the birds out of their misery and then had the presence of mind to sort everything out before Ella and I came home. There wasn't a feather in sight, just a bowl of chicken joints in the fridge. 'I felt it would have been wrong if they'd gone to waste,' she said quietly.

Ella, who'd been smart enough to figure out in a short space of time that chickens weren't ideal pets, took the news remarkably well but for a few days was concerned about what she was eating.

Even so, given our own sensibilities let alone our daugh-ter's, we couldn't risk a repeat performance and set about constructing a fortress that would not only frustrate Charlie and Megan but also defeat forest foxes, ring-tailed wild cats, and other loose dogs. I rebuilt the lean-to door and finished it off with a fat bolt. We cemented steel posts into the rock, put up fencing eight feet high and buried the base of it with a bank of rocks. Even a wild boar snouting about for loose corn couldn't break in. I also used some chicken wire and wood from old palettes retrieved from the dump to build a portable ark so we could put our brood to work scratching around in the orchard, but I got carried away and it ended up weighing a ton. Given the amount of wood it contained my ark was bound to float, but that was hardly the point.

Antonio's brother Xavier (pronounced Habeeay) had, by this time, offered his help. He had free-range black Vilafrancas, a beautiful local breed, which we thought were perfect, and he said we could have five hens and a cockerel.

'Make sure you get some young hens,' he advised as we went into his bustling chicken run. They all looked the same to me, save the few large cockerels. 'And the best way is to grab a leg.'

'That one, Dad. Get that one.'

' Which one?'

'The black one.'

Soon the whole coop was in a flap and Xavier had two chickens which he handed to me. We popped them into crates covered with upturned boxes and then I managed to grab one which was moving a little slower than the rest. Xavier and Maggie had a hen each, too, which just left the cockerel. By this time the young males had, very obligingly, figured it was perhaps wise to congregate in the far corner of the run, so we surrounded them and easily just picked one up. Xavier then flatly refused any money, so we made a mental note to offer our labours for a day come the grape harvest.

The next morning we were woken by our young cockerel's

muffled reveille coming from inside the lean-to. Excited, we rushed down the track to release our new chickens into their run.

'That one looks a bit scruffy,' said Maggie. 'I'm pretty sure it's an old one.'

So that's why it had been moving so slowly. 'Might not be. Might be just a bit off colour that's all.'

As if he knew it was expected, the cockerel clambered on to the biggest rock, pulled himself up to his full height and issued a rousing 'Cockledoodledoo-oooeeerrr!'

'Is that normal?' We roared with laughter, and then stood, our arms around each other, admiring them as they strutted about getting their bearings, their blue-black feathers gleaming in the sun.

'So, what are we going to call them, Ella?' Then Maggie quickly added, 'But best if you don't give them your friends' names, mmm?'

'Why not? That one can be—'

'Because, darling, because . . . er . . . it would be more fun to have silly names, wouldn't it?'

'Like what?'

Maggie looked at me for inspiration.

'How about Eggwina?' I blurted.

'That can be your one, Dad.'

'OK. Which one's my one?'

'The small one with a floppy thingymebob that's limping.'

Maggie was grinning, in that eyebrows raised, head on one side, womanly sort of way.

'Just you wait and see. She may, just may be a little long in the tooth.'

'Hens don't have teeth.'

'But, but, she'll show how, won't you, Eggwina?' I turned my attention to the largest hen, 'And this one,' I said, pointing, 'can be Thatcher the Hatcher.'

'I sense a theme developing,' said Maggie. 'What about the cockerel?'

'Archie. Likes crowing. Doing time.'

The children were starting to lose interest and so we left the chickens to enjoy their breakfast and went back to the house for ours. Bizarrely, the three other hens, almost identical and impossible to tell apart, ended up sharing two names – Bottomley and Widdecombe.

It was a good feeling to have finally got our chickens, and all safe behind our splendid new fortifications. We'd planned it out and thought of everything. Then, over supper with friends, an alarming mystery unfolded. Benet, Marta's husband, lent across the table, fixed me with a sideways stare and asked if escapologist Charlie had gone walkabout the day before.

No, I replied. Why?

One of his chickens had been taken, he said. He'd acquired five Vilafrancas at the same time as us, only now he only had four and a pile of feathers. The puzzle was that there had been no breach in his chicken run defences.

Listening to the story I assumed that his five-foot fencing was no match for an athletic fox on a daring daytime raid.

Eight-year-old Charlie, who'd lost quite a bit of his spring, couldn't have managed it even if he'd wanted to. Anyway, I stressed to a disbelieving Benet, he'd been tethered to a fig tree and snoring in the sunshine. Not guilty.

A few days later I was in the kitchen making tea for Maggie and a visitor from the village (who'd called by to ask for private English lessons) when there was a yell for me to come outside. Both of them were craning their necks and pointing up into the blue sky.

'What is it?'

'LOOK!'

I nearly fell over. An eagle was circling just above us, or rather just above our chickens who were obliviously scratching about inside my mobile ark which was on the vegetable garden terrace just in front of the house.

'But you should have seen it a second ago,' said Maggie. 'It glided right over us just above the tree tops!'

It was, needless to say, huge.

As I've mentioned, we knew there were large birds of prey about, but we'd only glimpsed them soaring at altitude. They were always distant, never a threat – but now it was close, far too close. That night we fretted about what risk there was to little Joe Joe, and knew that with Archie forever proclaiming 'Cockledoodledoo-ooeerr! I'm over here!' the eagle would be back. The next day we put wire across the top of the chicken run, got into the habit of looking upwards regularly and never letting Joe Joe wander too far.

We dusted down the binoculars again and double-checked

in our bird books until we were pretty sure the uninvited guest was a short-toed eagle, one of a pair which we have seen countless times since, but not that close again. Often we've heard them calling to each other before we spied them, sometimes flying quite low and fast on the borders of the village and not many metres from Benet and Marta's chicken run. Talking to locals we also realised that the vast, dark bird we'd spotted very occasionally gliding effortlessly down the valley from the mountain ridge, just to the fringe of our farm but no further, was in fact a golden eagle. There have been kites and buzzards too – once twelve of them spiralled on a thermal above the house for several minutes. And we were stunned to hear how, one day that summer at the busy village swimming pool, a large bird of prey landed by the water, looked around, took a few steps then flew away.

Some uninvited visitors to Mother's Garden that first summer left their calling cards.

When we reported to Pere that we'd found what looked like horse poo on the land he frowned and said we'd better fence our vegetable patch. Another neighbour couldn't be relied upon to keep his three horses tethered or corralled and a lot of people had complained about the damage they'd done to gardens and crops. Pere's patience was clearly wearing thin with this man. 'They have eaten my vegetables – that is why I have the wire fence. You cannot trust him to keep the horses away.'

We had a day of hand-wringing, fretting about what the

best form of defence might be, but, of course, we kept putting it off and eventually put it to the back of our minds and got on with tending Maggie's burgeoning vegetables, nurturing the vines and trying to keep the grass down. Even if the horses came on to our land again they were unlikely to venture near the house and, anyway, we didn't want to put up ugly wire fencing all over the place.

About a week later we were woken in the small hours by the clatter of hooves right under the bedroom window.

'Horses!'

Maggie leant over the balcony while I tore downstairs semi-naked and burst out of the front door waving my arms like my hair was on fire. Not a wise move. The horses bolted – and went straight through the vineyard at a gallop. It was too dark to see what damage had been done, so we went back to bed where we lay for the rest of the night waiting for them to return and picturing untold devastation. The next morning we found some lettuces had been eaten and trampled, but Maggie felt she had got off lightly. Thankfully the vines, which were just starting to produce bunches of grapes, looked to have withstood the shock remarkably well. Nonetheless I rang Pere for the owner's telephone number and then, without thinking how I would muster enough of the right words to express our displeasure, rang and advised his very pleasant wife of what had transpired. Even if she didn't understand everything there was no mistaking the tone.

Instead of fencing the garden I walked the north boundary of our land that faced the hillock where the horses were kept.

Much of it was an impassable mix of cane, brambles and trees along a fairly wide gully, so it was relatively easy to see that their only way through was via some tall pines – our usual route if we were walking cross-country to see Pere and Nuria. I tied rope between the trees and adorned it with red ribbons just for good measure and congratulated myself that it looked tough enough for the job. Pretty too. But it was my Maginot Line, with the trio merely switching their invasion plans and looping round to the east, before leaving more hoof prints and fertiliser across the abandoned hazel terraces. But maybe the bellowing that caused the night stampede wasn't such a bad idea after all. They've never (famous last words) been near the house or vegetables again.

One night, when we were both working into the early hours doing chores about the house, the dogs suddenly started going berserk.

'There must be something outside,' said Maggie, who opened the bedroom window to have a peek and found herself exchanging stares with an enormous hound that was standing with two identical silver-backed beasts close to the barn. They moved round to the back of the house before I had a chance to look, but I managed to see them a few seconds later as they raced with loping strides up the track to the top terraces.

'You're not thinking what I'm thinking are you?' I asked. 'There aren't wolves in Spain are there?'

We went straight on to the internet and were stunned to read that the Iberian wolf was alive and well – and making a bit of a comeback. One report, dated 1998, said the species was expected to spread back into Catalonia by the year 2000. But they meant the Pyrenees, surely? The animals we saw were huge and identical, but perhaps it was a trick of the full moonlight.

The next day, Nuria asked if we had been disturbed during the night. Something had terrified the horses – the three who'd visited us – which were tethered close to her and Pere's house. Their distress had woken her. And, she said, there was something else. A dreadful howling.

For the next couple of nights our dogs had to settle for a late night wee just outside the front door, from where I nervously scanned the darkness with a torch. There was no way I was going to venture round into the olive grove with them and relieve myself while admiring the stars if something unpleasant was on the prowl from the vast forest wilderness across the lane.

I spread the news (with hindsight rather recklessly) around the village, but most people were sceptical.

'Honestly, we saw them,' I pressed, my fleeting glimpse of the hounds turning into a pinpoint identification. 'And the internet report said it could be possible.'

'Did you know, though,' said Oriol calmly, 'that the man who lives down the valley has three dogs, three big dogs?'

'So?'

'Two of them are white, the other is black and white. They escape sometimes.'

*

When we moved lock, stock and offspring, that meant Charlie and Megan too, of course, and it was fascinating during those first days at Mother's Garden to watch our springer spaniels getting their bearings and vacuuming up the scents of Spain. We wondered how different it must all smell.

They suffered badly with ticks initially – and to our great consternation we even found a couple on the children, one behind Joe Joe's ear and another on Ella's clothing. Once that shock was over we got advice on how best to deal with the blood-sucking parasites, made clear that the long grass ban for the children (on account of snakes) was now doubly impor-tant, fitted the dogs with special collars and checked all four of them daily. It was undoubtedly a very unpleasant, unex-pected setback to the great outdoors adventure, but the danger abated and we found that if we were sensible about where we went and what we wore the risks were greatly reduced. I, for one, stopped yomping through the undergrowth in sandals after glimpsing a snake beating a retreat ahead of me.

That aside, the dogs lives settled into a blissful pattern of regular walks, food and lying flat out in the shade of the trees – a fig for Charlie and a walnut for his sister Megan – but there were hazards when the nuts and fruits began to fall. Whenever he went off on one of his occasional explorations that could last several hours, Charlie would inevitably come back smelling, well, like a Spanish sewer, but as the heat inten-sified the shade of the fig and walnut leaves seemed preferable to reckless exertion.

We were amazed and delighted by the amount of fruits

produced by Charlie's huge tree that first summer – so many that we were able to sell quite a few kilos to a couple of health food stores. The old dog would open one eye as much to say, 'Oh for goodness sake,' as I hitched my bottom along branches in an attempt to pluck any fat fruits that were attracting the white admiral butterflies and looked set to fall. If they hit the ground they exploded, although it didn't bother the normally nervous Charlie because he ate quite a few of them, which, come to think of it, explains a little irregularity he endured that summer.

But the tree climbing was starting to get a little bit silly (fig trees, with the elephant hide bark, look robust but are notorious weak) and I'd also had a nasty practical lesson on Newton's law of gravity when the branch against which I'd lent my ladder had become so much lighter that as I picked the fruit the ladder fell over. So instead I set about designing something that became known as the Kirby fig tickler, a highly technical means by which I could pick the fruit before they fell and without the need to risk my neck. A patent is being sought, but in the meantime here's the design: take your daughter's pond dipping net, bend the end until the net ring is at right angles to the pole, then select a straight cane of ample length and fix by means of electrical tape to the end of the pole. Next, poke the fig tickler straight up into the branches until the target fruit is in the net and the ring is pushing against the stem. Begin to tickle, and by that I mean push and shake, but not too robustly or there is a severe risk of the ripe fig being propelled out of the net and hitting you in the face.

With the able assistance of Ella, whose huge summer holiday spanned July, August and half of September, and who had to be pacified with a new, far larger pond net, we had hours of thrills and spills under Charlie's tree.

At the same time as all this was going on, the plum trees behind the house were also weighed down with fruit, and we were able to add several boxes of these to our shop sales. Matters weren't anything like as plentiful with the other fruit trees, though. The quinces were numerous, even if we didn't know what to do with them at first, and one pear tree and a couple of apples seemed to like us. But generally the orchard was big on leaf curl and very low on produce.

There were, however, plenty of other things to smile about. The vines looked healthy and the bunches of grapes were forming bang on schedule thanks to Maggie's judicious sunrise applications of sulphur powder and copper sulphate solution and our ceaseless weeding and rotovating. Between the olive trees in the grove behind the house Maggie's vegetables were going great guns and (there's no easy way of saying this) her watermelons were raising a few eyebrows, thanks in part to my efforts on the watering front. The potatoes were prolific (another crop that brought in a few sheckles), the salad crops were splendid, and we worked through copious recipes for courgettes over those summer months.

There had been talk early on of trying to emulate Maggie's mum's asparagus production – her asparagus sandwiches are to die for – but the idea of creating a bed and planting some roots faded that first April when we tasted wild asparagus, served up by Conxita in a scrummy *tortilla*, or Spanish omelette.

'It grows here,' she explained.

'Really?' we said. 'We haven't seen any.'

'It's not obvious, but we have a little on the land. You will find some on your farm, I'm sure.'

So off we went, very excited, to trawl every inch of the ten acres of Mother's Garden in a wild asparagus hunt that slowly turned into a wild goose chase. No kidding, but we found just one shoot – and evidence that someone had been there before us which was even more depressing. How dare anyone come on to our land and help themselves? Then, for about a week, we kept seeing cars with Barcelona number plates parked in the forest and smiley people walking along clutching bunches of the pencil-thin shoots. It was obviously a gross injustice. On the general scale of things it could have been described as inconsequential, but somehow it wasn't and to say we were miffed would have been an understatement.

Maggie tried to forget about it by clearing out around some old roses on the terrace just ten yards from the front door. I'd gone into my cave – sorry, barn – to reorganise my 'might come in handy one day' corner, when all of a sudden she called me. There, within a five-second dash of our kitchen was a cluster of wild asparagus just waiting to be gently fried in olive oil, seasoned and feasted upon. OK, there were only a dozen or so shoots, but it was so, so pleasing. And, if that wasn't enough, that weekend while we were sitting on the *balsa* wall at twilight chatting to Alex and his wife Remei, who were out for a stroll with his parents, we spotted Pere and Nuria drifting hand in hand through our vineyard. They were each holding a fat cluster of asparagus – and presented one to us.

One minute our dogs were the least of our worries. The next Megan started blooming, and we were walking around with our heads in our hands. Just when we thought the workload had reached a critical level we had to convert our lounge into a canine maternity ward and the house needed fumigating. Thanks to the breeze and the radar of at least one local free-range dog, there were suddenly seven very cute but increasingly voracious little Megans cavorting around doing lots of unsavoury things with gleeful abandon.

Charlie was never a suspect since he'd been firing blanks from a very early age. Inconceivable. No, we were fairly certain the culprit was Drai, Pere and Nuria's sly old hound who may have been greying round the muzzle but was never happier than patrolling the valley gripped by far more than just wanderlust. We'd seen him sloping off not far from where Megan was chained up and feared we may have made a ghastly mistake to think it was all right to leave her out during the day when we were only a couple of yards away in the house.

Paternity was never in doubt once the pups came into this world bearing a remarkable resemblance to our neighbours' Heinz 59 labrador cross. Pere and Nuria began by demanding a blood test, but one glance at the offspring and their dog (who looked incredibly guilty) and they capitulated.

We liberally sprinkled advertisements in shops and vets around the area and tried desperately to gloss over the diluting of the bloodline by emphasising Megan's impressive hunting lineage. Everyone who came to view the pups looked bemused as we tapped the pedigree, explaining that her grandfather was none other than top dog Sandringham Spot (one of Prince Charles's favourites apparently) while trying to explain what 'field trial champion' meant.

One by one the pups went, almost all to hunters, save a jet black female we named Biba and for whom Mother's Garden was to be home.

Cruel Harvests

mother's garden

That first, sultry summer, when the blue sky was sublime and Mac's prediction of no rain for two months came true, we had to change the pattern of our days, making the most of the cooler hours of early morning and dusk to water the vegetables and harvest what was ripe. Attempting anything too strenuous in the middle of the day was dumb and dangerous, so lunches drifted on in the shade of the trees, and the clear water of the balsa brought relief when even sitting contemplating your navel seemed too taxing – or the incessant flies prompted one too many slaps to the face. Then, late into the evening, there were moments of magic as the setting sun tinged everything with a terracotta hue and we chugged back and forth with the rotovator, or picked tomatoes, courgettes and aubergines while the children delighted in hunting for snails. Thinking back, those were among the best of times, harvesting, rejoicing in the simplest things, being outdoors and so far away from the old lure of a sofa and television, and marvelling at how happy the children were. We were tired but content, and the aches and pains were soothed a little in the twilight.

Our visitors' book was filling up fast too. Later, we worked out that seventy people had come to the farm that first year, and only a small number of them were day visitors. Maggie's mum Beryl had been the first back in the February, then, from May onwards, it was pretty relentless, with the pizza oven and barbecue pressed into service more times than I can remember, and the spare room occupied more nights than not. We enjoyed some special times, and it was that summer when cousins Rosa and Leila worked with Ella designing the Mother's Garden tree and colourful lettering which combined to become our trademark. Everyone was wonderful and eager to help, and we relished the company of family and some of our closest friends. But on reflection it was too much and gradually it took its toll as we tried to keep up the work rate early and late in the day and socialise as well.

By the end of August we were running out of steam, but were also mindful that the almond harvest was upon us and that the grapes would be ready within a few weeks.

Suddenly it was a huge fillip to have willing hands to help us, and as the almonds were knocked from the trees they were laid out on a net in front of the barn where Ella sat chatting for hours with young visitors Elaine, Lucy and Katie as they all steadily dehusked the nuts. They entertained themselves by putting the cleaned nuts into scarves tied round their tummies and saying they were pregnant. When a scarf was full and they were plump they would declare they were having a baby and gave birth to the nuts on to wicker panels which we were using for sun drying.

We all did several hours of the ridiculously slow work on the nut shift, but it was a novelty and a satisfying way to pass an hour or two in conversation. It was indicative, though, of how we were still a long way from getting a firm hold on the financial reality. More than half a year had slipped by and we were too befuddled trying to learn, trying not to make arses of ourselves in the eyes of the locals and grappling with a raft of new experiences to focus on a few home truths. Our flimsy safety net of about ten thousand pounds was very slowly but surely diminishing.

Not to worry, we told ourselves. The grape harvest will bring in several hundred pounds, and you only had to walk through the lower vineyard that September to be enthused. The vines were laden with fat bunches of darkening grapes which we, farmer Maggie Whitman and her willing worker Martin Kirby, had grown. It was impossible to put a price on that feeling.

The harvest was glorious too. The weather was kind, our local friends gathered aplenty and before we knew it Mac and Conxita's trailer was full and trundling off to the cellar where, for good measure, a quality check showed our grapes' sugar content was pleasingly high.

The top vineyards, though, were a different story. We'd laboured up there just as hard throughout the year, but as

Alex had warned us they produced precious little – there were nearly double the number of vines but they yielded only twenty per cent of the much younger lower vineyard. The advice from some quarters was to pull them out and replant, but something held us back, a reluctance to destroy or change anything until we knew more. Our instincts told us to give them a chance.

All the same, a few months later, when we were looking for a better deal for our grapes, I made the mistake of brushing them aside as an embarrassment.

'I'm very sorry I'm late,' I flustered as Maggie introduced me to a young man from a small local cellar who'd come to cast an expert eye. I'd been in town when he'd rolled up and I found them chatting in front of the house.

Keen to help cement a deal I plunged straight in. 'Maggie's the boss when it comes to the farm and no doubt you've had a look. But can I just say that I'm so sorry about the top vines. I know they have precious little fruit and look dire, but here surely,' I gesticulated beyond Maggie's alarmed expression in the general direction of the lower vines, 'is what you are looking for.'

'Actually,' the young man said softly, kindly while Maggie looked in pain, 'actually, I'm interested in the grapes from the old vines, not these younger ones.'

'Really?' I started to shrink. 'Only I thought—'

'It's a case of quality rather than quantity,' Maggie interjected, without adding 'you blithering idiot'. 'The older the vine the better the grapes. I'll explain later.'

In late November, when the days were still pleasantly bright, we took our last harvest of the year from Mother's Garden. Helped by friends from England we racked the olives from the trees and took them to the mill. Many of the trees were fruitless and we knew that until we fed and pruned them they were never going to provide an income, so we resolved to trade our six sacks of olives for twenty litres of oil. The future was bright, though. We had more than a hundred trees, a vital part of the jigsaw. With care we could be in serious business the next year.

As we rolled into December, we borrowed Mac and Conxita's tractor and plough and gave the vines a feed of well-rotted muck. The weather was unseasonally warm and just twelve days before Christmas we sweated as we cleared a bank of tall grass and then fretted that our bonfire might be fanned by the breeze. There were hard frosts at night but by early afternoon the undergrowth was tinder dry again.

Then, with awesome agility, the climate made some rapid seasonal adjustments and over a weekend our little world changed colour. A colossal storm tore across the Mediterranean from the east and deposited more than two feet of snow on our corner of Catalonia. Temperatures plummeted to minus twelve degrees Centigrade and life ground to a halt. There was no blizzard, no howling gales, just two days and two nights of relentless snow, turning Mother's Garden into a winter wonderland that would have had Bing Crosby bursting into song. Hazel branches cracked under the weight and we dressed for the Arctic.

The hill village with its steep streets, one of which is a mini version of Steve McQueen's San Francisco, became an ice- and snow-bound disaster area. Even Robbie the Range Rover couldn't cope, so we turned back and headed along the gentler lane to the nearest town to see what was left on the shelves of the bakeries and little stores there. The main road across the mountains to the coast was closed for a week, so we ferried Nuria and Marta to the town to stock up, and as I waited in the car for them I remembered how, on the same street a week before, I'd seen a camper van with British plates and had remarked to myself how sensible they were to escape the northern winter.

Our power supply came and went, but the snow didn't. It cloaked the olive trees and filled our wellies as we helped the children to make a suitably corpulent snowman with a carrot nose, forcing me to dry out by the ever-roaring fire in my long johns like an extra out of 'The Beverly Hillbillies'. Ella was having a whale of a time and it was all manifestly beautiful under a clear sky when all the weak rays of sunshine could do was make the brittle top crush of snow sparkle like a million gems.

But as our woodpile diminished at an alarming rate so did the sense of fun. We were set to return to Beryl's farm in Norfolk for Christmas and I'd set aside until the last minute the task of stocking up on firewood for friends who'd volunteered to farm sit for us. In the end I was forced to wade through the snow looking for old hazel we could dry out beside the fire. Running an open fire and woodburner relentlessly meant I had to make innumerable journeys onto the redundant terraces of hazel where invisible brambles waited in the snow to trip me up as I dragged boughs back to the house. It was seriously unpleasant and occasional blasts of Anglo-Saxon could be heard reverberating around the valley. Frantic for solutions I hit on the idea of using Ella's sturdy wooden sledge, which followed me faithfully to the top of the land only to sink without trace once it had been loaded with wood.

Eventually, the snow fell from the branches, but with it came the leaves of the olive trees and everyone knew there would be a terrible price to pay for our knee-deep winter blast, the likes of which hadn't been seen here for decades. Spring came and for a while everyone waited to see if the trees would recover. We were told the older ones with established roots would probably survive but that the younger ones might be decimated. Either way the day would come when the dead wood would have to be trimmed to encourage new growth. By Easter the extent of the damage became clear. The young grove of forty trees behind the house only had two that showed any signs of life. Worse still, the timeless avenue of old, twisted olives from the road to the house, and which continued along the track to the top of the land, was a brown shadow of its former self. So we braced ourselves, rang Alex and asked for his help. We knew that if we left the trees untouched our olive harvest would be negligible for donkey's years to come, but with expert pruning we may be harvesting again in two or three years.

Alex duly turned up, walked the land muttering, 'Itz a

disaster, a disaster,' and then warned us to be brave. There was a Catalan saying, he said, which is that you have to be very hard on the olive tree to reap the best harvest.

Even so, both of us were beside ourselves with despair as, one by one, most of the trees were reduced to a cold line of posts, stripped even of what little green leaf was battling to survive on the canopy of mostly bare branches. With Maggie weeping I ran up the track and stupidly asked Alex if he knew what he was doing. He calmly explained it was the only option. 'I have left a few trees which might bear some olives so you may get some oil,' he said, 'But there is no other way. You'll see – by the end of the summer the new growth will be as high as you can reach and it will all look very different.'

So it proved, but a dark cloud descended that winter which took months to clear. We learned of olive farmers further inland losing virtually everything, their groves slaughtered by the bitter cold. At least most of our trees were still alive, but clearing the debris after the pruning was very depressing work. The swirling pattern of the rings at the heart of ancient olive wood can be as compelling as the embers of a fire, but when you are forced to spend days gathering up cut branches from around the stumps of once proud olive trees you pray you never see it again. If there was any solace to be found it was in the growing mountain of iron-hard firewood we had seasoning in the sun in readiness for another hard winter.

Then came more disheartening news. There would be no money for the grapes until at least the autumn because the cellar had to sell the wine first. As we began again the process of pruning the vines and preparing the land we decided to search for another buyer for the next harvest. And looking at the three bare vineyards it was demoralising to think of the weeks of toil ahead given how feebly equipped we were. The only way we were going to find the time and energy to tackle other areas of the farm was to drastically reduce the number of weeks we'd devoted to the vines that first year. We needed a tractor but couldn't afford one. Then, without being asked, Dad rang to say it had been on his mind ever since he'd witnessed the trailer load of cow poo debacle, and that he was determined to trump up some money to buy an old one for us.

'*Va be*! *Va be*!' the farmer kept repeating as he patted the old tractor's dented mudguard and gave me a stare that dared me to doubt it 'goes well'.

'*Sí, sí,*' I said, straining my brain but failing to find the words in Catalan to say, 'I'm sure. Don't doubt you for one instant. So . . . why are you selling it then?'

After a year of wrestling with the language I'd reached the point where I could get by up to a point, but I didn't have anything like the linguistic dexterity to dabble in irony. It wasn't the time, either, to retreat and ask Ella to do the deal. This was palm-spitting, man-to-man stuff.

Nor was it the moment to confess I was merely a farmer's husband and that Maggie was the boss. We'd tried that one before on other people but the men usually persisted in addressing me not her. And this old boy looked definitely of the old school.

Our invaluable friend Delfi came to my rescue. Back in the September I'd taken up the offer from the mayor to run a twice-weekly English class in the village hall as a way to prop up our crumbling finances and had made some useful contacts in the process. Delfi was one of my star pupils – a vineyard owner who'd volunteered to help us find a tractor that fitted our needs and came within our budget of under £3000. He stepped in after I recounted the series of wild goose chases when we'd looked at tractors which were either too wide for our vines, too feeble, too knackered, had no brakes or the price mysteriously rocketed the second the owner twigged we were English.

'Iz no kaput,' said Delfi, making me wince at my teaching ineptitude. 'I ask you try it, yes?'

'*Sí, gracies.*'

The Spanish built Massey Ferguson 135 looked at least thirty years old and had its fair share of blemishes, but at least it was the right price (600,000 pesetas, 3600 euros or about £2200), right size and width and came with a harrow. The large rear tyres were new too. We agreed I'd put it through its paces at the farm in two days' time.

'Iz good, very good,' Delfi kept saying as we walked back through the village which, I shamefully admit, made me ponder for a split second if he was getting a cut. But then he reverted to Catalan and reassuringly stressed we should ask for a new battery and a full service before agreeing to buy.

For all my efforts to look like a Spanish farmer on the day of the test drive the old man changed his mind and wouldn't let me get behind the wheel of his tractor for the short trundle down the road to our farm. Instead I was forced to cling to the back of it, scrambling for a foothold. Word seemed to have got out and the normally deserted main street was crowded with (I couldn't help thinking) locals keen to see the foreigner being taken for a ride.

On the journey down the valley to the farm we barely breached 5 k.p.h. and it wasn't clear whether the farmer was an extremely cautious driver, or he didn't want to draw attention to some fatal flaw. His accent was so strong that I only ever fathomed 'Goes well!' as he gabbled away throughout the trip, and, to be fair, it didn't seem to have any obvious problems as, a short while later, I chugged back and forth up and down the vineyard. Then, that evening, Antonio said he knew of the tractor and that it was a fair price.

We agreed, and rang the village mechanic who was handling the sale. The next day he rolled up at the farm, smeared up to the elbows in engine oil and keen to shake my hand. He said he'd give the old girl a complete service, whack on a new battery and get her to us as and when, which, true to the local way of doing things, seemed to be an open-ended arrangement. But to our delight she was with us within the week. We cleared out the wood store to provide her with a shelter and agreed she should be called Nell, after my grandmother.

If the Christmas blast of snow and ice was anything to go by it looked as if 2002 was set to be a year of unusual weather. Everything seemed to be out of kilter. The figs were late, the plums and quinces were sparce by comparison to fruitful 2001, and while some of the other fruit trees showed a marginal improvement our potato crop failed almost completely on account of some decidedly dodgy seed spuds.

Maybe it was the time we were now giving to entertain and monitor Joe Joe who was covering the ground at an ever-increasing velocity, or the fact that we were starting to turn our attention to creating the long-discussed new kitchen, but we achieved less in the garden too. Maggie's carrots, onions, leeks, garlic, cucumbers, peppers, lettuces, tomatoes and broad beans all measured up, and even the newly planted strawberry bed provided Ella and Joe Joe with ample sweet temptation despite being besieged by self-set spinach. But there were no watermelons and precious few courgettes and aubergines like we had enjoyed the first summer.

Time and time again the clouds burst and saturated the land, and one morning, after a colossal night-time downpour that starved us of sleep, I took Joe Joe on a little adventure to see if, finally, the dry riverbed half a mile from the farm had come to life. As the pushchair bounced down the bare stone track through the forest towards the swimming hole we became aware of a distant roar that grew and grew as we approached the base of the valley.

When we first discovered the swimming hole during our first summer at Mother's Garden it was a place of beguiling stillness in the lee of the vast, almost vertical mountain ridge. It was a deep gully through red rock that had been worn into soft abstract shapes and where a deep pool of dark water was home to, among other things, a shoal of little fish and snakes that hung motionlessly in the water like twigs until they spied you. When the temperature nudged a hundred degrees for a few days we saw some boys jumping fifteen feet into the pool from the little bridge that spanned the void. But despite the heat we weren't tempted. The shadowy depths were all but stagnant, fed only by an occasional trickle weaving down from the mountains through the bare boulders of the otherwise lifeless riverbed. Besides, it was clearly dangerous for young children. So instead of swimming we preferred to picnic beneath a holm-oak or potter about looking at the wildlife and musing about the force of water needed to sculpt the rocks. But when did it happen? There had to be occasional cascades to keep the wide bed above and below the pool so clear of vegetation. When the valley had been cloaked with deep snow we expected, finally, to find the river in flood, but even then there was barely a tinkling sound.

So as Joe Joe and I dropped down the last few yards of track and tasted the mist thrown up by the torrent it was fascinating to finally hear that sound of the mountains and to witness the force that had been dormant for so long. The water level seemed to be about five feet higher, and the pool was a swirl of currents littered with debris carried down by the flood.

A couple appeared strolling along the track. They'd been told the river was flowing and had walked the two kilometres from the village to see for themselves.

'Nice, isn't it?' I said. 'Impressive.'

'Yes,' The man replied. 'It is good. But sometimes it is amazing. Eighteen years ago it was tremendous – ten feet higher than the bridge!'

Our biggest farm concern as the year wore on was the fate of our grape crop.

The rain continued to fall regularly through normally dry months, right into the summer. By the middle of August, when the land would normally be parched and hard, a stream was running down our farm track to the lane, and the grass was as green and keen as if it had been the first flush of spring. Repeatedly, the hitherto reliable, almost seamless Mediterranean sunshine was blotted out by leaden clouds, with the mountain landscape being illuminated instead by flashes of lightning – or night storms that prompted our old dog Charlie to lie between us rocking our old brass bed with his panting, which felt a bit like trying to sleep on a steam train.

So I lay awake worrying (in that middle of the night free-wheel fashion) about the roof, the crops, the vagaries of the weather, the portents of global doom, and the risk of damp getting into Nell's electrics. But, most of all, Mum was on my mind. It was clear, after her prolonged illness and desperate disability brought on by the series of strokes nineteen months before, that she was close to death.

She finally, mercifully, took her leave on 20 August. We flew back as her family united, drew close and worked through the emotions and practicalities. Then her many friends joined us at a clifftop Norfolk church to bid her goodbye – a serene day full of memories of her vitality and indomitable spirit, when someone eloquently reflected how it was as if a caged bird had been set free again. Mum had seen Mother's Garden, of course, when we'd first bought it back in September 2000, but there had been throughout our first eighteen months at the farm a deep sadness that someone so fond of Spain – her regular holiday destination where she felt so at home and where the family fact or fable of ancestral Spanish blood in our veins was always retold – was not able to sit in the shade of an olive tree, witness our good fortune and farces alike and be entwined in some way into the happy memories of this time.

We returned to Catalonia to find that the cocktail of wet blasts and searing heat had done its worst, and it became abundantly clear from talking to our neighbours that every vineyard across this patchwork land was blighted in some way. The word on everyone's lips was *pudrit*, which means mould, a haze of grey fungus that can envelop grapes on the vine and render them worthless. The big question was, how much would things deteriorate through September before the harvest?

We were horrified to think that our labours may have been wrecked, particularly since the old vineyards seemed to have found a new lease of life and were offering up at least double the amount of grapes from the previous year. And the stress levels were higher because, through Delfi, we'd made an approach to Torres, the leading Spanish wine label, to buy our modest harvest. If push came to shove we could always return to the same cellar as the year before, but a contract with

Torres would be a huge boost, not only bolstering slightly our meagre income from the vineyards but also proving that we were able to come up to their standards.

One of the Torres managers, Manolo, a towering Frenchman who'd grown up among the Champagne vineyards to the east of Paris and who also spoke Spanish and Catalan fluently, came to take some samples for analysis. We dabbled in all three languages, then watched nervously as he wandered through the vines selecting a few grapes here and there and popping them into a bag.

'We shall see,' he said as he leapt back into his 4x4. 'I will ring you.' A few days later he was true to his word and we were in. 'I will come again and tell you when to pick, but it is not likely to be for some weeks yet.'

And still the rains came and went. There was evidence of *pudrit* on some bunches of grapes, yet there was little we could do but wait. Only when the call to harvest came would we know just how badly we'd been affected.

So we kept busy, arranging for a delivery of crates from Torres, borrowing some more from Delfi, sorting out who'd be on hand to help pick – and gathering in our almonds.

'What we need,' said Maggie, 'particularly given what we're facing with the grapes, is a quicker and easier way of gathering and sorting the almonds. There's a metal rod thing with a rubber end which is supposed to be a more effective way to belt the trees.'

'I think I saw someone using one when we first looked around the farm.'

'Exactly, so no more flailing around with long sticks for hours on end or climbing trees. I'm going to buy one. Oh, and Antonio's kindly offered to lend us his electric dehusking machine if you could go and get it.'

The results were amazing. The previous year's efforts, which spanned weeks, were condensed into a few days, and our metal rod with a rubber end – we still don't know what it's called – was a revelation. Instead of setting three or four people armed with long sticks on to one tree, which either achieved precious little or sent the sharp pointed nuts whizzing dangerously in all directions, we found that one person could persuade the tree to give up its fruit by communicating with it through the medium of a bludgeon. One or two well-aimed blows to the main branches and it literally rained almonds onto your head (ouch) and into the nets. Then it was back to the barn where Antonio's riddler made very light work of all but the most stubborn husks.

As for the grapes, we waited and waited, and were alarmed to hear of harrowing stories of entire crops being left to rot on the vines because of the mould, or of trailer loads of grapes being turned away from cellars. Farmers queuing to deliver their harvest were seen crossing themselves.

Finally Manolo said our time had come, but stressed we were only to select the best grapes – those fully ripe and free of *pudrit* – or risk the humiliation of our harvest being rejected. The evening before we were due to harvest he walked between the vines pointing, 'This one, yes. This one no. This one . . .' We got the message. We rang the crew, namely good friends

281

Mac, Conxita, Roger, Angela, Marta, Benet, Nuria and Rachel, and told them to be ready for a war of attrition. They arrived full of smiles just as I was returning from running Ella to school and Joe Joe to nursery. We listened to Maggie's briefing on what Torres wanted, then spread out across the lower vineyard. There was a strange silence for a while with none of the happy banter of the previous year, which was hardly surprising as we all quickly experienced the depression of searching through the dew-sodden leaves and picking a seemingly perfect bunch of grapes only to find that the unseen side of it had been enveloped by mould. I kept hearing mutterings of despair from people around me, and after an hour our clothes were soaked and our sour hands were stained by grape juice and stinging. But while it was tortuously slow going, it was also clear that we'd escaped the worst excesses of *pudrit*. Our vines were laden with fruit and it seemed every one had been blighted in some way, but with careful selection there was a significant amount that we felt should pass the Torres quality controllers. People kept calling Maggie across for her opinion and very slowly the pile of full crates grew and grew. I stopped picking and in a fit of paranoia carried out a second check before loading the crates into our trailer. Then, as our team of pickers moved on to the top vineyards, Maggie and I bounced off down the track to the main road to face the Torres test.

With no *pudrit* to be seen among our grapes the checkers moved swiftly to the sugar content analysis. It was lower than 2001 – hardly surprising given the haphazard sunshine – but acceptable. Phew. Then, to our astonishment the weighbridge showed we'd beaten the previous year by about a hundred kilos.

We raced home to impart the good news and to rejoin the fray – and to discover that not only had the much older vines done a far better job of staving off the *pudrit*, but they'd also quadrupled their output. Our crop had surpassed our wildest hopes. We were exhausted, elated and more than a little inclined to get pizzicato.

But it was out of the question. The next morning we moved on to Marta's vineyard where, during a similar ordeal, we all agreed we'd try and lend a hand to three people we were indebted to – Antonette, Antonio and Xavier.

Antonette, a short, stout man of few words but with a ready smile on a face weathered by at least three decades tending vines, had spent a morning at our farm back in January helping to prune the oldest plants and giving a masterclass as well. Antonio, one of those handsome Latin guys who can look cool on a moped (but also has a flame red Triumph), had always offered advice and machinery when we'd been in need, and during the snow siege had roared up our drive on his tractor to check all was well. And his brother Xavier, who'd gifted us our Vilafranca chickens, had also gone out of his way to organise our house and car insurance for us. All three had vineyards and were racing against time to get the grapes to the cellar.

It was just before eight and chill when I climbed up through Antonette's stepped vineyard to glance at the sunrise before joining in the harvest. I was also trying to get my bearings. I'd got a lift with Marta, and her Citroën had bounced along for an inordinately long time through the tangle of tracks that twist and turn across the folds of the far larger, more open valley beyond our own. It was a stunning spot. The vines were guarded by lines of ancient olive trees whose trunks fanned out at the base like lava rock. Wet spider webs sagged across furrows in the clay soil like Bedouin tents and the turning leaves of the vines sparkled with dew. They were a mix of reds and greens – miniature maple leaves in the glory before the fall.

Then it was heads down and off we went, working as a team of nine and moving fast along the rows. These, like at Mother's Garden, were very old untrained vines, each with shoots fanning out in all directions rather than neatly held by wire in narrow lines. Within a minute my front was soaking yet again as we bent and searched for the fruit among the stems. Within the hour my trainers were caked with mud, my hands were sticky and stained and I'd sliced my thumb with the secateurs.

As the sun began to dry the scene and wet our foreheads with sweat we broke for breakfast. We were picking Carinyena grapes, but interspersed with them were a handful of Muscat vines and as we made our way back to the cars Antonette picked bunches of the green grapes for us to eat. I tried in vain to tune in as the farmer, seated on the grass with his wellied feet splayed before him and doorstep sandwiches on his lap, exchanged Catalan banter with his old friend

Agusti, Antonio and Xavier's father. I rewrapped my wound in my handkerchief and back we went, working apace and picking three-and-a-half metric tons in five hours. The more important sum at the end of the session, though, was to count my fingers.

Maggie took my place in the fray the following day when the team moved on to Antonio's, and then I gave a little help to Xavier whose harvest was interrupted by rain but, against the odds, proved to be the best of all. The abiding memory of my brief endeavours on his farm was the eerie sound of the caterpillar tracks on his old Fiat tractor, clanking and clawing across the wet ground towards me like a tank.

Not all the good grapes from Mother's Garden made it to Torres. Back in May another local friend, Oriol (like Delfi a student at my English class), came to the farm to cast an eye over the vines. My ears had twitched when I heard he worked with one of Spain's leading wine makers, and, being the wonderful guy we've since discovered him to be, he happily agreed to talk to us. He duly trundled up the track in his car, bearing a gift.

'I've brought this for you,' he said coyly, and handed me a bottle of red wine without a label.

'What is it? Oh, you made it?' I suggested.

'Yes. I hope you like it. The grapes come from vines which are a hundred years old.' Then he added, 'Have you given any thought to making your own wine?'

We grinned. It was a hopeless ambition. There was still far too much to do and learn. But we still talked about it and imagined how there might be a Mother's Garden label one day.

'Well, yes, but have we enough grapes?' asked Maggie. 'We only got about seven hundred kilos last year.'

'Yes, it's possible, just a little wine for yourselves. Maybe this year you will get a little more grapes than last year and you can keep some back for winemaking. I will help you make it if you want to.'

Blimey. With Oriol holding our hands we might just be able to do it, and given the amount of money we were spending on wine it had to be worth a shot. A couple of days later, once the children were in bed and the chores were done, we pulled the cork of Oriol's bottle and quaffed the best wine that had ever passed our lips.

Later, on the eve of our harvest, he returned with a hefty 200-litre barrel that took some manoeuvring into the barn, and advised us it was for the fermentation. He said we'd need to keep back about 200 kilos of grapes to make about 100 litres of wine. Then out of the blue one of his friends, who was built like Obelix, the cartoon Gaul, brought round a 400-litre barrel. It seemed a little excessive but we were in no position to argue. Obelix seemed to think I'd have no trouble carrying one end but before I could air a niggling doubt about that it rolled out of the back of his van. Supporting his end with one arm he waved with the other for me to grab my end as it emerged. I (and it) dropped like a stone. Fortunately the barrel wasn't damaged and before I'd pulled myself together Obelix had manhandled it into the barn on his own.

The grape harvest came and went and our attention turned to winemaking. Visiting friends were pressed into service pulling the grapes from the stems, then Ella had the honour of squidging the first crushed grapes between her toes. This was all glamorously performed in a large blue plastic bowl whose normal role in life was to serve as Joe Joe's fireside bath. Maggie took the plunge too, but I figured that in the interests of the final bouquet I'd just watch.

It was a time to forget the rigours of the harvest and to savour an exceptional experience, and it was wonderful that the treading of the grapes coincided with Beryl's stay. That made it a very good time for Maggie, which was so heartening to see because the strain of that summer and the (nonsense) niggle that she'd achieved less in the garden than during the first year had combined to take the wind out of her sails. Had she produced half what she had in that second year it would still have been a triumph given the host of other things going on, not least the building work in the new kitchen. You need to understand what a standard bearer Maggie is when it comes to quality. If she's going to tackle something she has to be able to see the goal in all its glory. And that conclusion, however distant, has to measure up or the job isn't worth starting because there are always others seedlings to water. And if a couple of leeks wilt in the heat there can be talk of a crop failure. I adore her for it, but it can all get a little mind-bending for both of us when, as has transpired at times, there are a multitude of tasks and few ends in sight, or when Maggie's energy levels and focus have been dented and distracted by something else she can't help doing to perfection – caring for others and making sure every visitor to Mother's Garden feels welcome and at home. She's brilliant at it, as countless people can bear witness.

So, as you can probably imagine, achieving so soon our dream of treading our own grapes was a huge fillip, and for a while the tiredness and aches were outgunned by glee.

Don't laugh, but we were both feeling our age a little – teenagers of the kipper tie seventies (allowed to stay up and watch 'The Waltons', and well aware who Bernie the Bolt was) who hadn't clocked on to the fact that they were, well, the seasoned side of forty and needing to understand they'd retained neither the flexibility nor stamina of the lithe young things they still thought they were. Maybe the physical shock to the system would have been the same whatever our ages, but the abrupt transformation winded us and torched the notion that we could stay up and party as well if we wanted to. Invariably, no sooner had the children been tucked up in bed than we felt an overpowering urge to follow suit, and that has never changed.

We poured the crushed grapes and juice into the two barrels Oriol and Obelix had loaned us (one for each grape variety) and began the twice daily ritual of pushing down the skins that had risen to the surface. Then, after a couple of weeks, we squeezed the skins again, this time in Oriol's little press with the children again lending a hand, and poured the part-fermented juice into a smaller 120-litre barrel we'd bought and laid in our storeroom. The residue was used to give our compost a little extra zest.

'How soon do you think before we will be drinking our own wine?' we asked, smacking our lips.

'Several months yet. Next year,' said Oriol. 'Now you must wait, always checking that the barrel is full and also taking out the residue at least twice. Then we will see.'

Facts of Life

mother's garden

*I*f someone had told me when we were living in Britain that sooner or later I'd be a Catalan civil servant, I'd have been as incredulous as if it had been claimed Wombles had been spotted on Wimbledon Common. But there I was, every Monday and Thursday evening, with the keys to the *ajuntament*, the village's imposing and very beautiful three-storey pink civic building, attempting a little linguistic bravado and actually quite enjoying myself.

But some nights it felt like I was dancing on quicksand.

There was one appalling day when, after the first of my two English classes seemed to have gone particularly well, I'd actually felt like a bona fide teacher. I'd waved off my ten beginners with a hearty 'goodnight' after an hour grappling with possessive adjectives and the tricky pronunciation of the letter H, which at one point made it appear as if everyone was participating in a halitosis spot check. It's not difficult to fathom why the letter is all but redundant here given the colossal garlic consumption. Anyway, they seemed to get the gist and had fun in the process, so I felt particularly good value at just three euros per student for the hour.

Then, before I could catch my breath, the ten intermediate students trooped into the room and plunged into some impressive, albeit a little ragged, conversation.

'Be careful with the letter T in "can't", Sergi.' I interjected. 'It's vital the T is clear otherwise you can be misunderstood and seem to be giving a positive answer. OK?'

Josep piped up, 'I know what OK mean – where it came from.'

'Means, Josep – I know what OK means. With an S. Really? Where does it come from?'

'American flying missions in the war – when they come back if no one killed they write "zero killed" – OK.'

'I didn't know that. It seems logical. Thank you, Josep, very interesting. Now on page—'

'Do you know what F-U-C-K fuck mean – where it came from?'

'Er . . . umm . . . n-n-n-no.' It suddenly started to get warm in the library room. 'Can't say I do offhand. But I expect you may all know what it means. Means, with an S, Josep. So, moving on—'

'It meanz Fornication Under Consent of the King. He told people they must do this to increase the population.'

'I'm not entirely sure "under" is the right word.'

291

'It was a long time ago, of course. I think.'

'Of course. Thank you, Josep. Now if you all have a look at page . . . page . . . one hundred and thirty-five you will see the irregular verbs.' I'd been completely thrown, so in an effort to change the subject as quickly as possible I opted at random to run through some past tense verb endings. Knowing Josep had a wife and two young children I thought it would get his mind off the matter if I asked him to tell the class when he was married.

'I'm not married.'

Oh bugger. You could have heard a pin drop. 'G-g-good use of the negative, Josep. Er, a-a-and how do you spell married, anyone?'

Oriol came to my rescue. 'M-A-double R-I-E-D.'

'Good. Very good. Thank you, Oriol. And when were you married?' I was desperate to get things rolling again and it was a cast-iron fact that Oriol was married. I'm never likely to forget it because his matrimonial status was the cause of my first English lesson blushes.

When I kicked off the classes in the autumn of 2001 Oriol and two women turned up after a few weeks. Soft-spoken Oriol, in his late twenties with jet black hair and a ready smile, sat next to Maria, a teacher roughly about the same age and equally gentle. In the nicest and subtlest of ways it became clear they were in love.

Then, as the students grew in confidence and grasped some basic vocabulary I encouraged them to share information about themselves like, 'My name's . . . I'm not married . . .' and so on.

I already knew Oriol and Maria had different first and last names, and they didn't usually arrive at the same time, but I started blinking rapidly as each in turn told the class 'I'm married.'

Proclaiming it was a good idea to practise I asked the class to repeat the sentence so I could double-check, and that night I told Maggie I was convinced my English class was a smoke-screen for an affair. My suspicions multiplied a short while later when Oriol told me he had to go to London to a wine conference and would miss a class, and then Maria didn't turn up either.

Needless to say, given the adage that assumptions are the parents of life's biggest balls-ups, I was shamefully wrong. Neither of them had seen fit (since everyone in the class except me knew, and I was asking them to reply in the first person) to explain they were married to each other. It was then I learned from schoolmaster Pere that it was traditional in Spain for a wife to keep her maiden name.

So after Josep's fornication theory I knew I could rely on Oriol to help get the conversation going again. I repeated, 'When were you married?' But he glazed over. He knew, but he didn't know in English. That didn't seem to matter to Maria who turned and fixed him with a withering look. By the time the church bell struck 10 p.m. and the class was over my nerves were shot to pieces.

I got embroiled in teaching thanks to football. I went to watch Barcelona on Pere's television one night and found myself sitting next to Quico ('Keeko') the soccer-mad Mayor.

At half time they turned towards me, said there were several adults who were keen to learn English and asked if I was interested.

'Who? Me? But I'm not qualified,' I said. 'I know my English. I worked as an editor, so at least I'm supposed to know it. But I've had no teacher training.'

'Try it,' said Pere, who very politely skipped the more salient point that there were no other English people in the village to ask.

'You will be given a contract with the *ajuntament*,' said Quico in Catalan, who by this time was grinning enthusiastically. 'You can use the library room.'

It was a mildly alarming prospect, but it was undeniably alluring – a little more income from any direction had to be welcome. It didn't take a degree from the London School of Economics to fathom out that unless we could come up with some other money-spinning ideas, however small, we'd find it impossible to invest in equipment or afford to develop the farm. In time that could prove frustrating and depressing. It was one thing to have just enough money to get by, but quite another to stagnate and not be able to improve our home or have a little cash to take the farm forward in ways that became clear as the months and year passed.

'You know what the problem is, don't you?' Pauline, her face dappled by shade from the fig trees, put down her beer and in a flash switched from smile to anxiety. A pleasant sojourn from the farm during a visit from my old boss Lawry and his wife suddenly got serious. 'It's all incredible and beautiful, but you're seriously undercapitalised.'

'What?' I yelled, laughing. 'You mean we're skint – that's what you mean!' Lawry smiled as I pointed at him. 'He said exactly the same thing – "you're undercapitalised" – just yesterday. Yes, we're low on funds and a dollop of dosh to get on with the derelict cottage and to tool up a bit more on the farm would be lovely.'

'You could press on with your plans.'

'Yes, we could, but if we haven't got it we can't spend it. A little more would be nice, of course. But we're working on it and we are forever thinking ahead what we could achieve. But the ticklish question for anyone thinking of doing something like this, is when does one decide there's enough 'capital'? Do you ever have enough?'

I was being overly defensive because they were, looking at our new lives with a clinical financial eye, absolutely right.

The only other back up we had were the endowment policies left over from our old mortgage, but which still had between five to eleven years to run and which were looking increasingly unreliable as the Stock Exchange nose-dived. They should have had a collective value of about seventy-thousand pounds at maturity, but that looked increasingly uncertain. Anyway, cashing them in would have been crazy. After that our only comfort was my twenty-two-year contribution to a company pension fund while with the newspaper.

So the invitation of gainful employment from Quico and

Pere was significant, both practically and psychologically. A door had opened.

We'd already discovered that life in our little rural Catalan community revolved around the *ajuntament*. The school, bar, restaurant, corner shop and bakery were all lush planets of gossip and character, but they all orbited the great hall where secretary Nuria was a fount of information and where the council and Mayor Quico held court.

From that day on Quico was a friend. Ever optimistic that I'd grasped what he was saying, he always rattled away in Catalan when we met for a predominantly one-way conversation at the school gate. We talked football, he asked me what was new on the farm and I occasionally gleaned a little more about what new village projects, besides English lessons, he and the council were cooking up – like the bright idea of a roaming herd of civic goats to clear ground in the surrounding countryside where in summer the fire risk didn't bear thinking about, or the huge new 350-seater theatre that was rising from the ground at the far end of the old football pitch.

It wasn't clear at all, initially, what pay I'd receive after signing up to be a part-time employee of the parish council because it was wholly dependent on how many people turned up. But the formal contract meant I was paying national insurance and getting health cover.

Shortly afterwards I thought I was going to need it.

Defying my forty-three years and losing my senses for a second, I rose majestically to head the ball during an impromptu men versus boys soccer match in a dusty corral, only to fall in a crumpled heap at Quico's feet.

I'd gone to collect Ella who'd been feeding the horses at Albert's farm just down the lane and inadvertently gate-crashed a well-oiled lunch party that was rolling merrily towards supper. Before I knew it I was roped into a high-octane kick-about that had alarming similarities with a crunching Sunday morning game I'd joined in Holland a few years back. That match had ended when a player was carted off to hospital with a broken arm, but not before several unfit men had come perilously close to heart attacks.

Quico, broad of girth and rarely without a cigarette, shouldn't be doing this, I thought, only to watch the Mayor waltz round everyone and thunder in a shot which would have delighted Barcelona's manager. 'Manchester United!' he whispered several times as he whistled past me. Needless to say I was on my knees long before him, and limped off home rubbing a badly bruised hip.

I should add that on the bright ideas front Quico and the council had something else up their sleeves. One balmy day we were shaken out of pastoral daydreams by a ten-second blast of the *Star Wars* theme tune that rattled the windows and was then followed by 'ATENCIO! ATENCIO!', and a statement that there was a stall selling trousers in the square that morning. Blimey. Up until then the music that preceded an announcement from the *ajuntament* half a mile away was always dulled by distance. Council worker Josep (as opposed to Josep who came to my classes) would be as indiscernible as a railway station announcer with a balaclava on back to front. Suddenly he seemed to be in the living room with a megaphone. And he'd changed his tune – gone were dodgy recordings of Mambo Number Five and Strauss to be replaced by some crystal clear galactic music and the theme tunes to *Born Free* and *Dr Zhivago*. Heaven knows what the decibel count had reached.

'You're coming over loud and clear,' I understated when we called in at the *ajuntament* to see the planner about our derelict cottage.

'Ah, *sí?*' said Josep proudly.

'What's changed?'

Josep, whose main role in life seemed to be to keep the rest of us in the picture, turned and pointed to a spanking new broadcasting system where before I'd seen him holding a battered microphone against the speaker of an old tape player.

'And,' his grin reached his ears, 'there are now eight speakers instead of three.'

I thought for a minute how a night-shift worker trying to sleep during the day might greet the news, but couldn't think of anybody. In a population of about five hundred I estimated half were retired, a quarter were farmers and the rest covered all other facets of village life. Maybe some of the senior citizens needed him to turn up the volume a bit.

Josep's pronouncements, one or two a day, were a long-established note in the age-old rhythm of life here, even if he elected to blast out popular hits and classics while other villages stuck strictly to Catalan music. We tried to figure out if there was some sort of pattern to his selection and it seemed he was trying to reflect the mood of the moment, even if to my mind he sometimes got it horribly wrong. Back in the December, when I was knee-deep in snow with baby Joe Joe on my back, struggling to carry an armful of firewood back to the house while Charlie our dog pulled me in the opposite direction, I waved my clenched fists in Josep's direction when he opted for 'I'm dreaming of a white Christmas . . .'

The English lessons proved a real bonus in more ways than one. In the course of an academic year it brought in several hundred pounds, but more importantly there were the contacts and new friendships that led to other things, not least our tie-up with Torres and the helping hand with our winemaking.

I liked every one of the very patient and good-humoured members of my class, all of whom knew at least two languages already and were keen as mustard. I'd let them practise occasionally on an unsuspecting visitor from England, at whom they'd lob probing questions like, 'Do you like your job? How many bathrooms have you got? Who do you prefer, Yasser Arafat or Ariel Sharon?' We ended my first year of teaching with supper under fairy lights strung between the walnut and fig trees in front of the house – a night when Delfi and Oriol brought the finest wine, Joe Joe cuddled up on Enriqueta's lap and Neus danced with Ella as Oriol played the guitar.

Even then, though, it was clear the teaching and our modest income from the farm were not generating enough income.

We may have had no mortgage, no water rates, minor heating costs and a miniscule car fuel bill compared to our old life in England, but we still had to find other ways to earn.

So, as always intended, I turned to writing and produced a few essays for my old newspaper and two major features for the *Daily Mail* Saturday magazine. It was undoubtedly a distinct advantage for me to have a profession that required nothing more than a computer and a phone line – if I could persuade anyone to buy my work on a reasonably regular basis. Freelancing is a notoriously fragile existence but by good fortune I secured in the second year a more regular, albeit very modest, income with a monthly chronicle about our new lives that was carried by the Saturday sections of the *Eastern Daily Press*, *Yorkshire Post*, *East Anglian Daily Times*, plus *Country Smallholding* magazine. There were also occasional pieces in other newspapers which all combined to keep some air in our rubber ring. And I was pleased and proud that such important regional morning titles wanted to run it.

The sums were starting to add up, but there was a new niggling stress – if we were going to realise our ambition of improving the house as quickly as possible we had to be far more resourceful. The old kitchen, with its broken brick floor, crumbling ceiling, two gas rings and dodgy mini oven, was getting well beyond a joke. There was barely enough room for a table, and in winter when we needed the open fire to keep warm things became horribly cramped. Even so, Maggie had somehow managed to produce copious quantities of preserves, pickles, fruit cordials as well as coordinating the feeding of legions of visitors, but it was ludicrous to carry on like that and she rightly aired her frustration, backed up by her mum. No argument. We desperately needed a far larger farmhouse kitchen. The obvious place was the only other downstairs room, the big so-called lounge which until then had been used more by the dogs because its small windows and rough, grey walls made it dark and uninviting.

As ever, Mac and Conxita helped to get us moving.

Mac rang to say some local friends of theirs had bought a derelict four-storey house in town and had offered to let them salvage what they wanted before the builders moved in to gut it. 'Come and have a look,' he urged. 'There may be some old doors, or sinks or the like. You never know. We'll have to be careful, though. It hasn't been lived in for years and could be dangerous.'

The house was on the busy main street where, beyond the shops, it narrowed and rose towards the primary school. The outside walls and tall windows were coated in grime. We pushed open the front door and, leaving Mac to forage under the stairs, I climbed to the first floor, where tall double doors opened into rooms with high ceilings and the walls had been delicately hand painted in a style typical of the nineteenth century – all strangely juxtaposed with dust-covered iron beds, wool mattresses and piles of newspapers and magazines from the sixties.

Conxita joined me.

'It was a wealthy family's house once, a long time ago,' she said. 'Some other people lived here much later on for a little while. They left about thirty years ago. But I think they only lived on this floor.'

Down the hall a makeshift, tiny kitchen looked out into a six foot square shaft that eased the darkness. There were hardboard cupboards, a cooker caked in grease, and plates and cups left to catch dirt on the shelves. At the back of the house Conxita opened shutters in the largest room to reveal that what at first looked like panels and mouldings were even more lavish wall paintings.

The next floor, which was split in two, had clearly been abandoned for much longer and was more shadowy and depressingly bleak. The back half, with stairs from the rear of the first floor apartment, was where the domestic staff lived, while the front half, accessed via the main staircase, provided accommodation for the farm labourers. Here, in a dark corner, there was a huge stone fireplace with smudges where hands had lent against the mantelpiece. Next to it was a shallow stone sink and rotten shelves for plates, all seemingly untouched since the last workers moved out countless decades before. I couldn't figure out the layout at first, but Mac explained how the house was probably run as he led me on up into the loft, where the large, high space was lit by ripples of sunshine slipping in between the tiles and where the uneven floor was covered with piles of old hand tools, bits of furniture and the frame of what looked like an aviary. Most things seemed riddled with woodworm. At the back there were old metal pots and stains on the floor where olive oil had been made, and against one wall lay scores of (unfortunately) empty wine bottles with labels from the thirties. Perhaps that was when the wealthy owners abandoned it, I thought. What must have become of them during the blood-letting of the civil war?

It was all utterly fascinating if a bit spooky, but I couldn't see anything that we'd want. Mac was more pragmatic. He told me to carry some of the tools downstairs and then took me back to the first floor where, after quickly pointing out a lovely old china sink in the loo, he steered me back into the little kitchen.

'We ought to take this gas cooker,' he said, kneeling and opening the oven door. 'It should clean up. Do you want it?'

We needed a cooker and this, with its four rings and oven, would be the right size, but I didn't even want to touch it. Before I could answer Mac began taking it apart.

By the end of the morning Mac and Conxita's trailer was loaded with old doors, tools, shutters, a corner cupboard, some wool mattresses (the stuffing of which was going to be mixed into their compost), the sink and the dismantled cooker.

Once it was out of its bleak home I looked at the gas range again. Maybe it would be all right. We took it back to the farm and set about scraping off the dirt. My oldest friend Mike who was over from Devon the next week set about it like his life depended upon it. The cooker came up like new. We fiddled about trying to reassemble it, updated the gas bottle valve and then discovered to our delight it all worked a treat.

'What are we going to call it?' I asked Maggie as we carried it into the already seriously overcramped old kitchen. 'How about Quico? Quico, the cooker.'

'Fine,' she replied. 'Now I want a new kitchen to put it in.'

Another tax we didn't pay was refuse rates. Instead we lifted the lid of our car trailer and lobbed all rubbish that couldn't be recycled into it, and once a week I trundled off to the tip. Maggie got used to the fact I could be gone a while, because it rapidly became clear to me that next to the skips was a rubble tip that was a treasure trove, liberally scattered with lovely old building materials we could use. When we left Norfolk I sold some old red bricks for fifty pence each. Here on the dump were piles of whole and broken red and sandy-coloured bricks, ages old and perfect for what we needed. I'd found some old bricks at the farm up by our well, but nowhere near enough for the pillars we had planned to support the kitchen work surface. So back and forth I went, carting not only bricks, but floor tiles, pieces of marble, a few doors, scaffold boards, old palettes, other wood to burn and, on two occasions, flawless porcelain bathroom sinks. I found a third sink, I'm unashamed to say, sticking out of a skip during an evening stroll through a local fishing port that was heaving with tourists at the time.

The tip trips always took a while because, of course, I had to dig about a bit – and keep a weather eye for the Romany in the blue van who wasn't at all pleased to see me the day our forays across the wasteland coincided. But I don't think we were looking for the same things. It was necessary to keep checking the tip because there were always fresh deliveries, such appeared to be the Spanish penchant to replace the old with the modern. There was building work going on all over the village and I was particularly chuffed when, having noticed scaffolding around one end of the church, I swung by the dump on my way back from taking Ella to school and found a small pile of sandstone bricks, just enough to create a feature either side of a new larger window that would lighten the room and give a wonderful view from the sink through the plum trees to the vegetable patch.

As for a sink, we had to splash out. We found a reclamation yard and picked up an excellent old porcelain double sink, five metres of marble for our work surfaces, 150 wall tiles plus a bidet and loo for our future bathroom, all for about 40 euros.

The old lounge turned into a war zone as, with Mac's help, we knocked a huge hole in the dry stone wall ready for the window and set about cutting channels for new wiring. Pawing over my wiring plan, all of which had to run back to a new switchboard under the stairs, from whence I planned to rewire the whole house, I confessed to Maggie that my earlier suggestion of us being in the new kitchen within a month might have been a tad wide of the mark. Four months later we moved in, and only made it in that time due to ster-ling contributions from Maggie herself (bricklaying, tiling, grouting), her cousin Chris the carpenter, our old mate Dave the builder (both on busmen's holidays), several other holi-day camp labourers – and, of course, my heroes Mac and Roger. Having two such capable and calm DIY stars living close by has been priceless. I think they both found me price-less too.

When Dave headed back with his artist partner Heather (who'd created a label for us based on our tree trademark and who delighted Ella by painting colourful designs on her bedroom walls), their car was loaded with four fat sacks of almonds which later went on sale at some East Anglian health food stores and delicatessens – a small trial in the run up to Christmas to see if in the future we could develop Mother's Garden produce sales in Britain. It went very well, with all but one store selling out before the holiday, but given the free transport and free labour of Heather and another Norfolk friend Jackie, we still had to judge how cost-effective it would be if all expenses had to be met. One thing was clear, though. The name Mother's Garden, the trademark and the label were all very effective and it was exciting thinking of ways to use them in some way. The organic movement in Spain was still very much in its infancy compared to some other european countries, but there were several local people who shared our principles and we knew they could be a source of ecological produce in the future if things took off and we couldn't gen-erate enough at Mother's Garden.

In the meantime an elderly neighbour who had access to a plot of land via our track suggested we might like to buy it. Once in a while we'd seen his yellow Renault 4 clawing its way up between our olives, but most of the time the two-acre plot on the brow of the hill was unattended. Buying it certainly had its attractions – there were fifty almond trees and about twenty-five olive trees. The downside was that it also had about seventy hazel trees that we didn't want, and it would be another lump of land to care for when we were struggling to cope with our existing ten acres, not to mention that we didn't have any spare money anyway. The temptation deflated when it became clear the farmer's opening gambit was more than double the going rate. But, given that the land was very sandy, had no water supply and that the man might, in time, notice we weren't in fact walking around with wads of euros in our pockets, we sent Alex to make it clear that, if the owner was reasonable, a deal could be on at some stage. There was also the worry that he would sell to someone who would start using chemicals on the land right next to our old vineyard, and carve up our track with heavy equipment. We are, at the time of writing, still waiting.

Another potential business idea materialised out of nowhere, based solely upon our nationality and apparent knowledge of wine: we had vines so it was assumed we knew what we were doing. Cristina, who ran the tourism office in the nearest town, had been coming to the farm regularly to brush up on her English and to give us some Catalan lessons. We'd become good friends and thoroughly enjoyed her company, gleaning so many things about local history, local attitudes and just generally discussing topical issues. One day she asked if we knew of any British wine importers who might be interested in a local cellar that was keen to export. The family in question had been tending vines for generations, but up until then their wine had been sold for blending and they'd never had their own label.

We'd already established that apart from the internationally renowned producers like Torres, the area was littered with little cellars producing fabulous wine that had never been exported. So, we thought, there was nothing to lose by going along for a tour and tasting.

It was all very intoxicating – and that was before the owner had pulled a cork. We squeezed into his car for a tour of the merlot vineyards, where the piercing cries of hawks were broadcast from speakers on poles to keep the sparrows and finches away, and where the sense of history made you swivel your head and blow out your cheeks. He told us that local cave art showed how vines had first been tended in that area two thousand years ago. The restored cellar, abutting the family house on the edge of the village, was a mix of old charm and new technology, and the wine, though still very young, proved to be full of character and promise.

There are still countless hurdles to clear, although we've found a buyer in Britain who shares our appreciation of the merlot vintage – and in the meantime a couple of other cellars have asked us to call by. It may all come to nought, or be just a tiny sideline, but it's all part of the learning curve.

The 'wildside camping' idea for Mother's Garden, however, fell apart when, after initial optimism that we'd put together what seemed a viable plan for a modest site, we discovered that the minimum the law required in terms of facilities included fencing, lighting, power points for every pitch, plus a reception area, bar and twenty-four hour security. It would radically change the character of the farm and we realised during a visit to another local site that to be viable it would have to be on a scale that would shatter our peace. 'Hi-de-Hi' wasn't what we had in mind.

So we have turned our minds once again to the derelict house beside the track, which has been home to our chickens, a few rats and an abandoned Seat that was crushed when part of the roof caved in. Once the house is rebuilt it could be a reasonable earner, but Archie and the hens are still in residence and we've got a mountain of work to do before we can begin to think about welcoming guests with the promise of eagles overhead and golden oriels in the olive trees.

It will happen, though, because at the beginning of 2003 we received a bequest from Mum's estate that we've decided to invest in some extra machinery for the tractor to pull about, namely a grass cutter and a little trailer and to have some plans drawn up for the building work. How far it will stretch remains unclear, but we might even try to build a bathroom in the farmhouse.

We became 'parents' again in 2002, when out of the blue two Canadian eighteen-year-olds moved in for three months and we were suddenly embroiled in such unpleasant dilemmas as how to get them out of bed in the morning.

'Hey, I'm sorry,' Stefan would say in his low, slow voice, squinting into the daylight after opening the bedroom door. 'What time is it?'

'Eleven o'clock – and we've got things that need doing around the farm,' I tried to say assertively. 'You've got to get up earlier.' Maggie was banging about in the kitchen and getting increasingly frustrated, yet neither of us knew exactly how to deal with the problem.

But we learned. And to be fair Stefan seemed to listen. He was always disarmingly philosophical.

'Yep. Yep. Noooo problem. But you've got to understand, we're teenagers, right? We can't help it. It's what we do.'

'Argh!' was all Gallagher, his girlfriend, could think to add from beneath the duvet. Stefan shrugged and beamed.

'Right,' I said, rudderless. 'Er, w-what do you want for breakfast?'

'Eggs!' Gallagher had suddenly shaken herself awake. She usually spoke at twice the speed and volume of her boyfriend. 'Can you do eggs? They've got to be right – no, on second thoughts, Stefan'll do it.'

'I will? OK.'

Theirs was the most unusual romance. Stefan was from Victoria in British Columbia while Gallagher was from Nova Scotia, almost as far apart as Canadians can be. They'd met while on gap year doing voluntary work in Britain and decided it wasn't going swimmingly, so high-tailed it to an Amsterdam hotel for a week. With funds evaporating fast, they accepted a lift to Barcelona where they asked a friendly passer-by who looked as if he might speak English – Mac – if there was a campsite in the city. Hence the road to Mother's Garden.

The young Canadians came to work on the farm in exchange for bed and board, which sort of worked but may have been helped if on occasions we were more, well, parental. At least that was what seemed to be expected sometimes. Not being particularly skilled at judging ages, especially our own, we saw them as being a bit younger than us while they had us firmly pigeon-holed in middle age, albeit as members of a fairly liberal, easy-going wing of the over forties club. Bizarrely, the whole experience turned out to be a rather sobering wake-up call for us as we were informed, very gently, by Stefan that we were indeed old enough to be their mum and dad.

When he was out of bed the good-humoured, softly spoken Stefan always worked steadily and conscientiously, and seemed unflappable. His was an utterly convincing display of young shoulders bearing a head seasoned over several lifetimes, able to tie a bow of wisdom into the end of most conversations, however brief.

'Maggie's going for a massage tomorrow,' I told him one morning. 'She'll enjoy it and she needs it. Anyway, she likes to be pampered.'

'Doesn't everybody?' said Stefan, taking a bite out of his 11 a.m. breakfast of peanut butter and jam on toast.

Gallagher meanwhile was an enigma, a sterner test for two parents used to under sevens. She was spontaneous, very affectionate, dependent and yet wilful. She was clearly going through a difficult time and as we grew to understand this her trust in us manifestly blossomed. She tried to do her bit, playing with Ella, attempting to mind Joe Joe without looking bored out of her brain, and then she'd have occasional frantic bursts of energy that prevented her from eating or talking until a job was done. The way she laid into the cloud of brambles around our septic tank was something to behold.

There was so much to smile about, too, especially their loud, uncontrollable mirth every time they spied someone with a mullet hairstyle, namely short on top and the sides but long at the back. This was all the more amusing because for much of their time at Mother's Garden Stefan's head looked like a little island of palm trees as, in an effort to give him dreadlocks, Gallagher spent hours teasing clumps of his hair and then slipping on short pieces of hollow cane to keep them apart.

We grew to love them both very much indeed and there was a whole lot of blubbering going on when, finally, they headed off – Stefan to walk the pilgrims' route across northern Spain to Santiago de Compostela, Gallagher to fly home to Nova Scotia with her leg in plaster after a rush of blood to the head about a flower out of reach up a sandy cliff that she just had to get for Stefan.

That Maggie should love, let alone like anyone who, after nearly three months of being fed and watered, tucked into something she'd brought along with her called a 'Kraft dinner' of macaroni and powdered cheese, insisting it had to be eaten straight out of a saucepan and declaring it was the best meal she'd had in ages, is perhaps a clue to the bond that somehow entwined us all.

They called us their Spanish parents, which felt rather nice.

Smiles Please

mother's garden

Canadian hasn't been the only Commonwealth accent drifting across the terraces at Mother's Garden.

'That was great!' documentary director Amanda would call with a flash of teeth, but with an intonation in her Australian lilt and a slight doubt on the fringes of her smile that told us what was coming next. 'Only could we do that one more time – from twenty-five yards back up the track maybe?'

It probably sounds completely loopy, but the sense of kismet about everything that has happened to us included the Channel Four experience when, after weeks of filming, our story kicked off the inaugural 'No Going Back' series in January 2002 and then was updated a year later.

It's weird looking back because, as some of our friends astutely pointed out, we didn't seem obvious candidates for a warts-and-all airing on 'reality television' – that strangely addictive genre of programming which can turn armchairs into a front-row seat in other people's lives as their quite normal but somehow fascinating foibles, along with their dirty washing and short fuses, are laid out like exhibits at a court hearing.

Nobody came right out and said it but of course it was also somewhat dubious that anyone should submit his or her family to trial by television when they were grappling with a monumental life change that was already an explosive cocktail of euphoria, trepidation, stress and exhaustion. The risk of it all going horribly wrong and the subsequent nationwide infamy and humiliation as countless millions settled down in the lounge with supper on a tray to watch your world fall apart didn't bear thinking about.

But we went ahead and did it all the same for reasons I'll try to explain. Perhaps some of you saw one or both of the documentaries, or vaguely recollect that while channel-hopping one winter's night you glimpsed a scruffy Herbert in a dusty Remo cap praying the pizza oven would work and eulogising dewy eyed about his new Spanish home. More likely people will recall Maggie turning into Mother Earth and persuading the once wilderness to offer up copious quantities of burgeoning fruit and vegetables while also caring (with a little help from me) for Ella and Joe Joe.

Well, it all seemed to touch a nerve. To our amazement millions tuned in to watch if anyone could pull off what on reflection may well be near the top of the charts of office day-dreams, namely jumping off the midlife merry-go-round and

314

high-tailing it to the hills in search of the good life – in our case without a grand money-spinning idea or any financial safety net, just an intolerable sense that the balance of our lives was wrong, and not wanting to regret later in life that we didn't have the nerve to tilt at least one windmill. So in that sense the 'No Going Back' series was temptingly real, and a little different from other television offerings like the utterly absorbing 'Castaway' social experiment with a time limit when everyone would go home, or an endurance game in a jungle or social and sexual sparring in a fortress house with television cameras above the toilets and a cash prize for the winner. There was no way either of us would sign up for anything involving cameras in the loo.

But why sign up at all? Because during that very heady time in our lives in the summer of 2000 we had already thrown caution to the wind and committed ourselves to letting go. We'd fallen in love with Mother's Garden and had set our hearts on having a shot at eking out a living here. The 'second thoughts' power leads to my brain were unplugged and at first glance the notion of our story being chosen, though highly unlikely, sounded fun and potentially lucrative. By the time we were told there was no fee, just expenses, Ricochet had locked on to our crazy plans and in a way it was flattering. We also learned that more than a thousand families had thrown their hats into the ring so there was a competitive edge too.

But none of these were significant reasons why we pressed on. We wanted our families and many friends to see and understand what we were attempting in an extraordinary chapter of our lives. I suppose, on reflection, we also saw merit in other like-minded people sharing our adventure, but that was a pleasing consequence not a driving force. And the fact that countless other people we didn't know would judge us wasn't a concern because we thought we would fade rapidly from their minds.

There was one last thing we did before we said yes to Ricochet. I rang a friend who works in television for his views on the production company and we researched what sort of programmes they had done. Once we knew they were responsible for the evocatively filmed 'River Cottage' series starring Hugh Fearnley-Whittingstall, that was it.

What was it like? Nerve-racking initially, but like all things the new can rapidly become the norm. Nothing, however, can prepare you for opening the bedroom window at 7 a.m. and finding a camera crew looking up at you or, six hours later, to have them take a keen interest in some decidedly dodgy DIY you wouldn't admit to your best friend let alone share with a nation of handymen.

And you can't fool them. After a few vain attempts to look and sound like Clark Gable I quickly lapsed into my normal round-shouldered posture and soporific voice, occasionally barking at the children and bellowing at the dogs to stop barking.

They weren't with us constantly, but visited us six times for up to a week for the first documentary, and although it didn't seem unduly pressured while they were around we were always shattered by the time they left.

They wanted us to behave normally, of course, but we found we could only do that if we had two things: heaps of patience and trust. I'm not sure what would have happened if we'd sensed there was an agenda, a determination on the part of Ricochet to find fault. There wasn't.

Had we not warmed immediately to the production team, especially regular visitors series producer Billy Paulett, director Amanda Blue and cameraman Will Millner, the wheel could have come off pretty rapidly. They saw enough of us to know the truth and we trusted them to tell it, which they did, save for a few minor bloopers which were comical not lamentable.

They were very professional and dedicated in every sense, impressively so, but also remarkably adept at slotting into our lives as much as possible. Now that's a skill. New friendships have been forged.

I'm relieved, though, that they never seemed to be around during one of the many Kirby debacles, like the day when, having lost the key to the barn I scaled the dry stone wall to clamber red-faced through a ventilation arch. Scrabbling for a foothold and trying to figure out how the hell I was going to get down again, I glanced into the barn to see two-year-old Joe Joe looking up at me perplexed and asking, 'What doin' Dad? What doin?' The toddler had had the sense to try the door that wasn't locked.

The toughest part of the filming without a doubt have been the interviews and trying to answer the sort of probing, sweaty-palm questions you get at job interviews, only now the topic wasn't your professional judgement but your views on the meaning of life, while the audience wasn't a panel of three people looking over their glasses from behind a desk but a large slice of the great viewing public.

This is where trust was the key. We knew they were going to take just a few lines from hours of questioning and we had to believe it would be a fair representation of what we said as a whole. And we were content at how in the second documentary they didn't pull their punches about how hard it had been on occasions, and were amused by the way our thrifty approach to life was portrayed. Did anyone else register the theme tune to 'The Beverly Hillbillies' as we were scrabbling around on the tip?

As for the public reaction, we were stunned. Being so far removed from Britain we felt detached and thought any hype and interest would rapidly evaporate. The first year we sat beside an open fire drinking wine while the documentary was screened. Then during the intervals and from the minute the programme ended the phone started to ring, and ring and ring. These, of course, were our nearest and dearest whom we expected to get in touch, but as the weeks and months passed more and more letters and emails started to arrive from all over the place. Some people even managed to track us down.

The second year we gave an email address and the floodgates opened. We've tried hard to follow up as many contacts as possible and apologise sincerely to those who were disappointed they didn't get a personal response.

And this book? At the outset it was only an idle dream that, at the time we rang Ricochet, barely amounted to a few pages of notes intended for occasional newspaper articles. One of the reasons for our move was to give me an opportunity to get down to some serious writing, although I wasn't thinking so much about this chronicle – rather some fiction that continues to bubble in my brain and may bear fruit soon. The idea of our journey to Mother's Garden becoming a full-blown memoir blossomed over those first months but, of course, we couldn't count on me achieving anything because we had neither a book to sell nor a publisher, and even if those high hurdles were cleared there was still the small matter of the public buying my work in sufficient quantities for us to earn anything. Not exactly what you might call a cast-iron business plan.

That it has happened is a joy, and whatever the outcome we have it forever, keeping secure a treasure trove of memories for us where, among the brightest jewels, we will always find our children.

A screwdriver and assorted Spanish electrical bits and bobs lay scattered across the kitchen table as I fiddled about trying to put a plug on a new extension cable.

'Now . . .' I said idly to myself, thinking what to do next, '. . . where am I?'

'In Spain, Daddy,' said Joe Joe helpfully as he breezed past clutching his Reliant Robin toy car, '. . . wiv Biba dog.'

'You're absolutely right,' I replied, patting Biba and sighing happily.

Joe Joe's observation was, of course, of the variety to fill any parent with a warm glow, and it rekindled strong memories of my emotions when his big sister Ella was just starting to turn glorious thoughts into words some four years before – 'Do all horses have cowboys?' – when I used to worry about how much I was missing. Now I know.

I'm nearly thirty hours a week better off when it comes to time that I could, and invariably do, spend with Ella – which means at least being within view or hailing distance even when we aren't doing something together or as a family. And I spend an inordinately large lump of time watching her with little Joe Joe or friends Paula or Chenoa, cavorting about the farm in the sunshine, letting their imaginations run wild and revelling in the space and freedom like both of us fondly remember doing in our own outdoor childhoods.

She's spreading her wings too.

In the ancient quarter of the nearby market town, where narrow cobbled streets snake up towards the castle ruins, and the higgledy-piggledy homes fuse into a honeycomb of urban life (Spanish style), all seems eternally peaceful. It's several steps away from the high street and marketplace with their bars and shops, and during the dark and increasingly cold evenings of late autumn and winter the alleys are empty apart from occasional souls heading home.

I should know. I've spent what must add up to several hours over the past year loitering on a corner beneath a dim lamp, studying the old houses, blowing into cupped hands when there's been more than a nip in the mountain air, and wondering how much longer Ella will be.

Pili's Sevillana dance classes are supposed to end at half past eight, but they never do. You only have to listen to the music and joy emanating from the studio on the top floor of her tiny house wedged in the corner of a blind alley to know that they – especially Pili – have lost track of time yet again as they rehearse for another public display.

Then, finally, out they burst, their teacher hugging and kissing them all while checking that their coats are buttoned, before I'm forced to jog off after Ella and her classmate Maria del Mar who, still fizzing with adrenaline, have foisted their bags on me and raced off down the hill skipping and shrieking.

Fiery Sevillana dancing with its flouncy, vibrant – or sometimes jet black – dresses, may be from the capital of Andalusia, but there are many people from southern Spain in this area whose fathers came north to find work in the now derelict lead mines. Twice this year the tireless Pili (incidentally from a family of nineteen children) has taken her all-female troupe of about ten young adults and ten girls to perform in an old mining village about five miles away where the white-washed cottages and church tower echo the very different culture of the deep south.

The second time was on a hot summer's evening, and having arrived very early as normal so Ella could be made up, and have her hair pinned into a bun and adorned with flowers and the traditional large decorative comb, I wandered through the village and exchanged smiles with a tiny old lady who was busy making lace outside her front door. The setting sun had turned the terraced houses pink and I cursed myself for not bringing my camera. An hour later I saw the woman again, on the balcony of the village hall in a line of women fluttering their fans and leaning forward over the balcony as they watched Ella and her friends dance.

Ella adores the dancing (and Pili) and has come on leaps and bounds. At another display, in front of about a hundred children on summer camp in a remote mountain village, the whisper went round that one of the dancers was English, but it seemed no one figured it was our kid.

People have no idea of her nationality either when she opens her mouth. About a year into our new lives we went to a pizzeria where Ella led the charge and ordered herself a drink. The barman didn't bat an eyelid and started chatting to her. Then we piped up and the barman did a double-take before asking incredulously if Ella was English too. He was astounded, and because of her accent was able to identify which village we were from. It's a common occurrence.

Her humbling linguistic dexterity, acquired within a few months of arriving, stemmed mostly from us throwing her into the deep end of the Catalan educational system. It sounds cruel and we felt terrible, but she's never been a clingy child and we were assured she wouldn't drown but would move rapidly from the doggy paddle to the breaststroke. So it proved. She swiftly became a local girl, perfectly at ease with her surroundings.

There are only twenty-five other pupils at the school. They

are split into three classes and the age range is from three (the kindergarten is included) to eleven. The hours are very civilised – 10 a.m. to 1 p.m., and 3 p.m. to 5 p.m., but they lob in a 9.30 start one week in the month with the Wednesday afternoon off, just to keep you on your toes and to give the teachers a clear half day for meetings and admin. The three terms are shorter than the English equivalents, but we don't have half-term breaks here. School ends in mid June and the hot summer holiday stretches away into distant mid-September.

Because she's in a class of nine the teacher–pupil ratio is good and the general investment in local education hereabouts is undoubtedly impressive. Several specialist peripatetic teachers support the permanent staff, although Ella's English teacher has, we suspect, found the challenge of carting coals to Newcastle a little strange.

While there have been less than thirty pupils in the village for some considerable time, the education authority still built a new school in 1999. In fact we've been reliably informed that the policy is only to resort to closing a village school once the number of children drops to six. Then they are bussed free of charge to the next school.

The downside is that Ella only has two children her own age in the school, a boy and a girl, so we are constantly exploring ways to widen her circle of friends. She has the advantage, though, of contact with visitors young and young at heart to Mother's Garden, and we have accepted that the fairly relentless comings and goings, though sometimes disorientating for her parents, positively broadens the stimulation in Ella's life and doesn't seem to perturb her.

It's been interesting to see how other language teaching is started at a far earlier age here – Ella studies Catalan, Castilian and English – even if we'd prefer that the teaching of all subjects was not quite so regimented and didn't lean so heavily on textbook exercises with almost nightly homework.

There's a fairly active parents' group that organises a host of out-of-school activities for the children, including for a chunk of the summer break, as well as social events and outings. But there are no school governors in a managing role and as far as we can make out the system of staff appointments doesn't involve the senior teacher or parents in any way. It seems to work on the basis that, during the long summer between academic years, a more junior member of staff must look for another posting if a more senior teacher decides they want their job. The staff have all been approachable and caring, and we've had the distinct advantage that the senior teacher Pere is our friend and neighbour. Lovely Remei, horticulturalist Alex's wife, is also on the staff, along with Isabel, whose olive oil expert brother Gerard (one of Joe Joe's favourite people) is set to marry our good friend Rachel from Barcelona. Ella will be a bridesmaid while Joe Joe the page will (fingers crossed) carry the cushion bearing the rings – both looking a million euros in matching silk outfits designed, made and hand painted by the bride.

In the meantime Ella's out-of-school activities (along with

the universal parental taxi service) have blossomed. Monday and Friday evenings remain clear for now, but for an hour on Tuesday evenings and again on Wednesdays Ella attends the music school in town. They use, incidentally, the tonic sol-fah (do-re-mi) system. The music school just happens to be a short distance from Pili's house, which makes life a little easier on a Wednesday because Ella has to then hot foot it to her 7 p.m. Sevillana class. It may sound excessive but she's been itching to get to grips with music – and it would be unthinkable to suggest she stops dancing.

So, after such hectic Wednesday evenings, when Ella is not spared homework, you can imagine that the 10 a.m. school start comes in quite handy on Thursday mornings.

Then after school on that day she takes her oils, brushes and little desk easel to the former convent in town which is now a rabbit warren of public rooms where a host of things seems to be taking place, for a two-hour art class with a highly respected, broad-smiling local artist.

As for Joe Joe, he seems to be acquiring quite a fan club. It's not unusual on a shopping trip for people we've never clapped eyes on before to greet our son warmly, and he's happy to switch languages for whoever's paying him attention. I have to admit to picking up a couple of Catalan words from him.

In spring carnival time Joe Joe, like his sister two years before, looked rather fetching in a bin liner. He flatly refused, though, to sport his silver cone hat that set off rather nicely the decorations on his carnival costume, advising me fairly directly, both in English and Catalan, that there was no way it was going on his head.

Then the tots from the day nursery, along with several similarly attired mums and a dad, spilled out of their classroom and sang songs as they climbed the stairs to the steep, narrow street.

I remembered it must have been about a year to the day that Joe Joe first nervously entered Marta's private nursery, run in the basement of her parent's home. But it is no ordinary basement. The house isn't in our village, but in the hilltop community just around the mountain and four kilometres from Mother's Garden, where the buildings cling together like limpets to a rock and where even the lowest rooms have windows that offer wonderful vistas and look down on vineyards and olive groves.

In that year Joe Joe had changed from a shy toddler to local celebrity, and as I followed the troupe through the village towards the primary school, countless people of all ages waved greetings and shouted '*Hola*! Joe Joe!'

He and all his friends looked bewildered for a while, understandable when your normal afternoon snooze is superseded by a route march up a one-in-six hill. But gradually they came to life with the older ones running, shouting and singing. In the normally almost deserted streets, where you might see a woman sweeping or someone walking, there were people on the doorsteps and smiling faces poking out of windows.

At the primary school all the pupils were waiting – all twelve of them. They had created a wonderful locomotive, two carriages and a coal wagon out of cardboard boxes and were clearly itching to start the tour of the village. It was at this point I realised the little ones, who'd already walked a fair old way, were facing another yomp – and still had to make their way back to Marta's at the end.

I loosened my shoulders in readiness for some serious child carrying, but Joe Joe was having none of it. He even upped the tempo and completed the procession several yards ahead of everyone else, hurling confetti with glee. When we got back to the school yard, perhaps sensing I was flagging, he led me to a table covered in half-eaten bars of chocolate. 'Ah,' I said. 'I take it you had some earlier?'

'Yep. Nice. In my tummy!'

He then discarded his bin liner and made a beeline for the sandpit where he informed several of his friends in perfect Catalan that he intended to join in.

I wondered how Maggie was getting on. She was back in our village following Ella (an aubergine) around the streets. Just a couple of weeks after we emigrated, when our daughter barely knew a word of Catalan, she'd been so brave and strong walking along in a bin liner costume among children she didn't know or understand.

'Do you want a drink?'

One of the other fathers in 'Joe Joe's village' urged me to fill a paper cup. He was a fireman, a really likeable bloke, whose son was also at the nursery. I reached for the first of several bottles and half filled the cup.

'Oh, you like *ranci*.'

'Um, it's, er, *ranci*, is it?'

'Wonderful. I hope you like it.' Then he smiled and waited for me to drink it.

I hadn't touched a drop of *ranci* since the day we bought the farm and Enric had introduced me to it and I'd made a mental note to avoid it at all costs in future.

I was remembering all of this as I obliged the fireman and downed the carnival *ranci*. It wasn't so bad. I smiled broadly with relief and he immediately reached for the bottle again.

'Oh, no, no, nooo, thank you' I gesticulated. 'Lovely. Absolutely lovely, but one's enough.'

On Mothering Sunday, while Ella was spending a few hours with Pili, Maggie and I took a picnic and pushed a sleeping Joe up the valley and into the forest.

It was good to take a break from the myriad of farm tasks.

We stroked the wild herbs to stir the scent and looked for the dog violets and grape hyacinths, while above us a golden eagle glided across the wilderness, caught a thermal and soared away towards the rugged face of the mountain.

We talked about how the children had been the main keys to our growing integration and acceptance. And we laughed at one particular memory.

It must have been towards the end of Ella's first academic year. The parents' group at the school announced there was going to be a Sunday coach outing to the model village near Barcelona, possibly with a beach stop on the way back. Ella was itching to go, but it was going to be a very long day so Maggie said she would stay at home with Joe Joe.

The model village was a curious mix of manicured gardens, a train ride around the boundary and a variety of tiny reproductions of Catalonian landmarks. We followed the meandering path through the maze of little buildings and then adjourned, first to the bar and then to the restaurant where, to my horror, the children (seated at a separate table) started getting seriously out of hand. The feeble partition wall separating the forty or so of us and a large party of senior citizens shook and the decibel count reached critical point, yet nobody seemed to be batting an eyelid. I chickened out and headed for the loo as the children raced into the main restaurant area and weaved in and out of the pensioners. But when I came back I got the strongest possible reminder of one key facet of life here – there is an extraordinary acceptance and love of children. Some of the little ones were perched on pensioners' laps, others were continuing the fun and games, and everyone, and I mean everyone, even the waitresses and waiters trying to get from kitchen to table with armfuls of food, was smiling.

We lined up for a photograph, then, back on the coach, we were told there was indeed time to stop off at a beach on the way home.

I didn't have a clue where we ended up, but it was one of those pretty little Mediterranean bays where, betwixt rocky outcrops and a puzzle of white wall holiday villas and apartments that reeked money, the fine sand was divided by a seam of thatched sunshades. Expensive, I thought, as I looked at the bronze, red, pink and lily white holidaymakers in various states of roasting. They were all but naked, but there was little doubt they were well heeled.

We hovered nervously for a few moments at the back of the sand as the children changed into their costumes and were plastered with sun cream. Several dads rolled up their trousers legs and a few produced handkerchiefs and proceeded to knot them.

Then we trouped through the thatched sunshades and sat in a row at the shoreline, letting the waves cool our feet and legs while we called to the children as they swam and splashed.

Just behind me a woman was lying on her stomach reading a paperback. I noticed it was Dickens' *Tale of Two Cities*. Her partner stirred, pulled himself up onto his elbows and noticed he couldn't see the sea anymore.

'What's going on?' he asked.

She nodded in my direction without looking up. 'It's Sunday, remember? The day the Spanish descend.'

Postscript

mother's garden

When it was agreed 'No Going Back' would be the title of the television documentaries we flinched, because we felt it gave the impression there was no way, come hell or high water, we would high-tail it back to Britain – that we were emigrating to start a new life with a steadfast refusal to look over our shoulders. Clearly not true.

Nothing is certain in this life and, back in the autumn of 2000 when filming began in earnest, there was a significant risk that within the year we would be back in Britain and among all things reassuringly familiar, licking our wounds and counting the cost of an ill-founded adventure. But for a fistful of good fortune and incredible help and support this could well have proved to be the case.

We were also uncomfortable that the title might suggest we'd found the perfect place and pace of life. This thought sat rather uneasily with the challenges ahead, our lack of knowledge and also our open-mindedness about the future. Faced with the family's changing needs, we might well move on again, backwards if necessary. While Mother's Garden and the peaceful community here in southern Catalonia are very much our home now they may well prove to be just another stepping stone in our lives.

Then we looked at it another way.

Even if we'd returned to Britain after a year there was still no going back to how we were. The documentaries and this book have charted our course, and there can be no doubt the experiences of recent years have had a profound effect upon our values and ambitions. With the old securities and routine left behind, Maggie and I have had to rely upon each other to an extraordinary extent and in the process have had to work a number of things out, but we agree it has been both an invaluable and enriching experience. Equally important have been the countless hours we have been able to spend with Ella and Joe Joe – precious moments in their lives we would have lost if time had been squeezed in the old way.

You may have twigged by now that this book isn't intended to be a practical guide in any shape or form (the opposite more likely), yet within it there are pointers to many of the stresses and unsavoury experiences, as well as the joys, that such a move can hold. Maggie and I felt it was imperative that any romanticism about the notion of doing likewise should be balanced with a candid account of our human failings and frailties, while also underlining the value of trying one's level best to integrate not congregate – oh, and retaining the capacity come thick or thin to laugh long and loud once in a while.

We were deeply moved by the messages of encouragement and offers of practical and physical help which flooded in after both programmes in January 2002 and 2003, all of which have been printed off and kept in a file which is as precious a record of this time as the documentaries. And we were astounded by how many people wrote seeking advice on how to fulfil their dreams of veering off the beaten track and heading for warmer climes. The reasons cited varied from health, to family, to a simple, insatiable urge to opt out. The questions came from people of all backgrounds and ages and were, or course, so difficult to answer because it's such a personal matter, such a huge step that is dependent on so many influences.

But most of all it was the messages from people with children that struck a chord. Parental uncertainty about a child's happiness and future is a factor that heightens the stakes so dramatically, and there's no denying the stress of what can only be a subjective judgement.

I know we would have dropped the whole idea if we weren't both in full accord and as sure as we could be about the community and environment we were moving to. Yet, even now, the distance that lies between us and our families and close friends in England remains the toughest test of all. This has been especially true for Maggie, one so in tune with her family and (as may well be true for many women) one who needs the strong bond of friendship. The telephone has partly filled the void, as has the stream of visitors that has included some of her favourite people, but being unable to whizz round to someone's house for a heart to heart, a good laugh or cry has been so painful at times – and painfully obvious to me, who, though utterly confident about our love, can never be a substitute for a close female friend at the times when it really matters.

As a Martian (men are from Mars, women are from Venus, remember) I've battled with the urge to hide or to try and make things better by doing something, or, worse still, arguing everything was rosy when it clearly wasn't, and I've also come to appreciate just how much harder it has been for Maggie. She's always relished the challenges in so many ways and has positively radiated happiness when we've balanced family life with achieving something significant on the farm. But there are days when it matters that her mum, family and closest friends are no longer just a few minutes away. On top of this, compounding her anxiety, has been Maggie's struggle to forge new, deep friendships here. She wouldn't agree but her Spanish is much stronger, and we have some wonderful female friends that we knew before we moved – notably Conxita and Marta whom we appreciate so much. But a common lament from Maggie has been that she couldn't express her feelings honestly and openly to them because she wasn't unconsciously fluent. There have been some new friendships of late, and that makes me so happy for the most important person in my life. But it would be a lie if I said this long-standing missing piece of the jigsaw wasn't still one of my greatest concerns. It was something we didn't discuss before the move, yet it is a significant fact of our new life that everyone considering following in our footsteps should bear in mind.

We also tell people that so many aspects of such a radical change of direction have to be right, but if by good fortune and a great deal of hard work they are, then the reward can be immeasurable. In the cases of couples with young ones, all we can do is send them our thoughts, to wish them all the luck in the world, to counsel that, whatever the emotive force for change, reason should prevail, and to hope they somehow find more time as a family, whether it's in Catalonia, Cumbria, Tuscany, Totnes or Timbuktu. Or, indeed, where they are now, because it may not be an issue of where, but of how they live. The best we can do is share our experiences. So here is our story and such is the ceaseless spinning of the world, we recognise that this book may in turn have some bearing on our own future.

Most of these pages have been written in my shambolic office corner of the farmhouse, but as life would have it these last few lines were not. It's 11 p.m. Ella is being looked after by our friend Marta just up the valley and is, I hope, sleeping soundly on a bed in her friend Paula's room. I'm in a hotel close to Tarragona Hospital, taking my break from watching over little Joe Joe who, a week ago, was rushed away in an ambulance suffering from bacterial pneumonia and bronchitis. Maggie and her sister Liz are with him now as, fingers crossed, there appears to be an ever stronger light at the end of a tunnel that has taken us on a sleepless, alarming journey through two hospitals and an intensive-care unit. Ever susceptible to chest colds, our two-year-old son slipped from happy squeals to acute illness with alarming speed as, in the most forceful way possible, the priceless value of time was defined for us.

It's an unthinkable close to this story, one that nobody would choose. But this book is done because there are literally no hours left if the publishing dates are to be met. I'm out of time and, anyway, for the moment the importance of it has evaporated in the heat of the strongest possible emotions and one consuming contemplation – how lucky I am to have Maggie, Ella and Joe Joe. We wait to see what tomorrow may bring.

(PS: A week later Joe Joe was back home, brandishing a clean bill of health and, shoulder to shoulder with Ella, taking the world in their stride, which was more than could be said for their parents.)

mother's garden

Websites

If you want to find out more about Mother's Garden, Catalonia or other information mentioned in this book log in to the following:

Keep track with what is happening down on our little Catalan farm by visiting www.mothersgarden.org

Discover more about Catalonia at www.gencat.es/catalunya/turisme/index_eng.htm

Find out more about the charity Imagine's work with African orphans and homeless people at www.imaginemozambique.org.

Explore the history and wines of Torres by visiting www.torres.es

Check out what other programmes are being made by the television production company Ricochet on www.ricochet.co.uk

And see what a clever bunny our logo and website designer Heather is on www.tartdesigns.com

THE OLIVE FARM
Carol Drinkwater

The Olive Farm is a double love story. It is a lyrical tale of the real-life romance between actress Carol Drinkwater and Michel, a television producer, and of an abandoned Provençal olive farm – Appassionata – which they fall in love with and buy.

And as the olives turn from green to violet, luscious grape-purple to a deep succulent black, we are drawn seductively into Carol and Michel's vibrant Mediterranean world. We experience the highs and lows of Provençal life: the carnivals, customs and local cuisine; the threats of fire, adopting a menagerie of animals and a ready-made family, potential financial ruin; as well as the thrill of harvesting your own olives by hand – especially when they are discovered to produce the finest extra-virgin olive oil.

Rich and resonant, *The Olive Farm* effortlessly captures the joys of living in a warmer clime, of eating fresh Mediterranean food, swimming in one's own pool, and sharing all this with the love of one's life.

Other bestselling Time Warner Paperback titles available by mail:

☐ The Olive Farm	Carol Drinkwater	£7.99
☐ The Olive Season	Carol Drinkwater	£7.99
☐ The Moon's Our Nearest Neighbour	Ghillie Basan	£7.99

The prices shown above are correct at time of going to press. However, the publishers reserve the right to increase prices on covers from those previously advertised, without further notice.

————————————— **timewarner** —————————————
paperbacks

TIME WARNER PAPERBACKS
PO Box 121, Kettering, Northants NN14 4ZQ
Tel: 01832 737525, Fax: 01832 733076
Email: aspenhouse@FSBDial.co.uk

POST AND PACKING:
Payments can be made as follows: cheque, postal order (payable to Time Warner Books) or by credit cards. Do not send cash or currency.

All UK Orders	**FREE OF CHARGE**
EC & Overseas	25% of order value

Name (BLOCK LETTERS) . . . .

Address . . . .

. . . .

Post/zip code: . . . .

☐ Please keep me in touch with future Time Warner publications

☐ I enclose my remittance £ . . . .

☐ I wish to pay by Visa/Access/Mastercard/Eurocard

Card Expiry Date ☐☐☐☐